JOHNSON BEFORE BOSWELL

Johnson before Boswell

A STUDY OF SIR JOHN HAWKINS'

Life of Samuel Johnson

BY BERTRAM H. DAVIS

GREENWOOD PRESS, PUBLISHERS
WESTPORT, CONNECTICUT

The Library of Congress has catalogued this publication as follows:

Library of Congress Cataloging in Publication Data

Davis, Bertram Hylton.
  Johnson before Boswell.

    Reprint of the ed. published by Yale University Press,
New Haven.
    Bibliography: p.
    1. Hawkins, Sir John, 1719-1789. The life of
Samuel Johnson, LL. D.   2. Johnson, Samuel, 1709-1784.
I. Hawkins, Sir John, 1719-1789. The life of Samuel
Johnson, LL. D.   II. Title.
[PR3533.H32D3 1973]   828'.6'09 [B]   72-12309
ISBN 0-8371-6691-8

© *1957 by Bertram Hylton Davis*

First published in 1960
by Yale University Press, New Haven

Reprinted with the permission
of Yale University Press

First Greenwood Reprinting 1973

Library of Congress Catalogue Card Number 72-12309

ISBN 0-8371-6691-8

Printed in the United States of America

PREFACE

SIX EVENTFUL YEARS elapsed between Dr. Johnson's death on December 13, 1784, and the publication of the biography which has endeared him to subsequent generations. But Johnson's admirers did not wait until 1791 to find him a place among the English worthies. In the weeks following his death the periodicals made public his letters, dug out hidden facts of his life, and preserved many of the anecdotes by which he is still familiar. Critics heaped praise upon the *Dictionary*, the *Rambler*, and the *Lives of the Poets*. By 1787 he had inspired numerous biographers.

In the rush to reach the public with an account of Johnson's life, the *Universal Magazine* had a decisive advantage. In August 1784 it had already published "Memoirs of the Life and Writings of Dr. Samuel Johnson," and it lost no time announcing that its account was still available to purchasers. Rivals followed quickly in the field. William Cooke's *Life of Samuel Johnson, LL.D.* was ready for sale scarcely two weeks after Johnson's death. At the turn of the year the *Gentleman's Magazine* published Thomas Tyers' "Biographical Sketch of Dr. Samuel Johnson," later printed separately, and the *European Magazine* published the first of five installments of an "Account of the Writings of the Late Samuel Johnson, with Some Anecdotes of His Life."

The two following years saw the publication of four minor and two quite notable works. Of the minor works, William Shaw's *Memoirs of the Life and Writings of the Late Dr. Samuel Johnson*, published in 1785, is the most significant. In 1786 a brief life served only to introduce the Jarvis edition of Johnson's *Dictionary;* and Joseph Towers' *Essay on the Life, Character, and Writings of Dr. Samuel Johnson,* published the same year, was too much concerned with Johnson's strictures on Milton to be of great interest biographically. Shaw's memoir, slight though it is, affords an occasional authentic glimpse into Johnson's life and character. On the other hand, it yields considerably in interest to the 1785 *Journal of a Tour to the Hebrides* (Boswell's preview of his *Life*) and to Mrs. Piozzi's *Anecdotes of Samuel Johnson,* published in 1786. In their own ways, both of these are outstanding contributions, not only to our knowledge of Johnson but to biographical literature generally, and the many editions through which they have gone attest to their continuing popularity.

Doubtless the most ambitious effort of these early years was the work which climaxed them in 1787. And by all rights Sir John Hawkins' *Life of Samuel Johnson, LL.D.* should have become a standard work. Hawkins was one of Johnson's oldest and most accomplished friends. As one of his executors he had access to Johnson's private papers. The book was more than two years in the making, and its 600 pages touched almost every phase of Johnson's rich career. Yet within eight months Hawkins' *Life* had been effectually buried beneath the abuse of its critics. It has not been reprinted since its second edition three months after publication, and it is known to most people only through the sneering eulogy which Boswell muttered over it.

Why did Hawkins fail?

To answer this question is in part the purpose of the present study. The answer is a story which begins almost with the hour of Johnson's death, and it will make clear, I hope, that the real object of the critics' abuse was not so much Hawkins' book as Hawkins himself. The book came under attack as soon as Hawkins' determination to write it became known. I have found it necessary, therefore, to describe in some detail the writing, publication, and reception of the *Life*. At the same time I have gathered under their main headings the charges leveled against it.

The primary purpose of the present book is to speak to these charges. If we are to bring Hawkins' *Life* back into notice, as I believe we should, it must be demonstrated beyond a reasonable doubt that the charges against it cannot be sustained in a fair hearing. The faults of the *Life* I have made no attempt to conceal, just as Hawkins' contemporary critics did not. But in citing the book's many virtues I hope that I may create a new balance which, however belatedly, will raise the *Life* to its proper position as a standard work on Johnson, second only to Boswell's.

In preparing this study I have had much help, for which I am happy to record my gratitude. My wife I must thank for her tedious job of typing and for her continuing patience and encouragement. To James Osborn, Herman Liebert, and Marshall Waingrow I am indebted for making a week in New Haven pleasant and profitable. Ernest Brennecke, George Nobbe, Otis Fellows, André von Gronicka, and James Shearer have offered a number of useful suggestions. Allen Hazen, William Sloane, and John Middendorf have studied the manuscript with particular care, and have rescued me from numerous errors of fact and judgment. To Donald J. Greene I owe a special note of thanks; indeed, so many of the ideas in this study may be traced back to him that I must ask his pardon for giving credit in the text only when I have made use of his invaluable study of Johnson's politics (New Haven, 1960). But to James L. Clifford, who first suggested this work, must go the fullest measure of gratitude. His many suggestions, sometimes for major revisions, I have almost invariably adopted, and with his customary generosity he has made available to me some of the results of his own research. My debt to his indispensable *Young Sam Johnson* I have acknowledged at frequent intervals throughout the text.

Finally, I wish to express my thanks to the Clarendon Press for permission to quote at some length from the Hill–Powell edition of Boswell's *Life of Johnson,* and to Mr. W. S. Lewis, the William Salt Library, the Pierpont Morgan Library, and Yale University for permission to quote from manuscript materials in their possession.

B. H. D.

Washington, D.C.
June 1959

CONTENTS

CUE TITLES

Boswell	*Boswell's Life of Johnson,* ed. George Birkbeck Hill, rev. and enlarged by L. F. Powell, Oxford, Clarendon Press, 1934–50.
Clifford	James L. Clifford, *Young Sam Johnson,* New York, McGraw-Hill, 1955.
ELH	*English Literary History.*
Gent. Mag.	*Gentleman's Magazine.*
Greene	Donald Johnson Greene, *The Politics of Samuel Johnson,* New Haven, Yale University Press, 1960.
John. Misc.	*Johnsonian Miscellanies,* ed. George Birkbeck Hill, New York, Harper, 1897.
JEGP	*Journal of English and Germanic Philology.*
Letters	*The Letters of Samuel Johnson,* ed. R. W. Chapman, Oxford, Clarendon Press, 1952.
Life	Sir John Hawkins, *The Life of Samuel Johnson, LL.D.* London, J. Buckland, 1787, 2d ed. 1787.
Lysons	Scrapbook of Johnsonian Clippings from Eighteenth-Century Newspapers, compiled by the Reverend Samuel Lysons.
Memoirs	Laetitia-Matilda Hawkins, *Memoirs, Anecdotes, Facts, and Opinions,* London, Longman, 1823.
MLN	*Modern Language Notes.*
MLQ	*Modern Language Quarterly.*

Cue Titles

MP	*Modern Philology.*
NQ	*Notes and Queries.*
Private Papers	James Boswell, *Private Papers from Malahide Castle,* ed. Geoffrey Scott and Frederick A. Pottle, privately printed, 1928–34.
Reade	Aleyn Lyell Reade, *Johnsonian Gleanings,* 11 parts, privately printed, 1909–52.
RES	*Review of English Studies.*
Scholes	Percy A. Scholes, *The Life and Activities of Sir John Hawkins,* London, Oxford University Press, 1953.
TLS	*London Times Literary Supplement.*
Works	*The Works of Samuel Johnson, LL.D., together with His Life, and Notes on His Lives of the Poets,* by Sir John Hawkins, London, J. Buckland, 1787.

Chapter One

THE RIVALS

*Biographers are very busy in preparing Materials for the Life of Dr.
Samuel Johnson. Many, we are told, are the Candidates, but the principal
which are mentioned are Sir John Hawkins, and James Boswell, Esq. his
itinerant Companion through the Highlands of Scotland.*

—St. James's Chronicle, *Dec. 14–16, 1784*

SIR JOHN HAWKINS has had the misfortune to be remembered for
two dubious distinctions. He blundered his way out of the famous
Literary Club by behaving rudely to Edmund Burke.[1] And Dr.
Johnson, with a license he seldom permitted himself, coined a new
word to describe him and left it for the delighted Fanny Burney to
mount in her diary: "Sir John was a most *unclubable* man!"[2] But
if Hawkins had been distinguished in no other way we may be certain that the London booksellers would not have approached him
after Johnson's death with their proposals for the double monument of an edition of Johnson's works and a full-scale account of his
life. Hawkins, in fact, was a man of numerous distinctions. The
booksellers went to him not only because as one of Johnson's executors he had access to Johnson's papers, or because he had already
resolved to write Johnson's life. He had belonged to Johnson's Ivy

1. Boswell, *1, 479–80.*
2. *Diary and Letters of Madame D'Arblay,* ed. Austin Dobson (London, 1904),
1, 59.

I

Lane Club and had been a member of the Literary Club for several years before his unhappy encounter with Burke. He had achieved some reputation as an editor of Walton's *Compleat Angler,*[3] and his lives of Walton and Cotton, prefixed to that work, were competent and popular. His *History of Music,* itself a monument, had established him as one of the foremost musicologists of his day—an amateur whom the professionals had reason to envy—and had proved him capable of intensive research, acute judgment, and sustained eloquence. A man of wide experience and acquaintance, he had been attorney, writer of Vauxhall songs, contributor to three editions of Shakespeare, critic, antiquarian, and collector; and for fifteen of his twenty years as a magistrate he had been Chairman of the Quarter Sessions for the County of Middlesex. Johnson had few friends who had done so much.[4]

So it was that in the dark hours immediately following Johnson's death Thomas Cadell and William Strahan,[5] representing a large number of London booksellers, waited upon Sir John, and in the sitting room of his home in Queen's Square agreed to pay him two hundred pounds for writing Johnson's life and directing their edition of his works.[6] There was good reason for their haste. For Johnson, the "Prince of Biographers," had left many celebrants in his court, and doubtless the booksellers were anxious to discourage competition and to preempt the services of the accomplished knight who had Johnson's papers in his custody. Eager to make public their

3. His edition was to be reprinted for over a hundred years.
4. It is surprising, therefore, to find an anonymous reviewer in *TLS* reprimanding Dr. Scholes for writing a biography of a "nonentity" (*TLS,* Jan. 30, 1953).
5. Thomas Cadell (1742–1802) was one of the most successful London booksellers. William Strahan had printed Johnson's *Dictionary.*
6. *Memoirs,* 1, 155–58. The actual written agreement was not drawn up until Christmas Eve: R. W. Chapman and Allen T. Hazen, "Johnsonian Bibliography: . . . a Supplement to Courtney," *Proceedings of the Oxford Bibliographical Society,* 5 (1939), 164.

agreement with Hawkins, they nevertheless waited until Johnson had been buried in Westminster Abbey on December 20, and then, in the *St. James's Chronicle* of December 21, they announced their project:

> In Justice to the Memory of the late eminent Dr. Samuel Johnson, the Publick are hereby cautioned against giving Credit to any Particulars respecting him, or any Posthumous Works pretending to be his, that may hereafter be published by anonymous Authours or Editors; and further are assured that an authentick Life of him by one of his Executors, and also a complete Edition of his Writings, consisting as well of original Compositions, as of those already in Print, are preparing, and will be published with all convenient Speed.

The official and sneering tone of this announcement could hardly fail to arouse those booksellers who were engaged in just such projects as the public were warned against. One of these, George Kearsley, was at that moment rushing William Cooke's *Life of Johnson* through the press.[7] In the next number of the *St. James's Chronicle* Kearsley argued (not unreasonably) that Johnson's executors had no right to complain of anyone publishing an account of Johnson's life, especially before they had seen it. A disinterested writer, he contended, would more probably be impartial than a person whose pen was guided by "lucrative motive," and he seized the opportunity to inform the public that his impartial biography would be ready for sale on "Monday next," December 27.[8]

The booksellers waited for the new year, and on January 6 inserted in the *London Chronicle* the first of a long series of advertise-

7. Cooke, editor of the *Beauties of Johnson* and of Johnson's poems (1785), had been a member of Johnson's Essex Head Club.
8. The book bears the date Dec. 28 but may have appeared on the 27th, in accordance with Kearsley's promise. It was published anonymously.

ments. The works of Johnson, they assured the public, would shortly be published with a "Life of the Author, collected from a Diary kept by himself, and other documents," and Johnson's editor and biographer would be "Sir JOHN HAWKINS, one of his Executors." While the advertisement said no more than was true, undoubtedly the booksellers would have been pleased to have readers assume that the "Diary, and other documents" would provide Sir John Hawkins with every essential of an authoritative life of Johnson. One reader, however, not only assumed nothing of the kind himself but seemed determined that no one else should make such a false assumption. In the Shakespeare editor George Steevens the booksellers had acquired a formidable adversary. If Steevens was noted for his scholarly attainments, he was at the same time notorious for his malicious delight in the discomfiture of his friends. "The Asp," as he was called, was understandably feared. During the Shakespeare Jubilee of 1768 Garrick had been much distressed by Steevens' harassing notes to the newspapers;[9] and Topham Beauclerk had once advanced the suggestion that a suitable close to Steevens' career would be death by hanging.[10] But if Steevens was harsh to his friends, against his enemies he was relentless. Since 1775, when without authorization he had published an address of Hawkins to the King,[11] he had been Hawkins' inveterate enemy. Tradition, in fact, attributes the disappointing sale of Hawkins' *History of Music* to the severity of Steevens' criticism,[12] and certainly the unsigned letters which he published in the *St. James's Chronicle* in January 1785 indicate, to say the least, an antipathy for Hawkins which must have been festering for years:

9. *Memoirs, 1,* 264–65.
10. Boswell, *3,* 281.
11. Miss Hawkins' account of the Steevens–Hawkins quarrel is in *Memoirs, 1,* 258–72.
12. John Bowyer Nichols, *Illustrations of the Literary History of the Eighteenth Century* (London, 1858), *5,* 428.

We hear that the Diary kept by Dr. Johnson, which is expected to afford such important Assistance to a Compiler of his Life, includes only the last twenty Years of it. His Method of Living, &c, during this Period, is not unknown to Thousands. For an Account of his Transactions throughout the preceding and eventful Term of almost fifty Years, there are said to be no Materials, such excepted as are understood to be in the Possession of Mr. Boswell, or were occasionally communicated by Dr. Johnson to his most intimate Friends, Sir Joshua Reynolds, Mr. Burke, Mr. Langton, Mr. Steevens, Dr. Burney, Mr. Ryland, and a few others.[13]

Had Steevens stopped here, the booksellers might have congratulated themselves on their good fortune. Unluckily it was not in Steevens' nature to stop, and in subsequent issues of the *St. James's Chronicle* he returned to the task of exploding the booksellers' claims. But it was the presumption of the booksellers in coupling Sir John's biography with Johnson's own writings that received his special attention: "The Rambler, &c. cannot be bought without a disgusting Incumbrance. It will resemble the Tax on Mrs. Siddons's Company. The Husband must be endured for the Sake of the Wife."[14] Since the public was "threatened" with several lives of Johnson, it should be permitted to choose for itself, and Steevens was quick to suggest what the choice should be. No member of the Literary Club but Boswell, he wrote, "could be prevailed on to undertake the Task of writing the Doctor's Life. The Publick may now be assured that this Work will be executed by a liberal and successful Pen, instead of being confined to the Hands of Catchpenny

13. *St. James's Chronicle*, Jan. 4–6, 1785. Steevens' authorship is attested in a letter from the printer of the *St. James's Chronicle* (*Private Papers, 16*, 72).
14. Ibid., Jan. 13–15, 1785.

and blasted Authors."[15] Of Boswell's methods Steevens had already noted the most significant details:

> His playful Importunities, and anxious Sollicitations, were alike prevalent with Johnson. If he failed once in an Enquiry, he renewed it at a more lucky Hour, and seldom retired without the Intelligence he sought. . . . Nor [did] his Curiosity [permit] one Circumstance to escape him that might illustrate the Habits, or exalt the Character of the Sage whom he respected almost to Adoration.[16]

To Boswell in Edinburgh such praise of himself and contempt for his rivals must have been heartening indeed. But the anonymous writer's knowledge of his methods was so intimate there was some danger the public would think that Boswell had written the letters himself. Boswell, moreover, was curious to know his admirer's identity. Accordingly, he took the triple opportunity to check idle speculation, to learn the name of the writer, and to advertise himself, and on January 18 sent off a letter which the *St. James's Chronicle* published on the 25th. He assured the public, on his honor, that he had not the least notion who the writer in the *St. James's Chronicle* was, but "his knowledge of the intimacy between Dr. Johnson and me is so particular, that were it not expressed with more elegance than I am master of, I should almost believe that this Essay was written by myself." He then entreated the writer to make himself known, either publicly or privately, and concluded by vowing that since Johnson's death he had not sent and would not send a single article without his signature.[17]

Although Boswell was unable to prod a confession from Steevens himself, the printer of the *St. James's Chronicle* shortly gave him the

15. Ibid., Jan. 15–18.
16. Ibid., Jan. 8–11.
17. Ibid., Jan. 22–25, 1785.

information that he sought. Meanwhile Steevens was preparing further attacks on the booksellers for encumbering their edition of Johnson with the heavy load of Hawkins' biography. "Surely," he argued, "if the Trade have studied their own Interest, and the Respect they owe to the Publick, their threatened Memoir of Johnson will appear as a detached Thing, to be received or rejected at the Discretion of their Customers." And having thrust the sword home, he could not deny himself the luxury of twisting it in the wound: "It is needless to mention Mr. Boswell's Abilities. They are indisputable."[18]

In his final communication Steevens reviewed his previous themes but gave impetus to them by a brisk lunge at Hawkins and by a pretended glimpse into Johnson's own intentions:

> It is evident from the Conduct of the late Dr. Johnson, that he designed Mr. Boswell for the sole Writer of his life. Why else did he furnish him with such Materials for it as were withheld from every other Friend? . . . Little indeed did he suppose that a Person whom he had made one of his Executors would have instantly claimed the Office of his Biographer. Still less could he have imagined that this Self-Appointment would have been precipitately confirmed by the Booksellers.
>
> Dr. Johnson intended the Destruction of all Papers that might afford Assistance to those injudicious and incapable Compilers of Memoirs whom he had but too much Reason to fear. A few scraps of petite Information are, however, said to have escaped his Diligence, and by what Means is not unknown.[19] The Quality of these Trifles is understood. . . . Where and in what

18. Ibid., Jan. 25–27, 1785.
19. In the margin of his scrapbook, Samuel Lysons wrote beside this sentence: "It was said that Sir J. Hawkins one day saw this Diary on Johnson's Table and put it in his pocket privately." Lysons' comment is not dated. For Hawkins' response to this rumor see *Life*, 2d ed., pp. 585–87.

Company our Author dined—how often he forgot the Return of his Birth or Wedding Day—when he began to chew Liquorice for his Cough—or take Opium to secure his Rest —are Particulars without which the World can sleep in Tranquillity. . . .

The Value of Mr. Boswell's Intelligence is unquestionably ascertained. It must be genuine, because received from the Deceased. It must be copious, as it is the Result of Enquiries continued through a Period of more than twenty Years. It must be exact, because committed to Paper as fast as communicated; and cannot fail to convey Instruction, as it will be enriched with a Multitude of original Letters by Dr. Johnson, on a Variety of Subjects.—Let the Opposer of Mr. Boswell prove the Authenticity and Consequence of his Materials in a Manner as satisfactory to the Publick. The Publick may then judge between our rival Biographers, and decide on their respective Claims to Confidence and Support.[20]

It is difficult to believe that Steevens was moved to this series of communications either by his fondness for the memory of Johnson or by his partiality for Boswell. When Boswell's own *Life* was on the verge of publication, Steevens mischievously informed Boswell that the public was no longer curious about Johnson, and by depreciating the book to others he made Boswell fearful of its sale.[21] Steevens, after all, had no reason to think that Hawkins could not write an authentic *Life* of Johnson. He did have reason to think that Boswell could write a better, as his knowledge of Boswell's methods and materials shows. But this knowledge was hardly the occasion for so violent an attack. In short, one is compelled to apply here Boswell's impressive evidence of Steevens' asplike nature, and say that his real motive was to deliver a death blow to an old enemy.

20. *St. James's Chronicle*, Jan. 27–29, 1785.
21. Boswell, *3*, 281, n. 3.

Unquestionably Steevens' attack was harmful to Hawkins. The *St. James's Chronicle* was a popular and respected newspaper, particularly in literary circles. And the Steevens letters do sound authoritative. Steevens' knowledge of Boswell was intimate and accurate; his knowledge of Johnson's Diary must also have appeared intimate and accurate, though eventually the publication of Hawkins' *Life* made it obvious that it was not. The public, however, could not have been aware of that in January 1785. Steevens, moreover, made certain that his strictures on the booksellers' venture received wider distribution by sending to the *London Magazine Improved* a number of the January letters, including Boswell's letter of January 18 and his own final letter to the *St. James's Chronicle*. With Hawkins' fitness as writer and editor thus publicly called into question—and the anonymity of Steevens' letters must have made it look as though Hawkins was under attack from various quarters —it is not surprising to find that the burlesque *Probationary Odes for the Laureateship,* published in June of that year, contained, and advertised on the title page, a mock "Preliminary Discourse by Sir John Hawkins, Knt." The discourse was a skillful parody of the prose style of Hawkins' *History of Music:*

> in volume the first of my quarto history, chap. I. page 7, I lay
> it down as a principle never to be departed from, that "*The
> Lyre is the prototype of the fidicinal species.*" And accordingly I
> have therein discussed at large both the origin, and various im-
> provements of the Lyre, from the tortoise-shell scooped and
> strung by Mercury, on the banks of the Nile, to the Testudo
> exquisitely polished by Terpander, and exhibited to the Aegyp-
> tian Priests.[22]

22. *Probationary Odes for the Laureateship: with a Preliminary Discourse, by Sir John Hawkins, Knt.,* 3d ed. London, Ridgway, 1785, p. vi. The preliminary discourse is best known for the epitaph with which it concludes:
> Here lies Sir John Hawkins,
> Without his shoes or stockings! (p. xv).

The *Probationary Odes* proved an extremely popular book. By 1787, the year in which Hawkins' *Life* was published, it had gone through eight editions.[23]

In addition to these attacks, Hawkins had to run a gauntlet of criticism in the weeks following Johnson's death, though much of it may never have come to his attention. As most active of the executors, he was blamed for withholding the full cathedral service at Johnson's funeral.[24] Dr. Burney was told that Hawkins had slandered Johnson.[25] Sir Joshua Reynolds was offended that, when acting as executor, Hawkins had charged his coach hire to Johnson's estate.[26] He was said to have illegally claimed for himself Johnson's watch and cane.[27] It was rumored that he had improperly removed one of the diaries from Johnson's apartment.[28] Many years later Edmond Malone was told that Hawkins had kept for himself

23. Many people, of course, would not have been affected one way or the other by Steevens' attack. Some, in fact, if we may consider the following poem representative, must have wondered what Steevens was shouting about:

> What a Pother is here about who's the best Claim
> To writing the Life of that *harmless Drudge* Sam!
> Rehearsing dull Scenes of so vapid a Part,
> Were to chronicle Beer of three Farthings a Quart.
> The Life of an Authour, in Garret or Cloyster,
> Is just like the Life of a Colchester Oyster.
> . . .
> (*St. James's Chronicle*, Feb. 24–26, 1785)

24. Thomas Twining, *Recreations and Studies of a Country Clergyman of the Eighteenth Century* (London, 1882), p. 129.

25. Ibid., pp. 129–30.

26. Sir James Prior, *Life of Edmond Malone* (London, 1860), p. 426.

27. Ibid.

28. Lysons, fol. 11r. *The Correspondence of Thomas Percy and Edmond Malone*, ed. Arthur Tillotson (Baton Rouge, 1944), p. 21. Malone's account of Johnson's Diary is curiously like Steevens' (p. 8): "It contains only an account of where he dined, what company he met, the state of his health, and such matters."

all of Johnson's books in which Johnson had made notations.[29] Under so many clouds of reproach was Hawkins' work begun. If men were unkind to Hawkins, fate was no more propitious. On Wednesday, February 23, 1785—hardly more than two months after Johnson's death—Hawkins' house in Queen's Square burned to the ground.[30] "Scarcely any article was saved," said the *London Chronicle* on February 26, and according to the *St. James's Chronicle* the house was plundered of many valuables during the fire, and Hawkins himself—the ex-Chairman of the Quarter Sessions for the County of Middlesex—was robbed of a gold watch and seals.[31]

The fire must have given the booksellers some uneasy moments. If scarcely anything was saved, what were the chances for Johnson's Diary and the other documents which had figured so largely in their advertisements? Anxiously Cadell must have looked to Hawkins, and before the *London Chronicle* could report a rumor that "several of Doctor Johnson's manuscripts were destroyed by the fire,"[32] the statement that Cadell desired was probably in his hands:

> Sir John Hawkins presents his compliments to Mr. Cadell with many thanks for his enquiries: he and his family are as well as he can expect: he has saved a box containing Dr. Johnson's papers and manuscripts all that is already written of the life is preserved and there is no want of materials for fulfilling Mr. Cadell's engagement to the public.
>
> Sir John recommends the advertising this information to the

29. James M. Osborn, *John Dryden: Some Biographical Facts and Problems* (New York, 1940), p. 267. The rumor heard by Malone may not, of course, have arisen until some time after Johnson's death. See also below, p. 38, n. 2.
30. *London Chronicle*, Feb. 22–24, 1785.
31. *St. James's Chronicle*, Feb. 24–26, 1785.
32. *London Chronicle*, Feb. 26–March 1, 1785.

public but that Mr. Cadell should do it in a better form than this note contains.[33]

Saturday[34]

As Hawkins recommended, the information was advertised to the public in a form better (though not notably better) than the note contains.[35] Meanwhile, for Hawkins, there was nothing to do but pick up what was left him and set to work again. Evicted by the fire, he removed with his family and his manuscripts to a house in Broad Sanctuary, Westminster, where he seems to have found at last the peace which the first two and a half months of his labors did not afford him. There was no further interruption. By October 1786 the *Life* was virtually completed; by December 8 of that year it was printed, and Hawkins was writing to his friend Bishop Percy that the eleven volumes of the *Life* and *Works* would be published early in the spring.[36] On the twelfth of February 1787 Hawkins

33. From the original in the Pierpont Morgan Library. One could wish that Hawkins had been a trifle more explicit in this apparently hurried note, for it is not without ambiguity. Hawkins might well have saved "a box containing Dr. Johnson's papers and manuscripts" and at the same time lost another box containing additional papers and manuscripts, or lost some papers which had been removed from the box to a place which a fire as sudden and swift as this one might have made inaccessible. When one considers that Hawkins' *Life* records documents and Diary entries the originals of which have never been traced, and that Hawkins' daughter had probably made copies of the Diaries so that the originals were no longer needed (*Memoirs, 1,* 188), the possibility that some of Johnson's manuscripts were lost in the fire should not be overlooked.

34. This is the only indication of the date, but the newspaper accounts make clear that February 26 is the only Saturday on which the letter could have been written.

35. *London Chronicle,* March 3–5, 1785. The information was advertised in at least five other newspapers.

36. Hawkins' letters describing his progress have been reprinted in Scholes, pp. 241–46.

presented the first set of the eleven volumes to the King,[37] and in March the books were made available to the public.[38]

37. *London Chronicle,* Feb. 10–13, 1787.
38. The first advertisements of the set did not appear until March 20, but it seems likely that the books were placed on sale earlier in the month. See, for example, p. 15. The *Life,* it should be noted, could be purchased separately from Johnson's *Works,* although the *Works* could not be purchased without the *Life,* which occupied Vol. 1.

Chapter Two

"HERE LIES SIR JOHN HAWKINS"

Your poor Trifler [Mr. Fush] has more than trifled away his life. He ended it by arsenick, somewhere in your town, about a week ago. But that is almost better than Sir John Hawkins. Boswell, and Co. will torture the poor Knight, half an inch at a time, to literary death. I would not be the Knight even for his coach and horses, which he seems to prize so much.

—*Sir Herbert Croft to John Nichols, March 11, 1787*[1]

ON JANUARY 9, 1787, the *Morning Chronicle*, in a short note, questioned whether the "numerous Johnsoniana" which had lately come from the press would not deprive the biographies of Hawkins and Boswell of the praise and attention they deserve, "if composed with ability." "Whenever Johnson is mentioned, the general exclamation is—Something too much of this!"[2] But there is no reason to think that the numerous Johnsoniana had glutted the public's appetite for Johnson or that it had any appreciable effect upon the reception of Hawkins' *Life*. Fortunately there is a measure by which we may judge not only the interest in Johnson but the initial success of

1. Nichols, *Illustrations*, 5, 213.
2. Possibly this was prompted by an article the day before in an unidentified newspaper (Lysons, fol. 11r): "Sir John Hawkins' *pondros* life of Johnson is now shortly to make its appearance. It is said to be extremely digressive, not unlike his History of Music, and to form memoirs not only of Johnson's life, but of Dr. Birch, and several of his cotemporaries; Boswell, and Mrs. Piozzi, are also preparing his life and letters, which we hope will conc[l]ude the long procession of dulness which has followed the *exit* of the unfortunate doctor."

Hawkins as well. When on March 13 the *St. James's Chronicle* published a letter from a correspondent who called himself "A Selector," it set in motion a process made possible in the eighteenth century by copyright laws which seem to us today incredibly lax.[3] The correspondent wrote:

> I am at present reading Sir John Hawkins's Life of Dr. Johnson, just published; and as I have been much pleased with the numerous Anecdotes contained in it of Dr. Johnson, of a great many other literary People, and among the rest, of the Editor himself, I here send you one of these *petites Pieces,* for the Entertainment of your Readers.
>
> Among the Heroes who figure in this multifarious Production, is the late celebrated Lord Chesterfield, from the Account of whom I have extracted the following Particulars. . . .
>
> If Mr. Baldwin, by the Insertion of the above, signifies his Concurrence in my Scheme, another Packet from me, in a Day or two, will, I hope, convince him that I am not dilatory in executing the Office of A SELECTOR

Mr. Baldwin, of course, concurred in the scheme and published the "Particulars" of Chesterfield along with the rest of the letter. Accordingly, "A Selector," by no means dilatory, had another packet ready containing Hawkins' account of Francis Barber in time for the very next issue of the paper. From then on, packets followed regularly. Five more were printed in March, to be followed quickly by four in April. How long "A Selector" might have continued no one can tell. But after the fourth April packet the paper printed a

---

3. Johnson,thought them lax too. The copyright laws in force in 1787 had been adopted in 1709, when there were so few magazines that no restrictions had been placed on them, and they were practically free to borrow at will. See Frederick T. Wood, "Pirate Printing in the Eighteenth Century," *NQ* (Nov. 20, 1930), pp. 381–84; (Dec. 6), pp. 400–3.

burlesque entitled "A Story in Sir John's Way,"[4] and whether or not "A Selector" was disheartened by the paper's sudden reversal of its treatment of Hawkins, he sent in a last packet (with the account of Johnson's death) which was printed in the issue for April 19. It was not his design, he confessed in this last communication, to turn reviewer; and he added, perhaps with more hope than trust, that the reviews would certainly "take Cognizance of Sir John and duly point out both his Merits and his Faults."[5]

Before the *St. James's Chronicle* had finished printing the extracts provided by "A Selector," the *London Chronicle* began printing a series of extracts of its own selection.[6] But it was in the magazines for March (published about the first of April) that Hawkins could have found his greatest satisfaction—assuming that there was a satisfaction in seeing his book plundered. To be sure, he might not have been pleased to see the *Political Magazine* reprint the account of Sir John Hill or the exchange of notes between Johnson and Andrew Millar without the formality of acknowledgment. But when (all with due acknowledgment) his strictures on Fielding and the anecdote of Sir Thomas Robinson were reprinted in the *County Magazine;* the account of Dr. Mead was reprinted in the *European Magazine;* the story of Birch's circuit of London and the history of taverns were reprinted in both the *County* and the *European Magazine;* the account of Goldsmith was reprinted in the *Universal Magazine;* and the memoirs of Samuel Dyer were reprinted in the *European Magazine,* the *Scots Magazine,* and the *Universal Magazine*—the flattery of such attention may well have seemed to Hawkins almost payment enough for the labors of more than two years. The *Universal Magazine,* moreover, proved nearly as warm a partisan as "A Se-

4. See below, p. 26, n. 31.
5. "A Selector's" contributions appeared in the *St. James's Chronicle* from March 13 to April 19.
6. Selections appeared in the *London Chronicle* from March 22 to April 14.

lector." In introducing what he called the "Instructive Memoirs of Mr. Samuel Dyer," the editor wrote: "In the life of the Late Dr. Johnson, just published by Sir John Hawkins, we find many curious and interesting Particulars of other Persons, who were happy in the Intimacy of that celebrated Writer. Among these, are Memoirs of Mr. Samuel Dyer. . . . These Memoirs are not merely amusing; they afford the most important Lessons in the Conduct of human Life."[7] In April the *Universal Magazine* further indicated its fondness for Hawkins by initiating a series of extracts from the *Life* which, in effect, constituted a brief biography of Johnson. The series was continued through six monthly issues and the midyear supplement.[8]

April, in fact—except for the reviews—was almost as successful a month for Hawkins' *Life* as March had been. It is true the *Political Magazine* offended again by reprinting the account of Goldsmith without acknowledgment, and in Dublin the *Hibernian Magazine* failed to acknowledge the exchange of letters between Johnson and Millar (which it had probably pillaged from the *Political Magazine* for March). The *Hibernian Magazine,* however, did acknowledge the anecdote of Dr. Mead, and the *Political Magazine* made amends by initiating a three-months' series much like that in the *Universal Magazine.* The *Gentleman's Magazine,* with much grumbling about what it considered Hawkins' uncharitable treatment of its founder, reprinted the accounts of Edward Cave and some of his associates on the magazine, while the *County Magazine* found the account of

7. *Universal Magazine* (March 1787), p. 141.
8. The editor's remarks introducing this series are notable for their judgment as to the relative merits of Boswell's *Tour* (1785), Mrs. Piozzi's *Anecdotes* (1786), and Hawkins' *Life:* "To the copious Memoirs of Dr. Johnson, in our Magazine for August 1784, we have since added . . . various Anecdotes of him . . . communicated by . . . Mr. Boswell and Mrs. Piozzi. . . . Sir John Hawkins . . . has just published the Life of his deceased Friend, in which as might be expected, we meet with many Particulars, both of the Doctor and others, no less interesting than those we have already selected."

Goldsmith to its liking. The *Scots Magazine* did not reprint anything from Hawkins in April, but went back to him in May for Birch's circuit of London and the account of the last two weeks of Johnson's life. In May the *Universal Magazine* and the *Political Magazine* were publishing the second installments of their series, and the *Hibernian Magazine,* as might have been expected, was reprinting unacknowledged what the *Political Magazine* had reprinted unacknowledged the month before. In the middle of the month the *Dublin Chronicle* featured a series which it called the "LIFE OF DOCTOR SAMUEL JOHNSON, *By Sir John Hawkins,*" but neglected to advise its readers that it was merely reprinting a review by Arthur Murphy in the *Monthly Review.*

After May, naturally enough, not much was extracted from the *Life,* although the series in the *Political Magazine* continued through June and that in the *Universal Magazine* through September. In July the *New Town and Country Magazine* went to the second edition of the *Life,* published in June, for Hawkins' account of how he pocketed two of Johnson's diaries; and the *Lady's Magazine,* with a nicer consideration of its readers than of Hawkins, reprinted without acknowledgment the tragic story of the heroine of Johnson's play *Irene.* In August the *Hibernian Magazine* did a little more rifling, and at the end of the year the *Town and Country Magazine* reprinted the history of taverns in its supplement.

Hawkins' *Life,* of course, was not the only book to be favored by the 1787 periodicals. Pugh's *Memoirs of the Life of the Late Jonas Hanway* and Gilpin's *Observations on the Mountains and Lakes of Cumberland and Westmorland* found their way into a number of magazines and one or two newspapers, though not into nearly so many as opened their pages to Hawkins. In fact, no book in 1787 can be said to have captured the public interest to the extent that Hawkins' *Life* did. It is everywhere—in the reviews, the magazines, and the newspapers; in the conversation at club meetings; in the letters that people wrote to their friends; in the diaries that they wrote to themselves. It is true that not all of the comment was flattering. But when periodical after periodical filled out its pages with extracts from the *Life,* it would be a great mistake to think that most of the public were not highly pleased with the display.

Hawkins' success is further attested by the need for a second edition within three months of the publication of the first. The success, however, was not enduring; nor was it entirely unqualified. The "Story in Sir John's Way" took some of the luster from the shining treatment accorded Hawkins by the *St. James's Chronicle,* while at the end of March the *Gentleman's Magazine* entered a number of complaints. In addition, there were probably numerous strictures which never came to Hawkins' attention, as in this letter written on March 23 from the Reverend Robert Potter to Edward Jerningham:

> I have not seen Gilpin's account of the Cumberland lakes. . . . But I have seen what surely no man ever wished to see, Sir John Hawkins' "Life of Johnson." How I hate a dull, cold, fastidious friend, who writes with the blackest water of Styx, held in an ass's hoof! I wonder they do not make a Bishop of this fellow. Poor Johnson! Under the idea of praise, how is his honest fame degraded by the injudicious and injurious accounts given of him by his friends![9]

Attacks like these were probably not very harmful; Hawkins' initial success remains a notable one, and we can hardly begrudge him whatever measure of pride he took in it. The real change came with the first days of May, when the April issues of the *Monthly Review* and the *English Review* made their appearance, and when a

9. *Edward Jerningham and His Friends: A Series of Eighteenth Century Letters,* ed. Lewis Bettany (London, Chatto and Windus, 1919), p. 358. Jerningham was a well-known wit, one of whose poems Hawkins mistakenly attributed to Johnson.

correspondent known as Philo Johnson breathed the first of two
fiery articles in the *European Magazine*.[10] From then on, London
was scarcely a habitable place for Hawkins.

> Thee, Johnson, both dead and alive we may note
> In the fam'd Biographical Line,
> When living the Life of a SAVAGE you wrote,
> Now many a Savage writes thine.

So quipped George Colman the Elder in the inevitable capitals
of the *St. James's Chronicle*.[11] Colman's poem epitomizes the attitude
of most of the reviewers toward Hawkins, whom, in the words of
Philo Johnson, they charged with perpetrating a libel on Johnson's
memory. This was only one of a number of charges, but it was one
of the most common and perhaps the most serious. The reviewer
for the *Critical Review* recorded no isolated complaint when he
wrote that Hawkins not only brought "Johnson's failings into open
day-light" but even magnified them. Such a man, the writer commented, could have felt "no sincere regard for his friend, or retained no respect for his memory."[12] In the *Monthly Review* the
dramatist Arthur Murphy wondered, if Johnson could arise and
read Hawkins' account, just where Sir John would "hide himself
from the indignation of an injured friend."[13] Even the reviewer in
the *English Review*, who did not share the general reverence for
Johnson, was moved to confess that if "St. Samuel" treated his
disciples "with arrogance and contempt while he was alive, they
have taken full vengeance on his ashes."[14]

10. The first review in the *Gentleman's Magazine* was published in the March
issue, but since it was largely concerned with pointing out Hawkins' indebtedness to the *Gentleman's Magazine*, I have not considered it among the
other reviews.
11. For June 12–14, 1787.
12. *Critical Review* (May 1787), p. 345.
13. *Monthly Review* (July 1787), p. 57.
14. *English Review* (April 1787), p. 259.

For a number of the reviewers such an approach to Hawkins permitted them not only to vent their righteous indignation but also to assume the coveted role of guardian of Johnson's fame. They fell to their task with a will. At least one, however, was not satisfied to object, as did the reviewer in the *European Magazine*,[15] that Hawkins held forth "as a public spectacle every caprice and human infirmity of a moral and respectable character,"[16] for this was to admit Johnson's frailty and let Hawkins off lightly at the same time. Since Hawkins had represented Johnson as a "vile compound of every vice that degrades humanity," wrote Philo Johnson, it was now the duty "of every man who honoured and respected the dead . . . of every man of genius and learning in the kingdom, to rescue his character from the unhallowed touch of his present historian, nor suffer the mangled carcase of his reputation to be thus hung in chains to all posterity."[17]

The flood of such eloquent invective could not easily be stopped. Hawkins' malevolence was given no quarter. But what angered Philo Johnson most was that Hawkins, having no courage to attack the living, made only the dead his victims, "contrary to every received principle that living authors are the objects of detraction, and that the dead are safe from their situation. . . . [T]he great solid principle that secures its [the *Life's*] condemnation, is the spirit of malevolence to the dead, which breathes all through it. Sir John

15. It must be remembered that, in addition to the two communications from Philo Johnson, the *European Magazine* published a regular review, and I distinguish the writers by referring to one as the reviewer and the other as Philo Johnson. Philo Johnson's articles, however, together constitute a review, so that I have considered them among the regular reviews.

16. *European Magazine* (May 1787), p. 319. The *European Magazine* reviewer was essentially in agreement with the reviewer for the *Critical Review* (see the preceding page). Like most of the reviewers, however, he was able to present his views in a distinctive way: "M. de Saxe says, that no man appears a hero to his valet; but certainly M. de Saxe would not have wished that his valet should write his life; though now—But we add not" (May, p. 319).

17. Ibid. (April 1787), p. 224.

Hawkins, with all the humanity and very little of the dexterity of a Clare-Market butcher, has raised his blunt axe to deface the image of his friend."[18]

The denunciation of Hawkins' attitude led inevitably to specific charges of inaccuracy, for frequently, said the reviewers, Hawkins was inaccurate because of his want of sympathy for Johnson. The *European Magazine's* reviewer defended Johnson from Hawkins' remarks on the anti-Walpole bias of the poem *London*, and he and Philo Johnson both took exception to Hawkins' comment that if Johnson's affection for his wife was not dissembled it was a thing that he had learned by rote. Arthur Murphy upheld the Essex Head Club against Hawkins' rancorous brand of a "six-penny ale club," and Hawkins' censure of authors who write for money elicited from the *Critical Review* the wry comment that Hawkins was himself receiving a consideration for "mutilating the Life of Johnson, and for misarranging his works."[19]

The reviewers then turned to the simpler errors of fact, or what they considered errors of fact. The *European Magazine's* reviewer corrected Hawkins' assertion that *Lexiphanes* was written by Kenrick, and Arthur Murphy (perhaps wrongly) insisted that Bonnell Thornton, rather than Richard Bathurst, was Hawkesworth's collaborator in the *Adventurer*.[20] Murphy noted, too, that the exchange

18. Ibid. (May 1787), p. 313. No one, obviously, would accuse Philo Johnson of raising a blunt axe against Hawkins. He handled his rapier with a courtier's precision, so that even the normally stoical Hawkins could hardly have kept from wincing. Indeed, the pseudonym Philo Johnson was not as appropriate as another would have been. For it was not so much love of Johnson that impelled this unknown writer as it was hatred of Hawkins. His animosity leaps out at almost every line. For this reason primarily, but also for the abilities displayed throughout the two articles, I think it a reasonable guess that Philo Johnson was Hawkins' persistent enemy, George Steevens.

19. *Critical Review* (June 1787), pp. 417–18.

20. The question of whether Thornton or Bathurst helped with the *Adventurer* remains unanswered. See L. F. Powell, "Johnson's Part in the *Adventurer*," *RES* (Oct. 1927), pp. 420–29.

between Johnson and Andrew Millar after Johnson had completed the *Dictionary* ("I am glad that he [Millar] thanks GOD for any thing") was an oral and not a written one, as Hawkins had said. A few other errors, some of them dates, were singled out. But in general, in their search for inaccuracies the reviewers fell back on the distortions which they attributed to Hawkins' lack of charity and perspicacity.

The charges against Hawkins of malevolence and inaccuracy were of particular interest to James Boswell, who in the spring of 1787 was in London, where he read the reviews in the company of Edmond Malone.[21] In May, Boswell inserted an advertisement in the newspapers intended not only to remind the public of his own efforts but no doubt to lend support to the reviewers, who, in repudiating Hawkins' *Life* were committing an act very dear to Boswell's heart.[22] His own *Life of Johnson,* he assured the public, was "in great forwardness," but had been delayed pending the publication of various promised works on Johnson, from which he had expected to obtain much information "in addition to the large store of materials which he had already accumulated." Although disappointed in that expectation,

21. *Private Papers, 17,* 27, 34.
22. At the King's Levee on Friday, May 11, 1787, Boswell was asked by the King how his writing progressed. BOSWELL. "Pretty well, Sir." KING. "When will you be done?" BOSWELL. "It will be some time yet. I have a good deal to do to correct Sir John Hawkins." KING. "I believe he has made many mistakes." BOSWELL. "A great many, Sir, and very injurious to my good friend." KING. "I do not believe Dr. Johnson was so fond of low company in the latter part of his life as Sir John Hawkins represents (describes, or some such word)" (*Private Papers, 17,* 29). At the Literary Club on Nov. 27, 1787, "Malone suggested an admirable thought, which was to have a solemn Protest drawn up and signed by Dr. Johnson's friends, to go down to Posterity, declaring that Hawkins's was a false and injurious Account." The suggestion was generally approved, but Sir Joshua Reynolds hesitated. "I resolved," wrote Boswell, "it should not sleep" (*Private Papers, 17,* 57).

he does not regret the deliberation with which he has proceeded, as very few circumstances relative to the History of Dr. Johnson's private *Life,* Writings, or Conversation, have been told with that authentic precision which alone can render biography valuable. To correct these erroneous accounts will be one of his principal objects; and, on reviewing his materials, he is happy to find that he has documents in his possession which will enable him to do justice to the character of his illustrious friend. He trusts that, in the mean time, the Public will not permit unfavourable impressions to be made on their minds, whether by the light effusions of carelessness and pique,[23] or the ponderous labours of solemn inaccuracy and dark uncharitable conjecture.[24]

But the reviewers were not to stop at Hawkins' inaccuracy and want of charity. They were quick to perceive that many of his 600 pages were devoted not to Johnson but to his friends, his works, and the customs and institutions of his day. In short, the book was swelled to such a size with its digressions that no reviewer could ignore them. The reviewer for the *New Annual Register* complained that it was "no easy task to separate the parts which properly belong to the hero of the story."[25] The *County Magazine's* reviewer concluded that the "many digressions relating to persons and things" would be as "*a propos* in any other life as in that of Dr. Johnson."[26] Nevertheless, he was ready to excuse the digressions (even though he found them the worst part of the book) by saying resignedly, "this is Sir John's way of writing." To some of the other reviewers,

23. The "light effusions" were Mrs. Piozzi's *Anecdotes,* just as the "ponderous labours" were Hawkins' *Life.*
24. *London Chronicle,* May 19–22, 1787; *St. James's Chronicle,* May 12–15, 1787; also at least one other newspaper (Lysons, fol. 23v).
25. *New Annual Register for the Year 1787* (London, 1788), p. 254.
26. *County Magazine* (March 1787), p. 234.

however, Sir John's way was synonymous with the absurd, and they refused to resign themselves to it. "In this bulky volume," complained the writer for the *Critical Review,* "we often lose Dr. Johnson. . . . The knight sinks under the weight of his subject, and is glad to escape to scenes more congenial to his disposition, and more suitable to his talents, the garrulity of a literary old man."[27] To this reviewer the digressions were nothing more than "idle gossippings." The *European Magazine's* reviewer pretended to find an error on the title page: "To the Life of SAMUEL JOHNSON ought to have been added, and *all his acquaintances;* for what properly relates to Johnson would hardly make a sixpenny pamphlet."[28] And Arthur Murphy went so far as to extract (with comments) the events of Johnson's life to compile a narrative which filled two articles of the *Monthly Review,* while in a third he proposed to "present the opinions, maxims, and reflections of Sir John Hawkins, together with his lives and anecdotes of other men, and all his miscellaneous matter, under the title of an Appendix to THE LIFE OF DOCTOR SAMUEL JOHNSON."[29]

The newspapers joined in the fun. "Idle gossippings" stirred the imagination of one periodical writer. Another found a prototype of Hawkins in the pedantic windbag Ned Poppy of the *Guardian.* A third solemnly reported that Hawkins was at work collecting anecdotes for the life of a popular criminal, Gentleman Harry.[30] But of course, if what the critics went on to say of Hawkins' style was true, he would hardly even have qualified as Gentleman Harry's biographer. Philo Johnson and the reviewer for the *Critical Review* compiled imposing lists of Hawkins' inelegancies. Few critics could restrain their laughter at Hawkins' praise of Johnson's own style for

27. *Critical Review* (June 1787), p. 417.
28. *European Magazine* (May 1787), p. 320.
29. *Monthly Review* (April 1787), pp. 274–75.
30. Lysons, fols. 59v, 60r, 60v.

its "immaculate purity" and "turgid eloquence." Parodies of Hawkins' style became common. The "Story in Sir John's Way" moved insipidly through one irrelevancy after another.[31] The writer for the *Critical Review* began his review with a mock series of *whereof's* and *wherein before's*.[32] And Arthur Murphy made an amusing attempt to account for Hawkins' style:

> Sir John most probably acquired his notions of language at his master's desk: he admired the phraseology of deeds and parchments, *whereof*, to speak in his own manner, he read so much, that in consequence *thereof*, he has been chiefly conversant *therein*; and by the help of the parchments *aforesaid*, missed the elegance *abovementioned*, and uses words, that *in them* we sometimes meet with, and being bred an attorney, he caught the language of the *said* trade, *whereof* he retains so much, that he is now rendered an incompetent critic *thereby*, and in consequence *thereof*.[33]

Though Hawkins' style was universally deplored, an occasional reviewer commended some of his criticism of the works of Johnson and others. There was some support, for example, for his indictment of Henry Fielding's "virtue without principle," and the *European Magazine's* reviewer praised his remarks on Johnson's poetic faculties, though not without the suggestion that Hawkins had cribbed

31. *St. James's Chronicle*, April 14–17, 1787. It was reprinted in *An Asylum for Fugitive Pieces*, 2d ed. Vol. 3, London, 1795, from which the opening lines of the parody are quoted: "I left Johnson in the evening. He had been very pleasant; there was nobody with us but *myself* and *him*; it was about seven o'clock when I parted from him, for I looked up at St. Dunstan's clock. It is a pity that these beautiful figures which strike the hours, should be defaced as they are."

32. *Critical Review* (May 1787), p. 340.

33. *Monthly Review* (July 1787), p. 70.

them from the *European Magazine* itself (for there was a recurrent suspicion that Hawkins had borrowed freely from other writers).[34] On the whole, however, the reviewers had too much to do pointing out his other imperfections to spare much time for his criticism. No doubt, if they had been asked, they would have agreed with Arthur Murphy, who remarked that Hawkins seemed to have no idea of the beauty resulting from a regular chain of causes and effects. "He thinks a play, like the life of an eminent man, may be written without order or connection." But it was hardly to be expected, he continued, that a person whose reading had been confined to "old homilies and the statute-book, should have a true relish for the beauties of composition." A ridiculous antiquarian, Hawkins would never be satisfied until his contemporaries wrote in the manner of a century and a half before.[35]

Reviews continued to appear until the first of October, but long before then the reviewers had exacted full justice on the "assassin of Johnson's memory."[36] Almost without exception he was indicted as malevolent and inaccurate. Absurdly digressive, he was incompetent both as stylist and critic, and his want of originality rendered suspect even those few parts of his book which rose above the poverty of the rest. The reviewers were thorough indeed; every approach was covered, and so infectious was their wit that a large segment of the public was quickly enrolled in their support.

Thus the one voice which spoke out in Hawkins' behalf was largely ineffectual. Did anyone ever imagine, asked Dr. George

34. A correspondent of *Gent. Mag.*, for example, accused him of taking the account of Zachariah Williams from the *London Magazine* (*Gent. Mag.*, supplement to 1787, p. 1157). See below, p. 54, n. 48.
35. *Monthly Review* (July 1787), p. 68.
36. As the *European Magazine's* reviewer styled Hawkins (Sept.), p. 200.

Horne,[37] that Johnson's was "a perfect character? Alas, no: we all know how that matter stands, if we ever look into our own hearts." "On the whole," he concluded, "In the memoirs of [Johnson] that have been published, there are so many witty sayings, and so many wise ones, by which the world, if it so please, may be at once entertained and improved, that I do not regret their publication." The reader was to adopt the good and reject the evil.

Dr. Horne's article rallied no forces. Hawkins, with a wisdom born, perhaps, of his long association with Johnson, would take no part in his own defense.[38] And instead of rushing to Hawkins' aid, many of the periodicals which had reprinted sections of the *Life* were now busily engaged in turning the general hilarity to account. It is not true, asserted the *St. James's Chronicle* on the second of June, "that Mrs. Hobart had an Intention of reading Sir John Hawkins' Book. The late Hours at which People of Rank go to bed, renders it wholly unnecessary to force a Sleep in publick Places." A writer for an unidentified newspaper reported that "A gentleman, lately arrived in town, has been for several days past afflicted with a *lethargy*, owing to the perusal of three chapters in Hawkins' *Life of Johnson*."[39] Another writer offered a practical suggestion for putting to use the famous willow tree planted at Lichfield by Johnson: "The branches only should be lopped off, and tied in bundles . . . and properly applied to the naked backs of his various biographers,

---

37. *Olla Podrida*, No. 13, Saturday, June 9, 1787. Horne (the Dean of Canterbury Cathedral) was, of course, defending all the memoirs of Johnson, but coming as it did in the midst of the furor over Hawkins' *Life* and just a few days after the publication of Hawkins' second edition, Horne's essay could hardly have been either written or read without Hawkins predominantly in mind.

38. *Life*, pp. 346–48.

39. Lysons, fol. 6ov. Since the *Life* is not divided into chapters, perhaps this writer had not seen the book.

taking care, that the largest bundle be appropriated unto the use and behoof of Sir John Hawkins, Knight."[40]

Such facetious sallies must have been good summer reading in 1787, and all in all they were harmless enough. Certainly Hawkins would have had reason to be pleased if the reviews had inspired nothing more ambitious or malignant. But that was not to be. When on the first of September the *Gentleman's Magazine* published the first installment of Richard Porson's three-part "Panegyric Epistle" on Hawkins' *Life,* it eliminated any hope which Hawkins may have had of finishing out a tumultuous year in peace. For the epistle, published under a pseudonym, not only reiterated the themes of the reviewers; it set the whole town laughing by ironically praising all the faults which the reviewers had singled out. "Have you read that divine book, the 'Life of Samuel Johnson, LL.D. by Sir John Hawkins, Knt.?' " Porson queried. For his part, he owned, he could not rest till he had read it quite through, "notes, digressions, index, and all," and now, in his sixteenth perusal, he was still discovering new beauties.[41] There was, for example, the great art with which Hawkins had inserted in the *Life* the substance of the other ten volumes of Johnson's works: "I cannot but laugh when I think what simpletons the booksellers are to sell the Life separately from the Works. Do they expect that any body will buy, at a great price, in ten volumes, what he may have so much cheaper in one?"[42] There were the strong proofs of Hawkins' learning: "we are informed, to our unspeakable comfort, that to *appose* means to *put questions;* and this is cleared up beyond a doubt by seven lines from Ingulphus."[43] There was the niceness of Hawkins' honor, for "he never borrows from an author without acknowledging the obligation. Witness

40. Ibid., fol. 90v.
41. *Gent. Mag.* (Aug. 1787), p. 652.
42. Ibid., p. 653.
43. Ibid.

Mr. Boswell, Mrs. Piozzi, the Gentleman's and European Maga-zines," and of course Joe Miller.[44] To crown all, there was Hawkins' style: *"the language is refined to a degree of immaculate purity, and displays the whole force of turgid eloquence."*[45]

With a solemn pledge, the panegyric closed: "I do hereby assure his Worship, that when any other friends of his die, whether he be disposed *to carve them as a dish fit for the gods, or hew them like a carcase for the hounds,* I shall be ready to exert my utmost powers in his behalf, against all his enemies open or secret."[46] And with one last cut at Hawkins' style, Porson appended to the third article, as he had to the first two, the pseudonym "Sundry Whereof."

After the severe but deft humor of the "Panegyric Epistle," the water closet scurrility of *More Last Words of Dr. Johnson,*[47] published in November, was anticlimactic at best. At its worst it was disgust-ing.[48] In any event, it wrote an ignoble *finis* to a year of Hawkins' life which began in hope and ended in ridicule and disenchantment. If by the end of the year the verdict against Hawkins was not unani-mous, it must have been nearly so. Had critics, wits, and much of their public been peering over the shoulder of Lady Eleanor Butler on February 9 of the next year, they could only have cried "Amen!" to an epitaph she etched into her diary: "Sir John Hawkins' life of Johnson. Wretched performance."[49]

---

44. Ibid. (Oct.), p. 847.
45. Ibid. (Aug.), p. 652.
46. Ibid. (Oct.), p. 849.
47. *More Last Words of Dr. Johnson . . . To which are added, Several singular and unaccountable Facts relative to his* BIOGRAPHICAL EXECUTOR, *formerly Chair-man of the Quarter-Sessions,* London, 1787. The title page gave for the author's name, "Francis, Barber."
48. *Gent. Mag.* said of it, quoting Deborah's opinion of the newly dis-covered foundling in *Tom Jones,* "Faugh! how it stinks! It does not smell like a Christian" (Nov., p. 996).
49. *The Hamwood Papers of the Ladies of Llangollen and Caroline Hamilton,* ed. Mrs. G. H. Bell (London, Macmillan), 1930.

Such agreement among Hawkins' critics is impressive. But reviews, with rare exceptions, are quickly forgotten. Even a satire as
trenchant as Porson's wanted the stuff for survival. It remained for
Boswell, in 1791, to give permanence to the charges against Hawkins, and his remarks in the introductory pages of his *Life* have
become the classic indictment:

> Since my work was announced, several Lives and Memoirs
> of Dr. Johnson have been published, the most voluminous of
> which is one compiled for the booksellers of London, by Sir
> John Hawkins, Knight, a man, whom, during my long inti-
> macy with Dr. Johnson, I never saw in his company, I think
> but once, and I am sure not above twice. Johnson might have
> esteemed him for his decent, religious demeanour, and his
> knowledge of books and literary history; but from the rigid
> formality of his manners, it is evident that they never could
> have lived together with companionable ease and familiarity;
> nor had Sir John Hawkins that nice perception which was
> necessary to mark the finer and less obvious parts of Johnson's
> character. His being appointed one of his executors, gave him
> an opportunity of taking possession of such fragments of a
> diary and other papers as were left; of which, before delivering
> them up to the residuary legatee, whose property they were, he
> endeavoured to extract the substance. In this he has not been
> very successful, as I have found upon a perusal of those papers,
> which have been since transferred to me. Sir John Hawkins's
> ponderous labours, I must acknowledge, exhibit a *farrago*, of
> which a considerable portion is not devoid of entertainment to
> the lovers of literary gossipping; but besides its being swelled
> out with long unnecessary extracts from various works, (even
> one of several leaves from Osborne's Harleian Catalogue, and
> those not compiled by Johnson, but by Oldys,) a very small

part of it relates to the person who is the subject of the book; and, in that, there is such an inaccuracy in the statement of facts, as in so solemn an authour is hardly excusable, and certainly makes his narrative very unsatisfactory. But what is still worse, there is throughout the whole of it a dark uncharitable cast, by which the most unfavourable construction is put upon almost every circumstance in the character and conduct of my illustrious friend; who, I trust, will, by a true and fair delineation, be vindicated both from the injurious misrepresentations of this authour, and from the slighter aspersions of a lady who once lived in great intimacy with him.[50]

It is difficult, if not presumptuous, to dispute an authority of Boswell's magnitude, especially when his testimony is only one, though the most brilliant, of a numerous galaxy. Since the publication of Hawkins' *Life,* much more than a century has passed—"the term commonly fixed as the test of literary merit"[51]—and Hawkins can hardly be said to have survived the test. The *Life* has not been reprinted since June of its first year, and there has been no clamor for its reprinting;[52] indeed, it is little known outside the circle of Johnsonians and other eighteenth-century scholars, who have tapped it frequently for out-of-the-way information. Time, in other words, would seem to have borne out Boswell's opinion. Thus anyone rising to Hawkins' defense must be foolhardy enough to challenge two opponents not accustomed to being beaten. Before he begins

50. Boswell, *1,* 26–28.
51. *Works, 9,* 241.
52. Hawkins' recent biographer, in fact, sees no reason for it to be reprinted. I am informed by Mr. Robert Hillyer, however, that in 1927 Arthur Machen wrote him of a projected edition of the *Life* which, for some reason, was abandoned. It should be mentioned here also that since the above was written the Macmillan Company has announced that it will publish an abridgment of the *Life.*

his task, however, he must give reason to believe that Boswell and the settled opinion of a century and a half may be mistaken.

The paradox of Hawkins' extraordinary career, Bertrand Bronson has written, is that in the last twenty-five years of his life—years of unusual achievement—"he was hounded by sneers and disparagement in almost everything he did."[53] The explanation of this paradox, I believe, may be found in the facts of Hawkins' career which I have cited in this and the opening chapter. When Hawkins and Steevens became enemies in 1775, a barrier was erected which Hawkins had always to surmount in order to achieve a modicum of success in his ventures. No doubt Steevens alone[54] could not have spoiled the sale, in 1776, of the *History of Music*. Hawkins would have been much better advised to issue his five sumptuous volumes one by one, rather than all together at a price that few could afford. But a carping and influential critic like Steevens may well have given pause to those who did have money to buy. No doubt Steevens in 1785 and 1787 could not alone have turned Hawkins and his biography into the jests of people everywhere. For this he needed help, and he found it because of another important fact of Hawkins' career. The prime mistake of Hawkins' life was doubtless the withdrawal from the Literary Club which he forced upon himself by his rudeness to Edmund Burke. The man who could not relish his membership in such a society was indeed unclubbable; Johnson's judgment was acute. But from that moment on, Hawkins had to beware the antipathy of members of the Club, particularly (after 1784) in matters where the sorely lamented Johnson was concerned. It is obvious that what Johnson's friends looked for in his biography was a monument, a cenotaph. The reviewers objected, it will be recalled, that Hawkins had revealed not only Johnson's virtues but his weaknesses as well, and they sprang in anger upon the man who

53. *MLN* (Nov. 1954), p. 522 (from a review of Scholes).
54. If indeed Steevens did attack the *History of Music*.

could so unfeelingly dissect their idol. Club members long before, of course, had taken sides. They sided, as was natural, with their own, and to James Boswell one after another—Sir Joshua Reynolds, Bishop Percy, Bennet Langton, Edmond Malone—turned over his memorabilia of Johnson and left Hawkins to rummage where he might. Club members thus were committed to a standard of taste in biography somewhat different from Hawkins' and to a biographer alien to him, and on the whole the reviewers were committed to them too. George Steevens, who probably wrote the articles signed "Philo Johnson,"[55] was a member of the Literary Club. Arthur Murphy was a member of the Essex Head Club, founded in 1783, and was intimate with much of the Johnson circle. The reviewers for the *Critical Review* and the *European Magazine* may also have been members of one club or the other, for their articles coincide at so many points with those of Murphy and Steevens that it is tempting to believe that the four men discussed their ideas together.[56]

This is not to accuse the Literary Club of conspiring against Hawkins. Boswell's difficulty in steering its members to a condemnation of the *Life* makes clear enough that so many independent minds could not easily be made to act as one.[57] Nor is it to impugn the motives of all those who saw so much in the *Life* to denounce. Doubtless their motives varied. A number of members were honestly concerned for Johnson's memory. Who can doubt that Steevens was burning to renew an old battle? Arthur Murphy was a wit, and there was no resisting the temptation the *Life* held out to him. Edmond Malone was Boswell's strongest partisan. But commitments to a rival biographer and to a specific standard of taste hardly

55. See above, p. 22, n. 18.

56. The *European Magazine's* reviewer, it should be noted, had been "acquainted with Johnson the last sixteen years of his life, and was often in his company" (July, p. 21).

57. See above, p. 23, n. 22.

permitted the critics to approach the *Life* with the clear vision of detachment. The book was as good as condemned before it left the presses. Hawkins has sat in judgment on wits and critics, said the reviewer for the *English Review*, and wits and critics will sit in judgment on him.[58] It is exactly what happened: as often as not the criticism was directed not against the book but against the man. Unclubbable, antiquarian, puritanical, dignified Sir John Hawkins —here was a morsel for a critic.

A morsel for a rival biographer, too. As I have said, the first attacks against Hawkins have all but been forgotten. It is Boswell who is today the standard authority on Hawkins' *Life,* whose measurement of his rival, not only in the passage already quoted[59] but in scores of places throughout his *Life,* is almost universally respected. It must be set down as one of the strangest of ironies that we should shape our opinion of Hawkins in the mould of Boswell's contumely. For Boswell could not look upon Hawkins with an eye unjaundiced. It was not only that Hawkins had referred to him as "Mr. James Boswell, a native of Scotland,"[60] though such slighting recognition rankled: "Hawky is no doubt very malevolent," Boswell wrote to his friend Temple. "Observe how he talks of me as if quite unknown."[61] To keep his readers posted on the inadequacy of the biographies which had preceded his was to boast of his own achievement and to set himself up, like the reviewers earlier, as the guardian of Johnson's fame. Unquestionably it was to Boswell's interest to make a shambles of Hawkins' *Life,* and in 1791 he could assail his rival with impunity, for the reviewers had long since

58. *English Review* (April 1787), p. 269.
59. See above, pp. 31–32.
60. *Life,* p. 472. One or two writers have pointed up Hawkins' neglect of Boswell by remarking that this sole allusion is contained in a footnote. Actually it is part of the text.
61. *The Letters of James Boswell,* ed. Chauncey Brewster Tinker (Oxford, Clarendon Press, 1924), *1,* 361.

satisfied the public that Hawkins' *Life* was absurd. That Boswell had good reason to consider his own work superior to Hawkins' none but a madman would venture to deny. His pride in his vast assemblage of Johnson's conversation and letters, however, was a blind which shut out the virtues of Hawkins' efforts, and he yielded to the impulse to win praise for himself by turning to ridicule the best that had gone before.

In his own day Boswell had the last word, and he is having it still. Today the somewhat scarce Hawkins' *Life* is a book to be laughed at rather than read. It is ironic that it should be so, and not just because we have been taught to laugh by a man who looked at Hawkins through the cataract of prejudice. Sir John Hawkins was Johnson's familiar associate at least fourteen years before the celebrated meeting of Boswell and Johnson in Tom Davies' back parlor. In 1784 he was one of Johnson's executors. Thus his acquaintance with Johnson spanned more than a third of a century, from Johnson's early struggles with poverty to the final struggles with conscience, sickness, and death.[62] Let us cherish our great men, said Carlyle. But we can hardly do so if we do not cherish the books in which they are preserved. Hawkins' *Life* is a first-hand account of the man who so impressed himself upon his age that Johnson and his times, for many, have become inseparable. We do not discard the Opie portrait of Johnson, or Reynolds' earliest portraits, because Reynolds lived to paint a better. It is time we brought Hawkins down from the shelf where he has been gathering dust these many years.

62. Hawkins' knowledge of the younger Johnson, in fact, has made him indispensable to those recent narratives of Johnson's early years, Aleyn Lyell Reade's *Johnsonian Gleanings* and James L. Clifford's *Young Sam Johnson*.

Chapter Three

PLAGIARISM AND INDEPENDENCE

Of Sir John Hawkins's long promised edition of Dr. Johnson's life and works, this at least gives us a favourable opinion, that it is not laid hastily before the publick eye to satisfy mere temporary curiosity. Sir John does not seem anxious to present the world with a mass of undigested materials.

—from an unidentified newspaper (Lysons, fol. 78v)

IF WE WERE TO JUDGE from the frequency with which the magazines borrowed from Hawkins without acknowledgment, we might very easily conclude that the people of the eighteenth century, if they did not actually condone piracy, were at least indifferent to it. On the contrary, they found the practice abundantly reprehensible, while at the same time they admired those publications which rose with sturdy independence above such palpable marauding. For Hawkins, writing in the wake of innumerable Johnsoniana, the opportunities to plagiarize were many, and we have seen that he was accused of lifting material from Boswell, Mrs. Piozzi, Joe Miller, and the *European, London,* and *Gentleman's* magazines. An attempt to clear him of this charge must claim priority; for though today we will not especially admire his independence, if we do not clear him we can hardly admire him in anything else. Such an attempt, moreover, affords a useful opportunity to assess the materials which went into the *Life.*

It should already be evident that much of Hawkins' book could not have been taken from printed sources. The assiduous attention of the booksellers to Johnson's Diary was not just a trick to catch the public. Such a trick would have had its reward when the *Life* was published. The Diary, of course, was not an exhaustive day-by-day account, like Pepys' diary or Boswell's journals, for Johnson was not so conscientious a diarist. Its entries were scattered and brief. Nevertheless, there is no denying its usefulness. With its help, for example, Hawkins could set the time of Johnson's early visit to Birmingham or recount authentically the unfortunate incident of Market Bosworth school. He had, in other words, an absolutely reliable index to numerous points in Johnson's career, and for that reason the Diary must be given a central place among his materials.[1] Certainly the booksellers were right to publicize it.

The Diary, moreover, was not the only one of Johnson's records that Hawkins had in his possession. The "Adversaria," folio volumes in which Johnson jotted notes for a number of his essays, effectually illustrated his method of composition. Invaluable to a biographer were a catalogue of Johnson's projected works, Johnson's plan of instruction for his school at Edial, a copy in Johnson's hand of the famous letter to Lord Thurlow, Johnson's diplomas, his corrected copy of *London,* and "a variety of notes and memorandums concerning [Mrs. Johnson] in books that she was accustomed to read in."[2] Two most important treasures were the original contract for the *Dictionary* and an account of Johnson's youth submitted to

---

1. Actually "Diaries" would be more accurate than "Diary." As Hawkins tells us, Johnson's *Annales* was "a variety of little books folded and stitched together by himself" (*Life,* p. 163). Of only one series of these records did Hawkins make no use. This was the section known as "Aegri Ephemeris," in which Johnson noted the "progress of his diseases" beginning about July 1784 (*Life,* p. 577).

2. *Life,* p. 89. Possibly Hawkins' possession of these books gave rise to the rumor, later heard by Malone, that Hawkins had kept for himself all of Johnson's books in which Johnson had made notations.

Johnson by his boyhood friend Edmund Hector. Finally, Hawkins had papers indicating that Johnson retained an interest in the copyright of the *Rambler* for a short time after its publication;[3] a copy of Madden's poem on Archbishop Boulter, with a note showing that Madden had given Johnson ten guineas for his help with the poem; an account of Dr. Levett "in a letter from a person in the country to Johnson";[4] and Johnson's translation from Sallust of *De Bello Catilinario* "so flatly and insipidly rendered, that the suffering it to appear would have been an indelible disgrace to his memory."[5]

These records, though not magnificent, were undeniably wealth. Hawkins, however, had an exceptionally valuable supplement to them. His own recollections of Johnson reached back at least a third of a century to 1749, when he joined with Johnson and eight others in "a club that met weekly at the King's head, a famous beef-steak house, in Ivy lane near St. Paul's."[6] With no specific confirmation by Hawkins of an earlier meeting with Johnson, it is impossible to state categorically that the two men were already known to each other when they joined together in the Ivy Lane Club. But there is abundant evidence to suggest that their acquaintance had begun earlier, perhaps at the very beginning of the decade. Such evidence must be examined. For to set Hawkins' first acquaintance with Johnson only a few years earlier is to stamp with authority the fullest account extant of a little-known epoch in Johnson's life.

It must be remembered that the Ivy Lane was Johnson's club, that he himself had formed it "to soothe his mind and palliate the fatigue of his labours" on the *Dictionary;* in short, to indulge himself in that "great delight of his life," conversation.[7] It was not to

---

3. *Life,* p. 326. Malone insisted that Johnson never sold his interest. See below, Appendix C, p. 189.

4. *Life,* pp. 396–97.

5. *Life,* 2d ed., p. 541. The translation is now in the Hyde Collection.

6. *Life,* p. 219.

7. Ibid.

be expected that Johnson, whose acquaintance was perhaps as wide as any man's in London, would have chosen his clubmates among strangers. This was not his way with later clubs. Satisfying his desire for conversation required a company of articulate and well-informed men, and it is only natural to assume that Hawkins, who then was little known, had already proved himself to Johnson. But when and how had he done it?

Two people as different as Hawkins and Johnson—one of them attorney, poetaster, and amateur musician, the other poet, biographer, journalist, critic, and lexicographer—could have met frequently throughout the decade of the forties on the common ground of the *Gentleman's Magazine.* Johnson's first contribution was in 1737, Hawkins' in 1739; and although Hawkins was never professionally affiliated with the magazine, he returned to it at intervals sufficient to establish a claim as amateur man of letters. In a letter written December 16, 1740, Edward Cave praised Hawkins' "dissertations" already published and solicited further contributions,[8] though the only contribution of that year ascribable with any confidence to Hawkins is an enigma published in August and signed with the initials "J.H."[9] Possibly, as L. F. Powell suggests,[10] the "dissertations" were Hawkins' first publications, the 1739 essays on honesty. In 1744 the magazine published Hawkins' eulogy of his friend Foster Webb and in 1748 his lengthy essay on Otway's tragedy *The Orphan.* In 1749 he was on good enough terms with Edward Cave to be consulted on the manner of inserting William

8. Scholes, p. 266.
9. In the *Life* (p. 48 n.) Hawkins explained that Foster Webb gave up writing enigmas after one of his was ridiculed by another *Gentleman's Magazine* correspondent. Hawkins was careful not to mention, however, that Webb's enigma was an interpretation of the August contribution with the very revealing signature "J.H." Hawkins seems to have given up writing them after that time also.
10. Scholes, p. 266.

Collins' "Song for Shakespeare's *Cymbeline*," though he was unable to win acceptance for his very sound advice.[11]

This is sporadic activity, to be sure, but it continued throughout the decade, and it was recognized favorably by the magazine's proprietor. The list of Hawkins' contributions, moreover, might well be augmented if one could see through the many disguises of pseudonyms and initials which make the magazine often such a puzzle.[12] But what is more striking than Hawkins' activity during this period is his profound knowledge of the magazine's contributors and policies.[13] Indeed, his recollections and comments are a vital contribution to our knowledge of a crucial period in English journalism, and their very intimacy suggests that Hawkins could hardly have been unaware of Johnson, whose pen, for a number of these years, was the magazine's chief support.

That Hawkins *was* deeply impressed by Johnson early in the decade seems apparent in his vivid description of Johnson's method of composing the Parliamentary Debates. Johnson's practice, says Hawkins, "was to shut himself up in a room assigned him at St. John's Gate, to which he would not suffer any one to approach, except the compositor or Cave's boy for matter, which, as fast as he composed it, he tumbled out at the door."[14] Johnson's speed of

---

11. *Life*, pp. 48–49. Cave published the poem in Oct. 1749, without reference to its context and with the substitution of the name "Pastora" for Collins' "Fidele." It should be added here that according to Scholes a number of lyrics composed by Hawkins and set to music by the blind organist John Stanley were published in the magazine at various times throughout the forties (Scholes, p. 233). My own search of the magazine, however, has not turned up either the music or the lyrics, which were published in 1742 as *Six Cantatas for a Voice and Instruments*, with a second series following three or four years later under the same title.

12. Hawkins' essay on *The Orphan* is signed "N.S." His eulogy of Foster Webb is not signed at all.

13. Hawkins' account of the contributors to the magazine alone fills a note which occupies the greater part of four pages (*Life*, pp. 46–49 n.).

14. *Life*, p. 99.

composition was phenomenal: "He was wont to furnish . . . three columns of the debates in an hour, written, as myself can attest, in a character that almost any one might read."[15] One can readily imagine the scene at St. John's Gate when Cave, the end of the month approaching, was urging his publication through the press: Cave amidst a group of his correspondents anxiously awaiting the messenger from Johnson's door; the boy suddenly bursting in, the ink drying as he waves the sheet in front of him; finally Johnson, the fit of creation thrown off, heaving his door wide and emerging like a giant from his castle. "As myself can attest"—perhaps Hawkins had been present at just such a scene as this. Certainly he was not likely to catch a glimpse of Johnson's manuscripts at any other time. Even if Cave had retained them after the Debates were published (and there is no evidence that he did), Hawkins, in those early days, would hardly have been interested in the manuscripts of Debates which were readily accessible to him in the *Gentleman's Magazine*. Later on, of course, the manuscripts would have been of very real interest to him. But later on they would have been of interest to another antiquarian, John Nichols, whose position in 1784 as proprietor of the *Gentleman's Magazine* would surely have led him to them if they were to be found among Cave's effects at St. John's Gate. When one considers the mountains of papers that a manuscript-saving habit in Cave would have accumulated for him in just a few years, one cannot help wondering if Cave, like most other editors, did not rid himself of the manuscripts once they were printed in the magazine. If he did, Johnson's manuscripts would not have survived beyond March of 1744, when his last Debates were published.

By early 1744, then, Hawkins would seem to have been attracted to Johnson. But perhaps the date of first acquaintance may be pushed

15. *Life*, p. 381 n.

back further still. In fact, Hawkins' hints, tantalizingly indecisive
though they are, point to an acquaintance very early in the decade.
Intensely interesting to Hawkins was Johnson's remarkable political
conversion—that change whereby, in a short time, Johnson became
reconciled to the Walpole and Pelham policies which in 1739 he
had denounced with all his energies:

> At the time when 'Faction Detected' came out, a pamphlet of
> which the late lord Egmont is now generally understood to
> have been the author, Osborne the bookseller, held out to him
> a strong temptation to answer it, which he refused, being con-
> vinced, as he assured me, that the charge contained in it was
> made good, and that the argument grounded thereon was un-
> answerable.[16]

Faction Detected was published in 1743, the year in which Hawkins
was most likely to receive the assurance he mentions from Johnson.[17] A pro-ministerial pamphlet, it was intended to convince
readers that the objections of the opposition were unreasonable and
factious. Hawkins, of course, does not suggest that Johnson required
a pamphlet of this sort to shake his anti-ministerial convictions.
Johnson, it must be remembered, had been composing the Debates
for the *Gentleman's Magazine* since July of 1741, and if he had remained the explosive anti-ministerial writer that he was in 1739,
the Debates would have been composed with a bias not unlike that
of the *Marmor Norfolciense*. Doubtless Johnson's convictions had
been gradually changing,[18] so that by July of 1741 Johnson, writing
for a magazine that asserted its impartiality, could look upon the

---

16. *Life*, p. 85.

17. The furor aroused by this pamphlet is reflected in the Weekly Essays
reprinted in *Gent. Mag.* for Oct. 1743.

18. There is no evidence, says Donald Greene, who has made the definitive
study of Johnson's politics, that after May of 1739 Johnson wrote anything
derogatory of Walpole (Greene, p. 134).

ministry with some detachment. What remained of his old prejudices led him to partake "of the short-lived joy that infatuated the
public" when Walpole finally resigned in February of 1742; but a
"few weeks, nay, a few days" dispelled the few remaining prejudices,[19] and Johnson thereafter was firm in Walpole's praise.[20]

With the help of this background, one more of Hawkins' statements should bring us to our conclusion. Describing Johnson's
antipathy to the ministry, he remarks,

> in the heat of his resentment, I have heard him assert, that,
> since the death of Queen Anne, it had been the policy of the
> administration to promote to ecclesiastical dignities none but
> the most worthless and undeserving men: nor would he then
> exclude from this bigotted censure those illustrious divines,
> Wake, Gibson, Sherlock, Butler, Herring, Pearce, and least of
> all Hoadly.[21]

Johnson's resentment, we have just seen, had certainly cooled by
1742, and it was not likely to have been heated any later than 1740
or, at the outside, the early part of 1741.[22] Hawkins, in fact, may
have been referring to 1739, for his discussion of Johnson's resentment is part of his criticism of the two political satires of that year,
the *Marmor Norfolciense* and the *Compleat Vindication of the Licensers
of the Stage*.[23] In any event, if Hawkins himself heard Johnson make

19. *Life*, p. 506.
20. *Life*, p. 514.
21. *Life*, p. 80.
22. No doubt Johnson could still (in almost the same breath) denounce
George II, and praise Charles II for his preferments in the church (Boswell,
2, 341–42). But George II was the executive, not the administration specified
by Hawkins. Boswell, it should be noted, verifies Johnson's change of heart
by saying that he came to think of Walpole as a "fixed star" (Boswell, 1, 131).
23. Perhaps it is significant that every one of the divines mentioned by
Hawkins was elevated to a bishopric before 1739, with the single exception
of Zachary Pearce, who, in 1739, was made Dean of Winchester with the
sumptuous living of £600 a year.

this assertion "in the heat of his resentment," there is every reason to believe that he had made Johnson's acquaintance by the beginning of 1741. "Johnson," said Miss Hawkins, "belongs to every period of my father's life."[24] Miss Hawkins is not always a reliable witness, but we need not quarrel with her here. The Johnson who later cherished the friendship of the "young dogs" like Boswell, Langton, and Beauclerk must have warmed in those early days to the young admirers, like Hawkins, who gathered at St. John's Gate and helped make the *Gentleman's Magazine* one of the most successful ventures of its kind.

Hawkins' personal knowledge of Johnson at this time lends his book a particular distinction. For Hawkins had the opportunity to observe Johnson at one of the most interesting periods of his career. Having failed in his last attempt to find security as a schoolmaster, Johnson had returned to London resolved, once and for all, to make the best of a skillful pen. It was, in effect, another beginning of his career, and of all Johnson's surviving literary friends, Hawkins is the only one who seems to have observed that career almost from the day of Johnson's return.

It is obvious, then, that Hawkins had much to contribute to his book from his own experience. An acquaintanceship of some forty years had ripened (Boswell's sneer notwithstanding)[25] into a real intimacy. Hawkins had been a charter member of Johnson's two most famous clubs, and Johnson, who loved old friends, thought well enough of the earlier club to revive it when it could sweeten his dying months. Mrs. Thrale noticed that Johnson, as with Garrick, would attack Hawkins himself but would never permit anyone else to do so,[26] and Frances Reynolds, present at a chance meet-

24. *Memoirs, 1, 85.*
25. See above, p. 31.
26. *Diary and Letters of Madame D'Arblay, 1, 58.*

ing of Johnson and Hawkins, observed with pleasure how fond of Hawkins Johnson was.[27] Finally, Hawkins' *Life* documents how frequently in his last months Johnson turned to his old friend for comfort and advice.[28]

To Johnson's papers and his own recollections, Hawkins added what he could glean from those friends of Johnson who were willing to help him. He may have had, for example, a letter from Dr. Adams, Master of Pembroke College and a fellow there at the time of Johnson's matriculation.[29] Nevertheless, there were inevitable gaps to be filled, and Hawkins naturally went to the stream of Johnsoniana that had flowed from the press after Johnson's death— to Cooke's *Life of Johnson;* William Shaw's *Memoirs of the Life and Writings of the Late Dr. Samuel Johnson;* Boswell's *Tour to the Hebrides;* Mrs. Piozzi's *Anecdotes;* and all the anecdotes and miscellaneous information of the periodicals, particularly the *Gentleman's Magazine,* the *European Magazine,* and the *St. James's Chronicle.* Most useful of all, however, were two brief works written almost immediately after Johnson's death: Thomas Tyers' *Biographical Sketch of Dr. Samuel*

27. *John. Misc.*, 2, 297–98: "As we were returning from the meadows that day, I remember we met Sir John Hawkins, whom Dr. Johnson seemed much rejoiced to see; and no wonder, for I have often heard him speak of Sir John in terms expressive of great esteem and much cordiality of friendship."

28. On Nov. 7, for example, Johnson wrote to Hawkins from Lichfield: "I am relapsing into the dropsy very fast, and make such haste to town that it will be useless to write to me; but when I come, let me have the benefit of your advice, and the consolation of your company" (*Life,* p. 575).

29. On July 12, 1786, Dr. Adams wrote to Boswell concerning (in part) Johnson's projected edition of Politian; "meeting with no great encouragement," Adams commented, "he dropped the Design." The wording in Hawkins' *Life* suggests that Hawkins had received a similar letter from Adams: "not meeting with sufficient encouragement, Johnson dropped the design" (*Life,* p. 27). Adams' letter to Boswell, now among the Boswell Papers, is in Waingrow ("Five Correspondences of James Boswell Relating to the Composition of the Life of Johnson," unpublished doctoral dissertation, Yale University, 1951), p. 62. John Taylor also furnished a few anecdotes.

Johnson,[30] and the *European Magazine's* anonymous "Account of the Writings of Dr. Samuel Johnson."[31] Tyers' sketch, though written in the most casual manner imaginable, evinces a lightness of touch and warmth of admiration which make it a delight to read, and it is by no means as inaccurate as often is thought. Tyers himself had known Johnson a good many years, and the indefatigable John Nichols seems to have kept him supplied with whatever scraps of Johnsoniana made their way into the office of the *Gentleman's Magazine.* The account in the *European Magazine*—which complements Tyers', since it is almost wholly concerned with Johnson's writings—is the most scholarly of these early works about Johnson, and it has been unduly neglected.[32] In fact, its scholarly precision, its intimate knowledge of Johnson, particularly of his *Shakespeare,* its vivid and easy style, and its praise of Boswell in the manner of the January letters to the *St. James's Chronicle,* make it difficult to avoid the conclusion that its author was the eminent George Steevens. One wonders if Hawkins, when he made use of this account and of various anecdotes contributed by Steevens to the periodicals, could have suspected that he was running up a debt to the man he had every reason to detest.

Hawkins helped himself to a number of things in these two works, lifting some of them bodily and adapting others to suit himself. His unfortunate printing of the oral exchange between Johnson and

30. This was first published in *Gent. Mag.* for Dec. 1784. Additions and corrections were published in subsequent months, and in 1785 the corrected sketch was published separately. It has been reprinted recently by the Augustan Reprint Society.

31. This was published in installments from Dec. 1784 to April 1785.

32. Even so distinguished a Johnsonian as R. W. Chapman seems to have overlooked it in compiling his monumental edition of Johnson's letters. Had he not done so he could more accurately have dated Johnson's letter No. 28 and identified the pamphlet of Sir Walter Raleigh which Johnson, in that letter, was requesting Dr. Birch to publish for the benefit of a blind friend. See also below, p. 111, n. 42.

Andrew Millar as an exchange of letters elicited from Boswell the just remark that to "have deliberately written notes on such terms would have been morose."[33] Hawkins' statement—"Johnson said that Chesterfield's accomplishments were only those of a dancing-master"—is perhaps an adaptation of Johnson's remark, as recorded by Tyers, that Chesterfield's "instructions to his son inculcated the manners of a dancing-master, and the morals of a prostitute"; if it is, Hawkins must stand accused of applying to the man what Johnson intended only for the letters.[34] Johnson's declaration, recorded by Tyers, that he "never saw the human face divine," was repeated by Hawkins, as was Tyers' own comment—"He was all his life preparing himself for death"—which found an appropriate setting in one of Hawkins' most perceptive and eloquent passages.[35] Tyers was the first to note that Johnson used to call the publisher Dodsley his patron, and that he wrote the *Life of Savage* in thirty-six hours, and the *Vision of Theodore* and the preface to *The Preceptor* each in one night—all facts repeated by Hawkins. From Tyers, Hawkins probably obtained two of his stories: one of Johnson's discovery, when he had completed the *Dictionary,* that the balance of the account with the booksellers was against him; and the other of Johnson's revealing his authorship of the Debates when a man at Gray's Inn boasted that by the style alone he could assign every speech to its speaker.

Hawkins' debt to the account in the *European Magazine,* though easily as great, was of a different kind. While it seems to have provided him with Garrick's poem on the *Dictionary* and with the extract from Fielding's *Champion* in praise of the *Life of Savage,* it

33. Tyers, p. 21; *Life,* p. 341; Boswell, *1,* 287, n. 2.
34. Hawkins, of course, may have had this remark from Johnson himself. Tyers' sketch, at any rate, was not the only possible source, for the remark was printed in *Gent. Mag.* as early as Aug. 1774 (p. 349). Probably it was one of those *bons mots* repeated in numerous companies.
35. *Life,* pp. 589–90.

provided something far more important—a ready guide to Johnson's works. Not only did it detail the year and month of publication
of the major works, but it also gave the first recognition to many of
Johnson's minor works.

In the *Life,* Hawkins said not a word of either of these accounts.
For some things from the *Gentleman's Magazine* he acknowledged
his indebtedness, but for others (whole letters and anecdotes, for
example) he had no word of thanks. Thus the question remains:
what was Hawkins' attitude toward this kind of lifting?

Probably it was much the same as Johnson's. Johnson, to mention
only one instance, found in either the *Universal Magazine* for August
1775 or the *Gentleman's Magazine* for September 1775 (since it
appeared in both), an account of Alexander Pope's personal habits
which he incorporated, without acknowledgment, into his *Life of
Pope.* It forms, in fact, one of the most interesting parts of that life.
Why should the magazine have had exclusive rights to the information? The law did not protect it, and when the magazine proffered
information about a figure of such abiding interest as Pope, it
could hardly expect that that information would not immediately
become part of the public domain. We see something of that attitude in the remarks with which Hawkins prefaced his own account
of physicians:

> [Johnson thought that] a very curious book might be written
> on the fortune of physicians. Such a book I should be glad to
> see; and if any person hereafter shall be induced to pursue
> Johnson's hint, he may possibly think the following remarks
> which have occurred to me in the course of a long intimacy
> with some of the most eminent of the profession, not altogether
> beneath his notice.[36]

36. *Life,* p. 236.

Had someone found the remarks "not altogether beneath his notice," there is no reason to believe that Hawkins would have expected the courtesy of an acknowledgment. The information was simply placed at the disposal of anyone who might find use for it. In similar fashion there was a growing pool of information about Johnson fed by the various streams of the newspapers and magazines, and while the pool increased in size and importance its origins were so rapidly obscured that they were often indeterminable.[37]

Borrowing from books was very different, not only because they were protected by copyright laws but because, to Johnson's biographers at least, working independently of the other biographers was a matter of pride. Later we shall see Boswell going to great lengths to avoid having to use material from Hawkins' *Life,* and no doubt Hawkins would have preferred the public to think that he was not indebted to his rivals. Nevertheless, there were riches that a conscientious biographer could not deny himself. In Cooke's *Life* there were the story (apocryphal, as Hawkins had to explain in his second edition) of the Russian translation of the *Rambler* and the anecdotes of the Shakespearean exchange between the dying Johnson and Dr. Brocklesby and of the seventy-pound annuity for Francis Barber, which Johnson delightedly styled *nobilissimus.* Cooke also furnished the texts of Johnson's letter to Edmund Allen written in the first moments of consciousness following an apoplectic stroke, and of various papers in the affair of Dr. Dodd.[38] In Shaw's *Memoirs* there was an account of Johnson's marriage which must have helped convince Hawkins that his own interpretation of that clouded period of Johnson's life was correct.

37. Modern writers, of course, are often happy enough to escape the tedium of careful documentation. In general, few but scholars document their sources conscientiously, and occasionally even they, as in Reade's "Final Narrative" of Johnson's early life, permit an introductory notice of indebtedness to suffice.

38. Cooke's *Life* also contained a useful catalogue of Johnson's works, though it was not as thorough a guide as that in the *European Magazine.*

Hawkins' attitude toward Cooke and Shaw was probably much the same as his attitude toward the writers for the periodicals. In any event, he could not have looked upon them as serious rivals in Johnsonian biography; large type, wide margins, and generous spacing permitted their memorials to pass as books but did not conceal the pamphlets which in fact they were. Boswell and Mrs. Piozzi were the rivals to be watched, and Hawkins would not have helped himself to any of their material unless he felt reasonably certain he could answer the inevitable charges of plagiarism.

Most of the charges he could answer well enough. The only thing in his *Life* which Hawkins unquestionably took from Boswell's *Tour* was the "Meditation on a Pudding,"[39] and here it is easy to see what his reasoning must have been. Even though it was delivered extemporaneously and recorded by Boswell rather than by Johnson, the "Meditation" was one of Johnson's own works. It is not beyond belief that Johnson, at some other time, repeated this parody in Hawkins' presence; at any rate, since it was one of Johnson's works, Hawkins would hardly have been willing to admit Boswell's exclusive title to it. To Mrs. Piozzi's *Anecdotes* the debt is not much greater. Perhaps he would not have identified the parson in Hogarth's *Midnight Modern Conversation* as Johnson's cousin Cornelius Ford if Mrs. Piozzi had not made the same identification. (At Hawkins' suggestion, John Nichols in the second edition of his *Anecdotes of Hogarth*, published in 1782, had rejected Ford and substituted the name of Orator Henley.)[40] Hawkins' statement that some of the characters in the *Rambler* were mistaken for living people may well have been prompted by Mrs. Piozzi.[41] And there seems no doubt that Hawkins' account of Johnson's regard for Molly Aston (though

39. *Life*, pp. 388–89; Boswell, 5, 352.
40. *Life*, p. 3 n.; *John. Misc.*, 1, 154; [John Nichols], *Biographical Anecdotes of William Hogarth* (2d ed. London, J. Nichols, 1782), pp. 172–73.
41. *Life*, pp. 381–82; *John. Misc.*, 1, 305.

it has been carefully revised) was taken from the *Anecdotes,* since both accounts mention Mrs. Johnson, and both print Johnson's Latin distich to Miss Aston.[42] Doubtless Hawkins considered the distich (again, one of Johnson's works) sufficient warrant for making use of the anecdote.[43]

Hawkins compiled his accounts of Johnson's contemporaries in much the same way as he compiled his narrative of Johnson. For many of these he drew upon his own recollections, but occasionally, having discovered a printed account which pleased him and suited his purposes, he inserted it in its entirety. Such was his account of Dr. Levett: "An account of him is given in the Gentleman's Magazine for February 1785. [It] is anonymous; I nevertheless insert it verbatim."[44] Hawkins' chief source for these accounts, however, was the 1784 edition of the *New and General Biographical Dictionary,* one of the richest of biographical treasure chests, and no doubt a favorite work of Hawkins. He used it in several ways. First of all, he took one account from it without change in wording, omitting only its final part: "Dr. Hawkesworth is a character well known in the literary world: I shall not attempt a delineation of it, as I find in the biographic dictionary an article for him in the words following . . ."[45] Next, Hawkins abridged two of the *Dictionary's* accounts, those of Nicholas Amhurst and Samuel Boyse: "[The Life] of Savage presents itself to view in the works of Johnson: those of the other

42. *Life,* p. 316 n.; *John. Misc., 1,* 255.

43. While Hawkins' and Mrs. Piozzi's accounts of Johnson's feat of strength on the stage at Lichfield are similar, certain details in Hawkins' not to be found in Mrs. Piozzi's suggest that each had the story from David Garrick separately (*Life,* p. 439 n.; *John. Misc., 1,* 224).

44. *Life,* pp. 396–97. George Steevens keeps insinuating himself into the book he attacked so viciously. Years later—in 1858—John Bowyer Nichols showed that the account of Levett had been written by Steevens (*Illustrations of the Literary History of the Eighteenth Century, 8,* 641).

45. *Life,* p. 220.

two [Amhurst and Boyse] are elsewhere to be found, and an abridgement of each of them is inserted."[46] Finally he rewrote three accounts in the *Biographical Dictionary*, those of Dr. John Hill (which the *Dictionary* had plagiarized from the *Universal Magazine* for January 1776), Dr. John Campbell, and Zachariah Williams, and for none of these did he make any acknowledgment. The amount of revision varies. Hawkins' account of Campbell, for example, extends to only a fraction of the length of the *Dictionary* article, but since just about all of Hawkins' facts may be found in the *Dictionary* and some of the wording is identical, the indebtedness seems apparent. In the *Dictionary* we read: "His house, especially on a Sunday evening, was the resort of the most distinguished persons of all ranks, and particularly of such as had rendered themselves eminent by their knowledge, or love of literature." And, somewhat later: "By this illness he was carried off, at his house in Queen-square, Ormond-street, on Dec. 28, 1775, when he had nearly completed the 68th year of his age." In Hawkins, these distant sentences, slightly modified by what seems to be his own recollection of Campbell's house, are joined in the following manner:

> His residence for some years before his death, was the large new-built house situate at the north-west corner of Queen square, Bloomsbury, whither, particularly on a Sunday evening, great numbers of persons of the first eminence for science and literature were accustomed to resort for the enjoyment of conversation. He died in 1775, having nearly completed the sixty-eighth year of his age.[47]

The account of Zachariah Williams was revised in much the same manner, though Hawkins' long acquaintance with Anna Williams enriched the account significantly. There is, to be sure, much less

46. *Life*, p. 157 n.
47. *Life*, pp. 210–11.

abridgment here than in the account of Campbell, so that on the whole it approximates the original fairly closely. Hawkins, in fact, liked one phrase so well that he permitted himself the liberty of taking it without change: Williams discovered that the variations of the magnetic needle were equal at equal distances east and west "by a kind of intuitive penetration."[48]

The revision of the account of Dr. John Hill must have afforded more enjoyment. Here, while he followed the original quite closely (the two accounts are the same length and contain the same information), Hawkins, amused by Dr. Hill's career, enlivened his account by turns of phrase which the more serious dictionary (or magazine) writer would scarcely have attempted. While the scholars of St. Andrews would hardly have been flattered by Hawkins' comments on Hill's degree, probably most readers would not have been displeased to find the generally sober Hawkins capable of occasional harmless raillery. Hill, says Hawkins, not naming St. Andrews, received his diploma "from one of those universities which would scarce refuse a degree to an apothecary's horse."[49]

The assumption behind Hawkins' failure to acknowledge these revisions is obvious enough. Acknowledgment was unnecessary, because the act of revision made the accounts essentially his own. An age like ours, which makes such widespread use of the *Dictionary of National Biography,* will hardly find fault with Hawkins' practice. Such dictionaries are the Spanish Main which authors have traditionally ranged in quest of gold. Indeed, they were compiled only

48. *Life,* p. 321. The *Gent. Mag.* correspondent who accused Hawkins of taking his information from the *London Magazine* would thus seem to have been mistaken. At any rate, I have found no account of Zachariah Williams in the *London Magazine.*

49. *Life,* p. 211. As Porson noted, Hawkins also went to *Joe Miller's Jests* for two anecdotes, neither of which concerned Johnson. I find only one of these (*Life,* pp. 347–48) in the unabridged Joe Miller edited by Andrew G. Dickinson, Jr. (New York, Henderson, 1903, *1,* 185–86), but think it quite possible that the other anecdote (*Life,* p. 192 n.) had the same origin.

to be plundered, and the more that is taken from them the richer they become. Hawkins went to the *New and General Biographical Dictionary* when his own memory or experience failed him, and he used it as we might expect a conscientious and honest biographer to have done.

Today, of course, the question of Hawkins' honesty is not likely to engage our deepest emotions. Our hearts will not go out to the *Gentleman's Magazine* because Hawkins neglected to acknowledge every anecdote or letter borrowed from it; nor will we glow with admiration because Hawkins' practice, in spite of the indignation of the *Gentleman's Magazine,* was exemplary—certainly for his time, and perhaps even for our own. Far more important is that a study of his materials reveals Hawkins to have been a biographer resolved to work independently or not at all. In Boswell's *Tour* and Mrs. Piozzi's *Anecdotes* were riches that must have tempted him sorely, and the wonder is not how much he took but how little. It is a reassuring study, for we can be sure of one thing, at least—that Hawkins' efforts are his own, that he stands, as Carlyle said of Johnson, on his own two feet. In Hawkins' day his chief recommendations as a biographer were his access to Johnson's papers, his ability to turn up out-of-the-way information, and his long association with Johnson. Today these are recommendations still, particularly since they plot the course of so large a part of the book. Thus if we bear in mind that, to his authority as Johnson's executor, an industrious Hawkins added a personal recollection of Johnson which reached back at least to 1749 and possibly to 1740 or 1741, we should be able to approach his book with rather more respect than was accorded it in those first days when the wits outdid each other in their attempts to put the "musical knight" in his place. The *Life* was by no means "laid hastily before the publick eye to satisfy mere temporary curiosity." It was a painstaking, full-length memorial of a very old friend; and its achievement becomes all the more remark-able when we consider that the elderly Hawkins did not follow the easy path of publishing only his personal recollections, but instead availed himself of almost every material that a biographer could honorably put to use.

Chapter Four

THE DARK UNCHARITABLE CAST, I

Nor could I, at any time, catch from my father any of that spirit of adulation which was subsequently excited in the breasts of those who foresaw that it would be creditable to have been of Johnson's acquaintance. My father judged of him as of his other friends, but certainly appreciated him most highly.

—*Miss Hawkins'* Memoirs, I, *88–89*

HAWKINS MAY HAVE BEEN writing a biography of an old friend, but his critics have amassed more than enough evidence from the *Life* to press home their charge that in reality he was malevolently defacing Johnson's image. Like a convex mirror (they might insist), Hawkins has taken in the whole scene but has reflected none of it fairly. Indeed, the Johnson they have found in the *Life* will hardly recommend himself to us. He was dirty and ill-dressed—"an habitual sloven," as Hawkins put it[1]—and at table his appetites, including an unmanly taste for tea, were indulged with a sensual disregard for the comfort of those about him. A slave to indolence, he neglected all order and regularity in living; nor could he be impelled to take up his pen except by necessity. Superstition troubled him, and politics drew from him only the familiar cries of opposition. Philosopher though he was, his "mind had acquired no firmness by the contemplation of mortality,"[2] and he was scarcely able to sustain

1. *Life*, p. 327 n.
2. *Life*, p. 365.

the shock of his mother's death. Unphilosophical also was his abnormal tenderness for the memory of a wife that he had learned to love by rote. Less tender of his friend Garrick, or of the poet Milton, he saw to it that Garrick was never elected to the Literary Club, and he exulted in the belief that Milton had been proved a plagiarizer. His charity was squandered on ne'er-do-wells like Francis Barber and Dr. Dodd, while he turned his back on the one relation who had any real claim to his regard.

Plainly this is an unflattering portrait of Johnson. But it is not so plain that it is drawn in the spirit of malevolence; and certainly it is not the whole of Hawkins' portrait. To be sure, one could wish that Hawkins had omitted certain strokes of it, or that he had mixed a few of his colors with greater subtlety. Not all of it can be shrugged off as harmless prejudice, such as his styling Johnson's taste for tea "unmanly." Some of it, like the statement that Johnson would never admit Garrick to the Literary Club, is obviously erroneous. Yet it would be difficult to prove malevolence in such an error. Garrick, after all, had to wait nearly ten years for admission, and it would have been a simple matter for anyone who knew Johnson's feelings[3] to extend this fairly lengthy period through the six remaining years of Garrick's life.[4] Still more was occasioned by a marked difference between the two men. It might be wished, for example, that Hawkins had commented sympathetically, rather than

---

3. As Hawkins did. See *Life*, p. 425, where Johnson consulted Hawkins about admitting Garrick to the Club and said, "He will disturb us by his buffoonery." By the time Garrick was elected, of course, Hawkins was no longer a member.

4. Though Hawkins was mistaken, Boswell's attempt to correct him was itself misleading; "However, when Garrick was regularly proposed some time afterwards, Johnson, though he had taken a momentary offence at his arrogance, warmly and kindly supported him, and he was accordingly elected, was a most agreeable member, and continued to attend our meetings to the time of his death." (Boswell, *1*, 480–81). Surely no reader of Boswell would suspect that Garrick had to wait as long as nine years to be elected.

severely, on Johnson's grief at the loss of his mother. In a similar situation, however, the stoical Hawkins would doubtless have concealed his own grief, and thus to him it would have seemed only proper that the philosopher Johnson should have done so too. We need not agree with him, but it is hardly fair to charge him with malevolence because his opinion differs from ours. With respect to Hawkins' attack upon Johnson's "ostentatious bounty" to Francis Barber, we must again distinguish between malevolence and something else. Hawkins' complaint was lodged against what he considered ill-bestowed favor to Negroes. For us, accordingly, as it was for many of Hawkins' contemporaries, the attack is to be regretted primarily on grounds of taste. In this matter Hawkins' judgment was inexcusably bad, and his prejudice led him into the related error of berating Johnson for neglecting the impoverished widower of one of his cousins, a man whose slight call on Johnson's charity had long since been answered. For the reactionary Hawkins, it would seem, any relation, no matter how distant, was preferable to a Negro. The liberal Johnson knew otherwise.

Hawkins' reactionary spirit was noted by a correspondent of the *Gentleman's Magazine,* who reproached him for controverting Johnson's "liberal sentiments" on the use of sizars and servitors at the universities—"distinctions as are certainly a disgrace to this liberal and enlightened age."[5] It is largely this spirit which accounts for Hawkins' attitude toward the efforts made by Johnson to obtain a pardon for Dr. Dodd, who had been found guilty of forging the Earl of Chesterfield's signature to an annuity. It was not that Hawkins deplored that humane spirit with which Johnson ran to the aid of a person in trouble. On the contrary, Hawkins recognized and

---

5. *Gent. Mag.* (supplement to 1787), pp. 1146–47. Johnson, it should be observed, disapproved of allowing the poor students to wait on the more fortunate some sixty years before the *Gent. Mag.* correspondent objected that the practice disgraced "this liberal and enlightened age."

respected the extent and depth of Johnson's charity, and his book abounds with examples of it which he obviously took pride in collecting. But Johnson's humanity was obedient to *every* call, and Hawkins felt that there were some calls which should not be obeyed. Such was the call of Dr. Dodd. As a former magistrate, Hawkins took the side of the law. He himself had had the task of examining the bill of indictment preferred by the Earl of Chesterfield against Dr. Dodd, though of course he had had no hand in the trial. But says Hawkins,

> The evidence on the trial, was so very full and clear, that the jury hesitated not in the least to pronounce him guilty of the indictment; and, no circumstance of alleviation appearing, they did not, as juries seldom fail to do where that is the case, recommend him as an object of that clemency, which his majesty is ever ready to exert, in favour of those who have the least claim to it.[6]

Hawkins, moreover, had a magistrate's respect for the decision of the court. When he said, "We live in an age in which humanity is the fashion," and proceeded to enumerate fourteen ways by which an offender might escape conviction or punishment,[7] he was doubtless dipping into his memory of times when, like other magistrates, he must have found the barbed wire of legal entanglement a real hindrance to conviction, or when decisions reached after long and arduous trial were set aside in a moment because sentiment prevailed over the reason of the law. For Johnson there was an appeal from law to the benevolent heart of man, just as in criticism there was an appeal from the rules to nature.[8] But it did not occur to Hawkins that the law might be harsh and unjust. The law had been established

6. *Life*, p. 521.
7. *Life*, pp. 522–23.
8. *Works*, 9, 248.

by the highest and most respected body in the land, and where it miscarried there would be found a jury to recommend clemency, and a king to exert it "in favour of those who have the least claim to it."

Doubtless such differences of spirit, temperament, or opinion led Hawkins occasionally into error, or at least into an argument he was left to carry on without support. True, they might have led him also—as Boswell would have it—into a malevolence which placed "the most unfavourable construction . . . upon almost every circumstance in . . . Johnson's character and conduct," for hostility is a natural consequence of difference. Had they done so, the malevolence with which he has been charged—the dark uncharitable cast— would make itself felt continually, and would force his readers to allow at almost every turn for the bias of his asperity. In the *Life*, however, no such allowance need be made. In reality, with the exceptions of those parts already noted, almost all the "malevolent" portrait of Johnson which Hawkins' critics presumed to find in the *Life* can be duplicated from other records, including those kept by Boswell himself.

Of Johnson's manner of eating, for example, Hawkins has left a brief but pointed memorial: "It was, at no time of his life, pleasing to see him at a meal; the greediness with which he ate, his total inattention to those among whom he was seated, and his profound silence in the hour of refection, were circumstances that degraded him, and shewed him to be more a sensualist than a philosopher."[9] If this seems to be an injustice to Johnson—and certainly it is a long way from flattery—it is worth reminding ourselves that no contemporary of Johnson has left us an attractive picture of his table manners. Mrs. James Harris, who was visited by Boswell and Johnson in 1775, complained that Johnson "feeds nastily and ferociously,

9. *Life*, p. 354.

and eats quantities most unthankfully."[10] Boswell's, of course, is the best-known record of this aspect of Johnson:

> When at table, he was totally absorbed in the business of the moment; his looks seemed rivetted to his plate; nor would he, unless when in very high company, say one word, or even pay the least attention to what was said by others, till he had satisfied his appetite, which was so fierce, and indulged with such intenseness, that while in the act of eating, the veins of his forehead swelled, and generally a strong perspiration was visible. To those whose sensations were delicate, this could not but be disgusting; and it was doubtless not very suitable to the character of a philosopher, who should be distinguished by self-command.[11]

If Hawkins' account is malevolent, where shall a word be found to describe Boswell's? One can almost think—such are their similarities—that Boswell has merely dyed the plain fabric of Hawkins' paragraph with the dark colors necessary to make the final work repulsive in the extreme. By being sparing in his details, Hawkins has spared some of our distaste as well.

Hawkins' description of Johnson's dress and appearance is again unflattering:

> the great bushy wig, which throughout his life he affected to wear, by that closeness of texture which it had contracted and been suffered to retain, was ever nearly as impenetrable by a comb as a quickset hedge; and little of the dust that had once settled on his outer garments was ever known to have been disturbed by the brush. In short, his garb and the whole of his external appearance was, not to say negligent, but slovenly,

10. Boswell, *2, 520.*
11. Ibid., *1, 468.*

and even squalid; to all which . . . he appeared . . . insensible. . . . [H]e saw that, notwithstanding these offensive peculiarities in his manners, his conversation had great attractions, and perhaps he might estimate the strength of the one by the degree of the other, and thence derive that apathy, which, after all, might have its foundation in pride, and afforded him occasion for a triumph over all the solicitude respecting dress.[12]

This initial description is supplemented with a note:

That he was an habitual sloven his best friends cannot deny. When I first knew him, he was little less so than Magliabechi, of whom it is said, that at meals, he made a book serve him for a plate, and that he very seldom changed his linen, or washed himself. . . . Johnson, as his acquaintance with persons of condition became more enlarged . . . corrected, in some degree, this failing, but could never be said to be neatly dressed, or indeed clean; he affected to wear cloaths of the darkest and dirtiest colours, and, in all weathers, black stockings. His wig never sat even on his head, as may be observed in all the pictures of him, the reason whereof was, that he had a twist in his shoulders, and that the motion of his head, as soon as he put it on, dragged it awry.[13]

This picture, of course, is no more attractive than the picture of Johnson eating. But it has been so often verified that it would be hasty to conclude that Hawkins' want of charity was, either consciously or unconsciously, distorting what he saw. Dr. Thomas Campbell found Johnson in "the most awkard garb & unpowdered grey wig on one side only of his head.[14] The delicate Mrs.

12. *Life*, p. 327.
13. *Life*, pp. 327–28 n.
14. *Dr. Campbell's Diary of a Visit to England in 1775*, ed. James L. Clifford (Cambridge University Press, 1947), p. 53.

Harris described Johnson as "more beastly in his dress and person than anything I ever beheld."[15] Miss Reynolds, whose tenderness for Johnson has never been questioned, noted that at one time his best dress was "so very mean, that one afternoon as he was following some ladies up stairs, on a visit to a lady of fashion, the Housemaid, not knowing him, suddenly seized him by the shoulder, and exclaimed, 'Where are you going?' striving at the same time to drag him back."[16] Boswell repeatedly mentions the "old shrivelled unpowdered wig, which was too small for his head," and his "black worsted stockings ill drawn up."[17] Boswell, moreover, once got himself into trouble by suggesting to Johnson that he might do well to dress a little better than was his custom.[18]

Though Hawkins' account of Johnson's dress will readily be seen to be more tender than that of Mrs. Harris, it may still be objected that there is a tendency in the account to make the worst of things. Hawkins emphasizes the unpleasant: Johnson *affected* to wear a wig; he was an *habitual sloven,* even *squalid;* these *peculiarities* in his manners were *offensive;* he *seldom changed his linen* or *washed himself;* he could never be called clean; he *affected* to wear the *darkest* and *dirtiest colours.* Boswell, however, admits the slovenliness, and Johnson himself never pretended to be fond of clean linen. He *did* wear dark-colored clothes, and probably the adjective *dirtiest* means no more than that they were of colors which would not easily show the dirt. Selecting clothes of such colors has probably been a common practice in every age. Carried to extreme, however, as Johnson's practice was, it takes on the character of an affectation. Foote told Boswell that the French were astonished at Johnson's "figure and manner, and at his dress, which he obstinately continued exactly

15. Boswell, *2,* 520.
16. *John. Misc., 2,* 261.
17. Boswell, *1,* 396.
18. Ibid., *2,* 475.

as in London."[19] Such obstinacy must have seemed affectation to the French; and in England it was affectation, too, though those who had become accustomed to Johnson would hardly have recognized it. If Hawkins was making the worst of things, at least he was siding with the truth.

Hawkins' attempt to account for Johnson's carelessness in dress ought not to go unnoticed. There is abundant evidence that the first reaction to Johnson's appearance was generally disgust, which promptly turned to admiration under the magical influence of his conversation. "Mr. Johnson is a man of a most dreadful appearance," Boswell confided to his Journal after his first meeting with Johnson. "He is a very big man, is troubled with sore eyes, the palsy, and the king's evil. He is very slovenly in his dress and speaks with a most uncouth voice. Yet his great knowledge and strength of expression command vast respect and render him very excellent company."[20] Reactions like this would not have escaped Johnson, who, in spite of his sore eyes, was one of the keenest observers of his time. Here, in such meetings as Boswell described, Johnson's undeniable pride in his conversational powers was fed in direct proportion to the initial disgust of his listeners. Success in overcoming that disgust, as Hawkins says, might well have "afforded him occasion for a triumph over all the solicitude respecting dress." Hawkins, far from being malevolent, has suggested a quite plausible reason for a trait which must have puzzled many of Johnson's friends.

Of Johnson's indolence Hawkins likewise says little that has not been confirmed again and again:

> In his studies, and I may add, in his devotional exercises, he was
> both intense and remiss, and in the prosecution of his literary

19. Ibid., 2, 403.
20. *Boswell's London Journal*, ed. Frederick A. Pottle (New York, McGraw-Hill, 1950), p. 260.

employments, dilatory and hasty, unwilling, as himself confessed, to work, and working with vigour and haste.

His indolence, or rather the delight he took in reading and reflection, rendered him averse to bodily exertions. He was ill made for riding, and took so little pleasure in it, that, as he once told me, he has fallen asleep on his horse. Walking he seldom practised, perhaps for no better reason, than that it required the previous labour of dressing.[21]

Johnson's "constitutional indolence" is frequently mentioned by Boswell, and Johnson himself once remarked that he "always felt an inclination to do nothing."[22] To be sure, Hawkins has made rather more of Johnson's indolence than Boswell has made. He did not agree with Johnson that no man wrote except from necessity and did not scruple to voice his disagreement. Nor did he scruple to make of Johnson's indolence a warning to those who might be similarly inclined:

> And here we cannot but reflect on that inertness and laxity of mind which the neglect of order and regularity in living, and the observance of stated hours, in short, the waste of time, is apt to lead men to: this was the source of Johnson's misery throughout his life; all he did was by fits and starts, and he had no genuine impulse to action, either corporal or mental.[23]

Hawkins then proceeded to cite the examples of Dr. Thomas Birch, Dr. John Campbell, Dr. John Hill, Henry Fielding, Tobias Smollett, Samuel Richardson, and Laurence Sterne—all men who, "by a good use of their time, were capable of great application and enjoying the benefits of society."[24]

21. *Life*, pp. 165–66.
22. Boswell, *1*, 463.
23. *Life*, p. 205.
24. *Life*, p. 206.

It may seem uncharitable of Hawkins to hold Johnson up to invidious comparison with seven of his contemporaries. But we must remember that it was comparison on one count only, and that Hawkins' purpose here, as often elsewhere, was a moral one. The "rising generation," which he mentions frequently in the *Life*,[25] was of real concern to him, as it may well have been to a magistrate who had witnessed his share of juvenile delinquency. One can see in Hawkins' picture of the indolent Johnson an effort to arouse in his readers an active contempt, not for Johnson but for indolence,[26] by demonstrating "that even the learning and genius"[27] of Johnson could suffer by it. One can also see Hawkins, in the passages just quoted, searching out the reasons why Johnson was the kind of man Hawkins felt him to be. The establishment of a relationship between Johnson's indolence and his "misery throughout his life" is by no means an idle conjecture. Anyone who has perused Johnson's *Prayers and Meditations* will have noticed how frequently Johnson resolved to bring "order and regularity" into his life, and how his invariable failure in these attempts left him dissatisfied and dejected. But Johnson's most miserable hours were those spent in solitude when, with nothing else to occupy him, he turned his thoughts upon himself. The type of order and regularity suggested by Hawkins would have crowded those hours with some of the many projects of interest to Johnson, and thus would have left no time for the type of reflection which inevitably made him miserable.

The more the reader peruses Hawkins' *Life*, the more he becomes

---

25. *Life*, pp. 157 n., 215, 217, 269, 371.
26. This interpretation is reinforced by a further statement of Hawkins' (*Life*, p. 350): "Johnson's intellectual faculties could never be unemployed: when he was not writing he was thinking, and his thoughts had ever a tendency to the good of mankind; and that indolence, which, in his hours of contrition, he censured as criminal, needed little expiation."
27. See below.

aware that Hawkins' principles of biography were identical with Johnson's. Dr Johnson maintained, wrote Boswell,

> that 'If a man is to write *A Panegyrick,* he may keep vices out of sight; but if he professes to write *A Life,* he must represent it really as it was:' and when I objected to the danger of telling that Parnell drank to excess, he said, that 'it would produce an instructive caution to avoid drinking, when it was seen, that even the learning and genius of Parnell could be debased by it.[28]

Johnson gave another reason for honesty in biography when Edmond Malone mentioned to him that some people thought

> Mr. Addison's character was so pure, that the fact, *though true,* [that he lent Steele one hundred pounds and reclaimed it by an execution] ought to have been suppressed. He saw no reason for this. "If nothing but the bright side of characters should be shewn, we should sit down in despondency, and think it utterly impossible to imitate them in *any thing.* The sacred writers (he observed) related the vicious as well as the virtuous actions of men; which had this moral effect, that it kept mankind from *despair,* into which otherwise they would naturally fall, were they not supported by the recollection that others had offended like themselves, and by penitence and amendment of life had been restored to the favour of Heaven."[29]

Hawkins was writing not a panegyric but a life, and no circumstance was alien to his purpose that might in any way illuminate Johnson's character, even if it illuminated a side of his character that Johnson's partisans preferred not to see. "In the performance of the engagement I am under," wrote Hawkins, "I find myself compelled to

28. Boswell, *3,* 155.
29. Ibid., *4,* 53.

68

make public, as well those particulars of Johnson that may be thought to abase as those that exalt his character."[30] Today, at long distance from Johnson's death, we can see that Hawkins was right. We will not be disturbed, as were some of Hawkins' contemporaries, if a memoir is not all eulogy. We will insist only that what is entered as fact be genuine, and that it be readily distinguishable from opinion.

Guided by these principles, Hawkins did not hesitate to mention Johnson's crediting for some time the story of the Cock Lane Ghost.[31] It was a fact which could not be ignored. For the same reason Hawkins could say of Johnson that when the proof sheets of William Lauder's fraudulent *Essay on Milton's Use and Imitation of the Moderns* were submitted to the inspection of the Ivy Lane Club, "I could all along observe that Johnson seemed to approve not only of the design but of the argument, and seemed to exult in a persuasion, that the reputation of Milton was likely to suffer by this discovery."[32] Some critics have been much offended that Hawkins should have had such a recollection of Johnson, and it is quite possible that Hawkins was mistaken. But as long as his memory told him that at the Ivy Lane Club Johnson seemed to exult in this persuasion, he would have felt compelled to record that observation, no matter whom it would offend. Similarly, he could not withhold his charge that in *London, Marmor Norfolciense,* and *A Compleat Vindication of the Licensers of the Stage* Johnson had adopted "vulgar prejudices" and was mouthing only the "cant of the opposition": "Johnson has taken a wide scope, and adopted all the vulgar topics of complaint as they were vented weekly in the public papers, and in the writings of Bolingbroke, flimsy and malignant as they are."[33] Though such

30. *Life,* p. 436.
31. Ibid.
32. *Life,* p. 276.
33. *Life,* p. 79.

a charge, coming from the pro-Walpole Hawkins, may seem to be only political bias, Greene's recent study of Johnson's politics demonstrates beyond question that Johnson *had* adopted "all the vulgar topics of complaint";[34] and of course we have already seen how quickly Johnson abandoned his role of political radical. Hawkins, we must note, was ready to make every allowance he could for Johnson's early radicalism. If Johnson voiced the cant of the opposition, he nevertheless was not a hypocrite:

> The truth is, that Johnson's political prejudices were a mist that the eye of his judgment could not penetrate: in all the measures of government he could see nothing right. . . . From hence it appears, and to his honour be it said, that his principles co-operated with his necessities, and that the prostitution of his talents, taking the term in one and that its worst sense, could not, in justice, be imputed to him.[35]

We must remember, too, that Hawkins was keenly interested in the change in Johnson's politics, and he could more readily convey his admiration for the later Johnson if he called our attention to the unpromising chrysalis from which he had emerged.

In these three accounts—of the Cock Lane Ghost, of Lauder's attack upon Milton, and of Johnson's early radicalism—if something was owing to Johnson, something more was owing to truth. So, too, with one last but very important part of the "malevolent" portrait for which Hawkins has been denounced. "I have often been inclined to think," wrote Hawkins, "that if this fondness of Johnson for his wife was not dissembled, it was a lesson that he had learned by rote, and that, when he practised it, he knew not where to stop till he became ridiculous."[36] Hawkins made it clear, we should note,

34. Greene, pp. 88 ff.
35. *Life,* pp. 80–81.
36. *Life,* p. 313.

that his conclusions about Johnson and his wife were conjectural. "I have often been inclined to think" is an informative preface to the statement just quoted. "As, during her life-time, he invited but few of his friends to his house, I never saw her . . . "[37] he confessed, with disarming honesty, a moment later. But by what process could Hawkins have reached a conclusion which seems, on the face of it, so libelous to his friend?

The process, as Hawkins makes clear, was natural enough. The marriage was not one of those which "inconsiderate young people" call love matches. After all, Tetty was old enough to be Johnson's mother, and they had no children. Moreover, she was negligent of some of the duties of a wife. By themselves these would not justify Hawkins' conclusion, but there were other more telling reasons. Hawkins knew of the temporary separation of Johnson and his wife, and of the nights Johnson, instead of going home, wandered the streets after the meetings of the Ivy Lane Club. Reports of the marriage not at all favorable had reached him by way of Garrick, Hawkesworth, and others, and in Shaw's memoir of Johnson he would have found corroborating testimony: "a suspicion of his conjugal infelicity . . . went abroad, and procured him much commiseration among his friends."[38] He himself had noticed that Johnson did not invite his friends to visit him at home. When one adds to all this the consideration that the austere and unemotional Hawkins would not easily recognize the warmth of affection in Johnson's repeated references to "dear Tetty," then it is not surprising that, having weighed this unpromising evidence, he should come to a conclusion which has shocked so many sentimental readers. But this was not lack of charity. Hawkins pondered the information available to him, and when it seemed to point to a match in which

37. *Life,* p. 314.
38. [William Shaw,] *Memoirs of the Life and Writings of the Late Dr. Samuel Johnson* (London, J. Walker, 1785), p. 110.

Johnson's fondness was a lesson learned by rote, he had no alternative but to say so.

Indeed, with respect to Johnson's relations with his wife, Hawkins proves to be a rather more honest biographer than Boswell. There is no reason to believe that he has suppressed any evidence; if he erred, he erred unintentionally. But Boswell's distortion was deliberate. Boswell knew, for example, that Mrs. Johnson not only drank to excess but took opium, and that she had contrived to keep Johnson from her bed.[39] He may have learned from Dr. Taylor, one of his chief informants, that Mrs. Johnson "was the plague of Johnson's life, was abominably drunken and despicable," and that Johnson had frequently complained to Taylor "of the wretchedness of his situation with such a wife."[40] Boswell had reason to believe, for he had read Hawkins, that there had been a separation between them, and he knew that though Johnson cherished the memory of his wife, he had contemplated taking a second wife only a little more than a year after Tetty's death.[41] Of the second wife, Boswell said nothing. And of the storms of Johnson's married life, he said only, "I have, indeed, been told by Mrs. Desmoulins . . . that she [Mrs. Johnson] indulged herself in country air and nice living, at an unsuitable expence, while her husband was drudging in the smoke of London, and that she by no means treated him with that complacency which is the most engaging quality in a wife."[42] While

39. Yale Boswell Papers, April 20, 1783, paper marked "Tacenda."

40. Clifford, p. 312.

41. Donald and Mary Hyde, *Dr. Johnson's Second Wife*, privately printed, 1953; in *New Light on Johnson*, ed. F. W. Hilles, New Haven, 1959. The Hydes conclude in this excellent essay that the truth about Johnson lies somewhere between the accounts of Hawkins and Boswell. James L. Clifford makes the following comment on Hawkins' reactions to Johnson's marriage: "I came to accept Hawkins and to reject Boswell. . . . Though Hawkins's remarks in this instance may have sounded uncharitable, they impressed me as representing a more probable condition" ("The Complex Art of Biography," *Columbia University Forum*, spring 1958, p. 37).

42. Boswell, *1*, 237–38.

this is thin veneer, it manages to conceal the scratches in the grain beneath. Boswell's picture, unquestionably, is romanticized. But this is the way of panegyric rather than of biography.

Boswell, of course, insisted that he was not writing panegyric: "I profess to write, not his panegyrick, which must be all praise, but his Life; which, great and good as he was, must not be supposed to be entirely perfect."[43] And when Hannah More pleaded with Boswell to mitigate Johnson's asperities, he replied: "He would not cut off his claws, nor make a tiger a cat, to please anybody."[44] Indeed, the fullness of Boswell's portrait—the alternating light and shade—is one of its great glories. Nevertheless, the tendency for a man of Boswell's devotion must frequently have been toward panegyric. He could not bring himself, for example, to recount Edmund Hector's fascinating story of the drunken evening Johnson spent with a relation, but dismissed the episode by remarking that Hector had known Johnson to be intoxicated but once.[45] Interesting, too, is Boswell's comment on a parody by Johnson quoted in Mrs. Piozzi's *Anecdotes:*

> Mrs. Thrale has published as Johnson's, a kind of parody or counterpart of a fine poetical passage in one of Mr. Burke's speeches on American Taxation. It is vigorously but somewhat coarsely executed; and I am inclined to suppose, is not quite correctly exhibited. I hope he did not use the word '*vile agents*' for the Americans in the House of Parliament; and if he did so, in an extempore effusion, I wish the lady had not committed it to writing.[46]

Boswell may have been unwilling to cut out the tiger's claws, but he was not averse to brushing some of the burs from his coat.

43. Ibid., p. 30.
44. Ibid., n. 4.
45. Yale Boswell Papers; Boswell, *1*, 94.
46. Boswell, *4*, 317–18.

It would be possible to have a good measure of respect for the case which Boswell and the critics made out for Hawkins' malevolence if we could convince ourselves that they had approached their task with even a modicum of objectivity. If the book was to be damned, it deserved at least a trial which would have included a reasonably systematic examination of the evidence. But Boswell and the critics were hardly more systematic than those dabblers in Johnson's *Dictionary* who, having heard the definitions of "oats" and "network," assume that the *Dictionary's* only function is to entertain a party of friends. A person whose ideas of Hawkins had been born and nourished on the pages of Boswell might blink his eyes in disbelief if he should chance to take up a copy of Hawkins and open it to the very first page:

> The general sense of mankind, and the practice of the learned in all ages, have given a sanction to biographical history, and concurred to recommend that precept of the wise son of Sirach, in which we are exhorted to 'praise famous men, such as by their counsels and by their knowledge of learning were meet for the people,—and were wise and eloquent in their instructions,—and such as recited verses in writing.' In each of these faculties did the person, whose history I am about to write, so greatly excel, that, except for my presumption in the attempt to display his worth, the undertaking may be thought to need no apology; especially if we contemplate, together with his mental endowments, those moral qualities which distinguished him, and reflect that, in an age when literary acquisitions and scientific improvements are rated at their utmost value, he rested not in the applause which these procured him; but adorned the character of a scholar and a philosopher with that of a christian.[47]

47. *Life*, pp. 1-2.

Is it possible to mistake Hawkins' purpose? This is the idea of Johnson which he would have his readers retain from the start. Johnson was scholar, philosopher, and Christian, a man who so greatly excelled in wisdom, knowledge, poetry, and morality that the mere attempt to display his worth may be considered presumption. It is a curious preamble to malevolence.

Nor do we have to read very far to find that the picture of Hawkins' malevolence illustrates the later pages no better than the first. On page 11 Hawkins informs us that Johnson's spirit was too great to sink under the weight of poverty. On page 15 he pays tribute to Johnson's professional qualifications: "If nature could be said to have pointed out a profession for him, that of the bar seems to have been it: in that faculty, his acuteness and penetration, and above all, his nervous and manly elocution, could scarcely have failed to distinguish him, and to have raised him to the highest honours of that lucrative profession." On page 16 he extols Johnson's ability to read quickly and perspicaciously, and to remember what he had read. On page 18 he makes clear that Johnson's reading at Oxford "begat in his mind those sentiments of piety which were the rule of his conduct throughout his future life, and made so conspicuous a part of his character," and on the next page that the profligacy of his cousin Ford could not efface Johnson's deep sense of religion or his reverence for the national church. On pages 35 and 36 Hawkins commends Johnson for his grateful remembrance of his benefactor, Gilbert Walmesley, and for the modesty of the advertisement inserted in the *Gentleman's Magazine* in the vain hope of enrolling enough pupils to continue his school at Edial: "That this notification failed of its end, we can scarce wonder, if we reflect, that . . . he had not the vanity to profess teaching all sciences, nor the effrontery of those, who, in these more modern times, undertake, in private boarding-schools to qualify young men for holy orders." On page 50 we read that Johnson was one of the most quick-sighted

men Hawkins had ever known "in discovering the good and amiable qualities of others," and that he was ever inclined to palliate
men's defects. And on the next page: "With all that asperity of
manners with which he has been charged, and which kept at a distance many, who, to my knowledge, would have been glad of an
intimacy with him, he possessed the affections of pity and compassion in a most eminent degree."

It is hardly necessary to continue. An extended examination of
this kind would only multiply examples of Hawkins' abiding admiration for his friend. Nevertheless, it should be of interest to look
for a moment at two or three of the better-known incidents of
Johnson's life, so that we may satisfy ourselves as to whether or not
Hawkins' interpretation of these incidents is notably more uncharitable to Johnson than other interpretations current in his day.

One of the best-known stories about Johnson concerns his quarrel
with the bookseller Thomas Osborne. As Hawkins tells it,[48] Johnson had been employed by Osborne to select some of the fugitive
pieces from the Earl of Oxford's library, recently purchased by
Osborne, for reprinting in the *Harleian Miscellany*. "Seeing Johnson
one day deeply engaged in perusing a book, and the work for the
instant at a stand, he [Osborne] reproached him with inattention
and delay, in such coarse language as few men would use, and still
fewer could brook." When Johnson attempted to justify himself,
Osborne called him liar, and in anger Johnson "seized a folio that
lay near him, and with it felled his adversary to the ground." This
transaction, says Hawkins,

> which has been seldom urged with any other view than to
> shew that Johnson was of an irascible temper, is generally re
> lated as an entertaining story: with me it has always been a

48. *Life,* p. 150. There are numerous versions of the story, the earliest that
I have found appearing in the *Westminster Magazine* for Nov. 1777, though
undoubtedly it was well known long before that. See Clifford, pp. 270–72.

subject of melancholy reflection. In our estimation of the enjoyments of this life, we place wisdom, virtue, and learning in the first class, and riches and other adventitious gifts of fortune in the last. The natural subordination of the one to the other we see and approve, and when that is disturbed we are sorry. How then must it affect a sensible mind to contemplate that misfortune, which could subject a man endued with a capacity for the highest offices, a philosopher, a poet, an orator, and, if fortune had so ordered, a chancellor, a prelate, a statesman, to the insolence of a mean, worthless, ignorant fellow, who had nothing to justify the superiority he exercised over a man so endowed, but those advantages which Providence indiscriminately dispenses to the worthy and the worthless! to see such a man, for the supply of food and raiment, submitting to the commands of his inferior, and, as a hireling, looking up to him for the reward of his work, and receiving it accompanied with reproach and contumely, this, I say, is a subject of melancholy reflection.[49]

Even the most perverse of readers would have some difficulty finding any malevolence directed against Johnson in this paragraph. On the contrary, the intensity of Hawkins' admiration lights the passage with a benevolent glow, while at the same time—and this is what is most remarkable—his indignation fires away at those who would put an unfavorable construction on this circumstance of Johnson's life.

In 1762—to mention another circumstance—Johnson accepted a pension from the government and thus left himself open to criticism from several sides. The canting remarks of the enemies of government would have been simple for Johnson to ignore. But in the *Dictionary* Johnson had remarked of a pension that "In England it is

49. *Life,* pp. 150–51.

generally understood to mean pay given to a state hireling for treason to his country," and while this may have been an amusing joke in 1755, when he accepted the pension seven years later he became a mark, not merely for wits large and small, but for those who honestly thought he had forfeited his principles in order to live in comfort. Johnson, says Hawkins, found himself in a predicament, but who "except the Great Searcher of Hearts" can know that he sacrificed his conscience?

> Or, seeing that the grant of Johnson's pension was confessedly unconditional, and bound him neither to the renunciation of any of his political principles, nor the exercise of his pen in the defence of any set of men or series of measures, who will have the face to say, that his acceptance of it was criminal, or that it was in the power of any one to pervert the integrity of a man, who, in the time of his necessity, had, from scruples of his own raising, declined the offer of a valuable ecclesiastical preferment, and thereby renounced an independent provision for the whole of his life?[50]

Once again we are confronted with the spectacle of the man accused of putting an unfavorable construction on almost every circumstance of Johnson's life, actually going to great lengths himself to warn others against an unfavorable construction.

Hawkins, to be sure, has one reservation which he cannot withhold. It is difficult, if not impossible, to justify Johnson both in the definition of *pension* and in his acceptance of a pension:

> in one instance or the other he was wrong, and either his discretion or integrity must be given up: in the former, he seems, in some of his actions, to have been wanting, in the latter never: not only charity, but reason therefore, directs us in the opinion

50. *Life,* p. 394.

we are to form of an act which has drawn censure on his conduct, and proves nothing more than that he was not equally
wise at all times.[51]

As usual, Hawkins is honest. And he is right. Johnson's definition
was indiscreet; he could not expect to have his definition and his
pension, too, and Hawkins has put on this circumstance the only
construction which, as he says, charity and reason can direct. Boswell's efforts to justify Johnson in both are obviously forced.[52] For
if Johnson was aware, as Boswell says, that pensions were sometimes "given and received on liberal and honourable terms," then
the definition was by all means indiscreet, for it tended to bring
into disrepute all those who *had* accepted pensions on such terms or
who would accept them in the future—including Samuel Johnson
himself. There must have been at least a few moments when Johnson wished that the printer of the *Dictionary* had had the wit to
strike out this definition, just as he struck out part of the definition
of *renegado.*[53]

Hawkins was quick to appreciate the immediate effect of Johnson's pension. Raised to a state of comparative affluence, Johnson
was now in a position to indulge that compassion which "many
whose real or pretended wants had formerly excited."[54] He always
went abroad with change in his pockets to distribute to beggars (a
practice he recommended to his friends), and he enlarged his house-

---

51. *Life,* pp. 394–95.
52. Boswell, *1,* 375: "His definitions of *pension* and *pensioner* . . . may be
generally true; and yet every body must allow, that there may be, and have
been, instances of pensions given and received upon liberal and honourable
terms. Thus, then, it is clear, that there was nothing inconsistent or humiliating
in Johnson's accepting of a pension so unconditionally and so honourably
offered to him."
53. Ibid., *1,* 296.
54. *Life,* p. 395.

hold by the admission, first, of Dr. Levett,[55] and, ultimately, of a bizarre assortment of permanent and transient guests. Some of them had "elbowed through the world, and subsisted by lying, begging, and shifting, all which he knew, but seemed to think never the worse of them."[56] Indeed, says Hawkins, "almost throughout his life, poverty and distressed circumstances seemed to be the strongest of all recommendations to his favour. When asked by one of his intimate friends, how he could bear to be surrounded by such necessitous and undeserving people, as he had about him, his answer was, 'If I did not assist them no one else would, and they must be lost for want.' "[57]

Johnson, of course, did not insist upon the gratitude of those he befriended. As Hawkins tells us, he could never approach his dwelling after an evening away without "the dread of finding it a scene of discord."[58] Mrs. Williams would complain of Frank's inattention to duty, and Frank of Mrs. Williams' domineering manner. Even the transients (who would have brought their children into the house during Johnson's absence) would whine that the food was insufficient or ill-prepared. And yet Johnson would not put them out.

> Nay, so insensible was he of the ingratitude of those whom he suffered thus to hang on him, and among whom he may be said to have divided an income which was little more than sufficient for his own support, that he would submit to reproach and personal affront from some of them, even Levett would sometimes insult him, and Mrs. Williams, in her paroxysms of rage, has been known to drive him from her presence.[59]

55. "Johnson in pity loved Levett, because few others could find any thing in him to love" (*Life*, p. 404).

56. *Life*, p. 408.

57. *Life*, p. 404.

58. *Life*, p. 408.

59. *Life*, p. 409.

Characteristically, Hawkins has left a final comment on what he terms this "pusillanimous" conduct of Johnson:

> The above facts and observations are meant to shew some of the most conspicuous features and foibles in Johnson's character, and go to prove, not only that his ferocity was not so terrific . . . but that he had a natural imbecility about him, arising from humanity and pity to the sufferings of his fellow-creatures, that was prejudicial to his interests; and also that he neither sought nor expected praise for those acts of beneficence which he was daily performing, nor looked for any retribution from those who were nourished by his bounty. Indeed, they were . . . incapable of being awed by a sense of his worth, or of discerning the motives that actuated him.[60]

Once again, of course, we are glimpsing the same indiscriminate bounty that attempted vainly to save the life of Dr. Dodd and provided a seventy-pound annuity for Francis Barber, and Hawkins is shaking his head to warn us against so reckless a generosity. But we would be doing Hawkins a real injustice if we did not see beyond the terms "pusillanimous" and "imbecility" to his profound admiration for the Johnson who could lavish his bounty, however indiscriminate, without any thought either of thanks or repayment. As a magistrate, Hawkins was concerned lest Johnson's bounty should encourage the worthless and the vicious; as a friend, he was concerned lest it should leave Johnson more nearly miserable than happy. If "pusillanimous" and "imbecility" seem like harsh words to describe this aspect of Johnson's character, it should be remembered that the outspoken Hawkins does not overlook the fact that the cause of Johnson's failure to act was "humanity and pity to the

60. *Life,* p. 413.

81

sufferings of his fellow-creatures."[61] His reluctance to exercise a
proper authority in his own household, however, meant that Johnson dreaded returning home at night. Was it uncharitable of Hawkins to suggest that there was just enough of the coward in Johnson
to keep him from a showdown with those unfortunates who as-
sailed his ears with their complaints and made a serf of him in his
own castle? Here, perhaps, Johnson was constitutionally given to
letting ill enough alone, and while he undoubtedly would have been
pleased with a few more of the comforts of home, I suspect that
both he and the ungrateful recipients of his bounty were perfectly
well aware that he could have issued them no ultimatum which
they could not have forced him to retract. No matter what they did
to him, he was not one to withhold his bounty and put them out
on the street—probably the only measure capable of getting him
the comfort he would have liked.

Before we condemn Hawkins for his opinion of Johnson's indiscriminate bounty, let us remember, also, that Johnson's attitude
toward beggars was an extraordinary one. While most of us might
in theory commend that charity which is open to all, in practice
we are likely to follow Hawkins' example and ignore the hand
held out to us, while we satisfy our consciences with the thought
that the beggar would only have wasted our money in drink. To
Johnson, a man who could argue against giving charity to beggars
was "a true Whig."[62] Yet Johnson himself once confessed that one
could give away five hundred pounds a year and do no good.[63]
And in the *Covent-Garden Journal* for June 2, 1752, Henry Fielding,
celebrated widely for his charitable heart, condemned bounty to

61. Moreover, Johnson's definition of *imbecility* ("weakness; feebleness of
mind or body") and the illustrative quotations indicate that in the eighteenth
century the word did not have the stigma attached to it today.
62. Boswell, *2*, 212.
63. Ibid., *4*, 3.

beggars as "a crime against the public." "It is assisting," he said, with a magistrate's experience to support him, "in the continuance and promotion of a nuisance."[64] Hawkins' own experience as a magistrate would have convinced him of the truth of this statement. Both as moralist and as biographer, therefore, he felt impelled to make clear his attitude toward this "foible" of Johnson.

Candour, wrote Dr. Newton, Bishop of Bristol, about Johnson's *Lives of the Poets*,

> was much hurt and offended at the malevolence that predomi-
> nates in every part. Some passages, it must be allowed, are
> judicious and well written, but make not sufficient compensa-
> tion for so much spleen and ill humor. Never was any biog-
> rapher more sparing of his praise, or more abundant in his
> censures. He seemingly delights more in exposing blemishes,
> than in recommending beauties; slightly passes over excellen-
> cies, enlarges upon imperfections, and not content with his own
> severe reflections, revives old scandal, and produces large quo-
> tations from the forgotten works of former criticks.[65]

These words have a familiar ring. If one were not warned, in fact, he might easily find himself assuming that Dr. Newton's statement had been extracted from one of the reviews of Hawkins' *Life* written in the spring or summer of 1787. The similarity is as signifi-cant as it is striking.

I think it not unreasonable to conclude that Hawkins and Johnson were criticized in similar terms because, as I have already suggested, their methods in biography were similar. Honesty is frequently offensive, and for Hawkins, as for Johnson, the first requisite of a

64. *The Works of Henry Fielding, Esq. with an Essay on His Life and Genius,* by *Arthur Murphy, Esq.* (new ed. London, 1808), *14,* 83.
65. Boswell, *4,* 285, n. 3.

biographer was that he be honest.[66] This meant that all evidence—
the favorable and unfavorable alike—must be accepted, and if sometimes the unfavorable seemed to accumulate with depressing rapidity, it was hardly the fault of the biographer. If the admirers of Parnell resented being told of Parnell's drinking, that was to be regretted; but as long as his drinking was a fact, Johnson would have
felt obliged to mention it.[67] The biographer should be a moralist,
too, for as Johnson said in the *Preface to Shakespeare*, it is always a
writer's duty to make the world better.[68] This meant that he must
not only collect his evidence but ponder it carefully for anything
that might be construed for the benefit of his readers, and if the
result was sometimes an example to be avoided rather than followed,
that again was hardly the fault of the biographer. Since idleness was
responsible for much of Johnson's misery, Hawkins would have
considered himself negligent if he had failed to depict the effects
of that vice.

Johnson's difficulty with the *Lives of the Poets* was that he was
trying to please a public of varying prejudices. One person might
resent the censure of Gray's poetry, another the attack upon Milton's
Republicanism, and a third the account of Pope's parsimony, while
still another might resent all three. Thus an indictment like Dr.
Newton's was to be expected. But attacks like Johnson's (or what

---

66. One exception to Hawkins' general honesty must be noted. In questions
involving his own honor or reputation, he is not always reliable. Thus his
explanation of his withdrawal from the Literary Club included no reference
to the encounter with Burke or to the reception accorded Hawkins afterwards, and his attack on the Essex Head Club doubtless concealed his annoyance at not being asked to join. His account in the second edition (pp. 585–87)
of his pocketing Johnson's Diaries may be accurate, but it is rendered suspect
because he changed a date in order to work in this defense of his own conduct.
On the other hand, it must be recognized that all these may have been ra-
tionalizations rather than downright dishonesty.
67. *Works*, 2, 19.
68. Ibid., 9, 253.

seemed attacks) upon favorites long dead seldom startle us like an attack upon a recent favorite. If time makes us see a little more clearly, it does so partly because it tends to disengage our passions. Johnson had time on his side; Hawkins did not. In 1787 Johnson's friends could still recall his majestic frame weaving through the crowds of Fleet Street, could still hear his sonorous voice ringing out its message of good sense, could still be warmed by the noble fire of his presence. In such an atmosphere, what was more natural than that charges against Hawkins similar to Dr. Newton's against Johnson should be brought repeatedly and with a fervor intensified by the still vivid memory of Johnson?

Today, so many years later, the mask of Johnson's nearness should no longer blind us to the merits of Hawkins' method. It is true, we do not find in his *Life* that sweetness of temper that is always brimming with love, just as we do not find it in Johnson's *Lives*. His appraisal of almost everyone, of almost every situation, has something of the judicial in it. Like other writers of the day, he was given to compiling lists of a man's virtues and vices, just as Johnson, having described Shakespeare's best qualities as a dramatist, went on to enumerate his worst. Perfection was not to be found in man, as a magistrate well knew. But if the magistrate in him sometimes made him appear cold, aloof, and even harsh, we cannot be too often reminded that the magistrate in him is at the same time his greatest source of strength. It was the magistrate that forced him to come to grips with all the important questions of Johnson's life: Johnson's relations with his wife, his pension, his idleness, his affection for the ungrateful and undeserving, to mention only a few. It was the magistrate that tolerated no hasty decision, but insisted upon the objective and thorough examination of all available evidence. It was the magistrate that preserved carefully the evidence upon which his decisions had been based. If in the long scroll of decisions reached by Hawkins there are some we cannot check with our approval, by the law of human fallibility we should recognize that this is natural enough. In any event, we should be grateful to the man who was not content merely to record the facts of Johnson's life, but never let slip the opportunity to gain an insight into Johnson's character by a sober evaluation of those facts. Finally, we should be grateful most of all that Hawkins has left us, untampered, the evidence available to him, for when we have reason to suspect his decisions we need only review the evidence ourselves in order to confirm or allay our suspicions. Such review, as I have been attempting to demonstrate, should redeem Hawkins from the censure of those who found him malevolent at every turn. Of course he sometimes disagreed with Johnson or took exception to his behavior. Of course he made mistakes in judgment. But these are very different things from being malevolent.

Chapter Five

THE DARK UNCHARITABLE CAST, II

I was deeply occupied with my father in the examination and selection of Dr. Johnson's papers, and can truly say, that the tenderest regard was shown to the feelings of every individual.

—Miss Hawkins' Memoirs, *1, 66 n.*

BOSWELL, IT SHOULD BE OBSERVED, did not trouble himself particularly with Hawkins' attitude toward Johnson's friends and other contemporaries. The "dark uncharitable cast" was intended to apply only to Hawkins' attitude toward Johnson. But it is clear that the earlier critics of Hawkins' *Life* meant to brand with the iron of malevolence not only his attitude toward Johnson but his attitude toward practically everyone upon whom he had "sat in judgment," as one critic put it.[1] Had the charge passed out of existence with Hawkins himself, we might with impunity dismiss it. But sung out so boldly in its own day, the charge has passed like a round from generation to generation, until it has come down to us almost without change.[2] It cannot, therefore, be dismissed. Fortunately it can be dealt with quickly.

1. *English Review* (April 1787), p. 269.
2. "There are," writes Dr. Scholes (p. 192), "... (as we would expect from Hawkins) some uncharitable judgements." Joseph Wood Krutch, *Samuel Johnson* (New York, Holt, 1944), p. 71, describes one of Hawkins' confessions as "characteristically cynical."

In his accounts of Johnson's contemporaries, Hawkins' purposes and methods are patently clear. While he frequently disapproves, he does not consciously misrepresent, though in such brief spans he is not always able to summon all the evidence for his opinions, as he was with Johnson. With Hawkins, to disapprove was to moralize, and sometimes he moralizes at such length that he misleads us into thinking that he has tilted the balance of his judgment rather toward the unfavorable than the favorable. Finally, on occasion an unusual choice of words (like Johnson's "imbecility") makes him appear a harsher judge than he is.[3]

Philo Johnson, as we have seen,[4] accused Hawkins of the unpardonable sin of irreverence to the dead. To attack the living was according to the rules, for the living could reply. But to attack the dead was despicable. It is true that Hawkins wrote of a number of people who by 1787 were dead, and some of them he may fairly be said to have attacked. Many of his readers resented his judgments on Goldsmith, and on Fielding, Richardson, Smollett, and Sterne (for he condemned all the major novelists).[5] The *Gentleman's Magazine* took offense at some of his strictures on Edward Cave. Most disturbing of all, to the Johnson circle at least, proved to be the account which the *Universal Magazine* reprinted as the "Instructive Memoirs of Mr. Samuel Dyer," one of the members of the Ivy Lane and Literary clubs. Malone called it greatly "overcharged and discolored by . . . malignant prejudices,"[6] and Sir Joshua Reynolds and Bishop Percy both used it as the occasion for a tirade against

---

3. "My friend, Sir John, is a matter-of-fact man," wrote Horace Walpole in 1776 (Scholes, p. 129)—a judgment no reader of Hawkins is likely to dispute.

4. See above, p. 21.

5. See above, p. 66, however, for evidence that Hawkins could also admire the novelists.

6. Prior, *Life of Edmond Malone*, p. 419.

Hawkins.[7] None of them, however, produced evidence to refute Hawkins' statements.

Nevertheless, moralist that he was, Hawkins may well have "overcharged" this portrait, though at this distance, with so little known about Dyer, it is difficult to tell how far Hawkins may have wandered from the truth. Hawkins did not deny either his sweetness of temper or his modesty; he insisted upon them. Nor did he fail to grant Dyer an intellect of the highest order. But he found in his sloth and sensuality the evils that led to intellectual failure and moral and material ruin, and here was a lesson not to be overlooked—that evil can break the promise even of greatness. The chief purpose of the account, therefore, was "to point a moral," and such was Hawkins' regard for the account that he was willing to allot ten pages of the *Life* to it.[8]

The account of Goldsmith[9] also deserves further consideration. Goldsmith's admirers have denounced it roundly and will doubtless continue to do so, and yet it affords a picture of Goldsmith essentially the same as those drawn by Boswell and others who had known him. Most offensive have been Hawkins' indictment of Goldsmith as an "idiot in the affairs of the world" for rejecting the patronage of the Earl of Northumberland; his remark that the members of the Club, since Goldsmith wrote for the booksellers, looked upon him as a mere literary drudge; and his statement that Goldsmith, in his dealings with the booksellers, "is said to have acted very dishonestly, never fulfilling his engagements." "Idiot," we can readily see, is one of Hawkins' unfortunately chosen words, though we would be unfair to Hawkins if we failed to note that he

7. Ibid., pp. 425–27. It is interesting that the account of Dyer should have been the only one singled out by Philo Johnson as worthy of praise. The *European Magazine* had reprinted it the month before it printed the first of Philo Johnson's articles.

8. *Life*, pp. 222–32.

9. *Life*, pp. 416–21.

considered Goldsmith an idiot only in "the affairs of the world." We can readily see, too, that Hawkins, who had questioned the wisdom of Johnson's rejection of Chesterfield's patronage, would find reason to rebuke Goldsmith for his rejection of the Earl of Northumberland's. Goldsmith, like Johnson, was failing to recognize his own interests. As for the attitude of the club members (which Johnson himself confirms),[10] Hawkins was quick to admit that Goldsmith fooled them all, for he wrote "one of the finest poems of the lyric kind that our language has to boast of . . . and surprised us with 'The Traveller' . . . ," which Johnson called the "best written poem since the time of Pope."[11] Finally we may notice that the doubts cast upon Goldsmith's dealings with the booksellers are based upon hearsay; Hawkins has not attempted to vest them with the dignity of fact.

Certainly there is not the lightness of touch in this portrait essential for making the awkwardness of Goldsmith really attractive to us. Hawkins was too practical a man to have much patience with a friend who managed his affairs as badly as Goldsmith managed his. Yet if we draw the screen of Hawkins' impatience we can still have an occasional sight of Goldsmith quite worth setting beside what we know of him from other sources. There is, for example, this recently authenticated glimpse of Goldsmith as storyteller: "He would frequently preface a story thus:—'I'll now tell you a story of myself, which some people laugh at, and some do not.' "[12] Or this of Goldsmith lending his aid to Hawkins' musical researches: "While I was writing the History of Music, he, at the club, communicated to me some curious matter: I desired he would reduce it to writing; he promised me he would, and desired to see me at his chambers:

10. Boswell, *3*, 252.
11. *Life*, p. 420.
12. *Life*, p. 418. According to Sir Joshua Reynolds, *Portraits* (New York, McGraw-Hill, 1952), p. 51, Goldsmith began one of his stories with "There lived a cobbler—some people do laugh at this story and some do not."

I called on him there; he stepped into a closet, and tore out of a printed book six leaves that contained what he had mentioned to me."[13]

If Hawkins was aware of Goldsmith's shortcomings—as who was not?—he did not, on the other hand, hesitate to give him the praise he considered his due: "Goldsmith is well known by his writings to have been a man of genius and of very fine parts."[14] In short, in the tradition of his day Hawkins was merely casting up the balance of good and bad, and whoever thinks him a harsh judge would profit from a glance at the *New and General Biographical Dictionary* of 1784. Hawkins himself, in the portraits of Amhurst, Boyse, and Hawkesworth, has given us an opportunity to study the method of the *Dictionary;* and if we compare Hawkins' abridgments—that of Dr. Campbell, for example—with the originals, we shall find that Hawkins has by no means preserved the bad in preference to the good. Indeed, whoever studies Hawkins' portraits in the *Life*—and let us still limit our discussion to the portraits of the dead—will find that Hawkins almost invariably says everything in a person's favor that he can. In fact, one will be surprised to discover how many persons Hawkins has praised almost without qualification. A partial list would include Dr. Bathurst, Dr. Lawrence, Dr. Mead, Dr. Nugent, Dr. M'Ghie, Dr. Campbell, Topham Beauclerk, Anthony Chamier, and George Psalmanazar. The names of those whose virtues are only slightly qualified would extend the list much further.[15]

It is worth spending a moment over this notion of Philo Johnson's that it is despicable to attack the dead. It is a notion which Boswell

13. *Life*, p. 420.
14. *Life*, p. 416.
15. Horace Walpole was impressed with Hawkins' fairness. In the margin of his copy of the *Life*, next to the account of Moses Browne, Walpole wrote, "It is handsome in Hawkins to say nothing uncandid of Browne who wrote against him." Walpole's copy is in the library of W. S. Lewis of Farmington, Connecticut.

himself was momentarily tempted to subscribe to, for in the manuscript of his *Life of Johnson* he recorded that the members of the Ivy Lane Club were Bathurst, Hawkesworth, "Mr. John Hawkins an attorney" and "several more persons of various talents and pursuits, of whom as many such as are dead have had their characters drawn by said attorney."[16] The infelicity of this statement could not have been Boswell's only reason for crossing it out. It must have occurred to him promptly that a number of dead people were not being handled very reverently in his own *Life*. Perhaps he remembered, also, that in his *Tour to the Hebrides* he had already quoted one comment of Johnson justifying a biographer's revealing the defects of the dead,[17] and that in his *Life* he was planning to quote another:

> JOHNSON. Sir, it is of so much more consequence that truth should be told, than that individuals should not be made uneasy, that it is much better that the law does not restrain writing freely concerning the characters of the dead. Damages will be given to a man who is calumniated in his life-time, because he may be hurt in his worldly interest, or at least hurt in his mind: but the law does not regard the uneasiness which a man feels on having his ancestor calumniated. That is too nice. Let him deny what is said, and let the matter have a fair chance by discussion. But, if a man could say nothing against a character but what he can prove, history could not be written; for a great deal is known of men of which proof cannot be brought. A minister may be notoriously known to take bribes, and yet you may not be able to prove it.[18]

Upon this, Boswell has commented, "What Dr. Johnson has here said, is undoubtedly good sense."

16. From the manuscript of Boswell's *Life*, Yale Boswell Papers.
17. Boswell, *5*, 238.
18. Ibid., *3*, 15–16.

But to leave the dead and go to the living. Here we may wonder. Certainly Hawkins was not particularly charitable to his two chief rivals in Johnsonian biography, Boswell and Mrs. Piozzi. He angered Boswell by terming him merely "a native of Scotland"[19] and by omitting to say that it was Boswell who first suggested that application be made to Lord Chancellor Thurlow for an increase in Johnson's pension so that he might recover his health abroad. He angered Mrs. Piozzi by denouncing her second marriage as a "degradation of herself" and a "desertion of her children."[20] He did not speak well of Burke, with whom he had quarreled at the club, or, in the second edition, of Steevens, whom he had every reason to despise, but he forbore mentioning either by name. He must have offended Dr. Taylor by his insertion of a Latin entry from Johnson's diary which revealed that Johnson had composed at least one sermon for Taylor. Hawkins, however, seems to have printed the entry only after much deliberation. The page has been twice canceled. In the first cancel Hawkins wrote, "In his Diary I find the name of one Clergyman whom he assisted."[21] Perhaps it would have been better to leave it at that. But Hawkins' profound dislike for the practice of delivering ghost-written sermons seems to have overcome his regard for the feelings of the individual he considered at fault.[22] In the second cancel he stated explicitly

---

19. *Life*, p. 472.

20. Hawkins could hardly have ignored Mrs. Piozzi's second marriage, which was a most important incident in Johnson's life. In denouncing the marriage he was, like many of Johnson's friends, defending Johnson's attitude toward it.

[margin: he was also speaking his own mind]

[margin: a part of Jn's attitude.]

21. See below, Appendix, D, p. 196.

22. Edmond Malone, who had seen the cancels, was of a different opinion. While he did not regret that Taylor was mentioned by name, he charged that at first Hawkins "had not the spirit" to make an open accusation, but after quarreling with Taylor revised the passage to include the name. Quite possibly Malone is right. However, there is no record of a quarrel, and Malone's conclusion about Hawkins' motive is obviously speculation. See below, Appendix, C, p. 191. Hawkins, we might note, was not the first to reveal Tay-

that in Johnson's "Diary I find this note: '77 Sep.22 Concio pro Tayloro,' " and with slight modification this was retained in the final version.[23]

On the whole, however, Hawkins' concern for the living is remarkable. He might have found it useful to attack the *Lives* of Johnson that preceded his, but his work is singularly free of any contempt for the *Lives* of Cooke, Shaw, and Tyers, for Boswell's *Tour* and Mrs. Piozzi's *Anecdotes*, or for the anonymous *Lives* of the *Universal* and *European* magazines.[24] And more than once Hawkins went out of his way to avoid discussing his contemporaries. Thus when he gave his account of the Ivy Lane Club he characterized all the members except Mr. Ryland and Mr. Payne, who were still alive,[25] and when he gave his account of the Literary Club he char-

lor's secret. Two years earlier the *Whitehall Evening-Post* (Jan. 1–4, 1785) had recounted a story of manuscript sermons being misdelivered to "Demosthenes" Taylor when they were really intended for his "illiterate namesake" at Westminster.

23. *Life*, p. 392 n.

24. In Aug., 1784, more than three months before Johnson's death, the *Universal Magazine* published "Memoirs of the Life and Writings of Dr. Samuel Johnson."

25. How unfairly Hawkins was maligned will appear from a passage in Arthur Murphy's *Essay on the Life and Genius of Samuel Johnson*, first published in 1792: "This list [of the members of the Ivy Lane Club] is given by Sir John, as it should seem, with no other view than to draw a spiteful and malevolent character of almost every one of them" (*John. Misc.*, 1, 389). Not counting Johnson, Hawkins listed nine members of the club, three of whom (including himself) he did not characterize. Thus there are characterizations of Dr. Salter, John Hawkesworth, Samuel Dyer, and Drs. M'Ghie, Barker, and Bathurst. The account of Hawkesworth, we have seen, was reprinted from the *Biographical Dictionary*, and in general it is favorable. The accounts of three of the others are quite complimentary: while Dr. Salter was "no deep scholar," he was "a man of general reading . . . well-bred, courteous, and affable"; M'Ghie "was a learned, ingenious, and modest man"; Bathurst was "greatly beloved" by Johnson "for the pregnancy of his parts and the elegance of his manners." On the other hand, the account of Barker leans toward the unfavorable: he was "an excellent scholar" and "a deep metaphysician," but he was thoughtless and slovenly, and Johnson snubbed him for his Unitarian principles. Finally, we have already seen that Hawkins expressed his disapproval of Samuel Dyer. In other words, Murphy's description—a spiteful

acterized only the three members who had died. Miss Hawkins recorded how she discovered among Johnson's papers a letter from Mrs. Piozzi to Johnson concerning her second marriage, a letter which Mrs. Piozzi would hardly have wished disclosed to the public. "I carried it to my father: he enclosed it and sent it to her, there never having been any intercourse between them."[26] Such consideration for others is hardly deserving of the epithet *uncharitable.* Indeed, the evidence suggests that a much more accurate estimate of Hawkins' *Life* was that penned by Elizabeth Carter in a letter to Mrs. Montagu dated June 22, 1787: "Have you read Sir John Hawkins's Life of Dr. Johnson? I have just finished it, and think it much less exceptionable than the other two.[27] Indeed there are but very few passages that are likely to give pain to any one. His character of Dr. Johnson is impartially, and very decently and candidly represented."[28] Coming as it does from a woman who had been Johnson's friend from his first days of struggle in London,[29] and who might have felt slighted because Hawkins failed in his *Life* to credit her with a work which was really her own,[30] this letter must command our respect. Mrs. Carter, we should notice, admired Hawkins' impartiality, candor, decency, and consideration for the feelings of others. These are the qualities essential for objective yet sympathetic biography—the very qualities which, in a time less torn with the strife of grudge and rivalry, might have gained Hawkins many more admirers as ardent as Johnson's "Eliza."

and malevolent character—can at most be applied to two of Hawkins' accounts. And even then it may still be disputed whether these were written out of spite and malevolence.

26. *Memoirs, 1,* 66 n.

27. Mrs. Carter was doubtless referring to Boswell's *Tour* and Mrs. Piozzi's *Anecdotes.*

28. *Letters from Mrs. Elizabeth Carter to Mrs. Montagu* (London, 1817), *3,* 270–71.

29. She was the "Eliza" celebrated in Johnson's Latin and Greek verses published in *Gent. Mag.* in 1739.

30. See below, p. 110.

Chapter Six

UNPARDONABLE INACCURACIES

Having read both Hawkins and Boswell [the Tour to the Hebrides], I now think myself almost as much a master of Johnson's character, as if I had known him personally . . .

—*William Cowper to Samuel Rose, June 20, 1789*[1]

WE SHOULD EXPECT of Hawkins, as of any other biographer, a high standard of accuracy—higher, certainly, than his critics would have us believe that he attained. Yet, complained Boswell, who was in a position to know, "There is such an inaccuracy in the statement of facts, as in so solemn an authour is hardly excusable, and certainly makes his narrative very unsatisfactory." Still more sweeping was the indictment of Boswell's friend Edmond Malone, who wrote to Lord Charlemont on November 7, 1787, that there was "scarcely a material fact" in Hawkins' book "truly stated."[2] If such charges are true, whatever else we find in Hawkins' favor, Boswell will continue to affect his followers (and rightly so) with his victor's contempt for a rival whom he wished to see not merely outclassed but actually disgraced.

It would be folly to contend that Hawkins was always accurate. A list of thirty or forty of his errors of fact could be compiled with-

1. *The Correspondence of William Cowper*, ed. Thomas Wright (New York, Dodd, 1904), *3*, 386.
2. Boswell, *1*, 524.

out difficulty, and it would not be exhaustive. And when to these we add the mistakes in interpreting Johnson's handwriting and in transcribing Johnson's letters and works, the list becomes so imposing that we may find ourselves throwing up our hands in despair and confessing that Boswell's condemnation of the book as "very unsatisfactory" was charitable indeed. In our own day a biography with so many errors would be quickly laughed into oblivion, and few would feel that justice had not been served.

But it is an all-important consideration that Hawkins was not writing in our day. The reviewers were unable to enumerate many of Hawkins' errors for the simple reason that most of the time they had no way of knowing whether or not he was wrong. In 1787 the tender and systematic preservation of the records of a man's life had not yet enshrined what was known of Johnson's history in a series of volumes available to anyone capable of making his way through a card catalogue or a bibliography. The many refinements we have given the bibliographical process in our day were quite unknown. Consequently, anyone setting out to compile a memorial was assuming a much more difficult task than his counterpart assumes today. His material was where he could find it. And when we consider that for much of it Hawkins was groping in the darkness of fifty, sixty, and even seventy years before, the magnitude of his task should caution us not to expect from him the record of accuracy we expect from our contemporaries. Of course, we must set him a high standard still, but in suiting it to his day rather than to ours, we are doing him no more than that justice which any author may reasonably demand.

Some of Hawkins' errors, like those of oversight, were readily avoidable, and one can only assume that with such a large mass of material at his disposal he was certain to overlook something. It is surprising, for example, to find him asserting that in 1732 Johnson was undermaster to Anthony Blackwall at Market Bosworth school, since John Nichols had pointed out, in an issue of the *Gentleman's Magazine* obviously used by Hawkins,[3] that Blackwall had died in 1730.[4] Hawkins should also have known (for it was common knowledge) that the author who attacked Johnson in *Lexiphanes* was Campbell rather than Kenrick, but on the other hand it was hardly fair of Boswell to rebuke Hawkins for an error he was quick to correct in the second edition, with which Boswell was acquainted. More difficult to understand is the confusion which Hawkins permitted concerning the date of Johnson's pension, for though he did not actually date it, he left the impression that it had been granted in 1760. Hawkins could have readily checked the date in the official records, or with any number of Johnson's friends; at any rate, the assignment of the pension to 1762 by the accounts in both the *Universal* and *European* magazines should have encouraged him to be explicit himself. A similar confusion in the relative dates of *Irene* and *The Vanity of Human Wishes* could have been avoided in much the same way. As for the poem *London,* Cooke's *Life* had stated accurately that Dodsley had purchased it for ten guineas, but for reasons not now ascertainable Hawkins trusted to a less reliable informant. It is likewise difficult to understand why Hawkins should have presented the exchange between Johnson and Andrew Millar upon completion of the *Dictionary* as formal, written notes. In Tyers' account (doubtless Hawkins' source) the remarks are transmitted orally by messengers, the only way, as Boswell pointed out,

---

3. *Gent. Mag.* (Dec. 1784), p. 893.

4. In the same issue of the magazine, Nichols had announced that only six sheets of the translation of Sarpi had been printed, though of course if Hawkins had reason to believe that the number was twelve he was justified in ignoring Nichols. Since no one has yet discovered the sheets, the correct number is still anyone's guess, but Nichols' insistence that there were six even after the publication of Hawkins' *Life* suggests that he was confident of being right. See Edward L. Ruhe, "The Two Samuel Johnsons," *NQ* (Oct. 1954), p. 433.

that they could have retained both their humor and their vitality.[5]

Clearly, Hawkins could have eliminated these errors, and it will be difficult to quarrel with anyone who insists upon calling them inexcusable. But of most of Hawkins' errors there is reason to be tolerant. It is true that recourse to a calendar would have kept him from placing in the year 1734 a Diary entry dated only "Friday, August 27th," for in 1734 August 27th did not fall on a Friday.[6] It is true that his misreading of Johnson's hand resulted in some absurdities and elicited from Boswell, with some justice, the remark that "it would have been better to have left blanks than to write nonsense."[7] Boswell does note, however, both here and elsewhere, that Johnson's was not an easy hand to read. And we ourselves should note that Boswell's own interpretation of Johnson's hand is not invariably happy.[8] Hawkins' errors, moreover, are not predominantly of this sort. Most of them do not impose upon our good nature when they ask us to tolerate them. The ascription of *Lexiphanes* to Kenrick, for example, seems natural enough when we consider that Kenrick had not only been an active vilifier of Johnson but had himself compiled a dictionary. A similar error was the ascription to Johnson of the translation of Crousaz's *Examen*. Johnson *had* published a translation of Crousaz's *Commentary*, an extremely rare work which Hawkins had probably not even seen; and since both the *Examen* and the *Commentary* were concerned with Pope's *Essay on Man*, the confusion was almost inevitable. Even Boswell, with Hawkins' error to caution him, ran into trouble here, as we shall see in a moment.

5. Boswell, *1*, 287.
6. *Life*, p. 163 n. The error may have been the result of careless proofreading.
7. Boswell, *1*, 208, n. 1.
8. As, for instance, when he quotes Johnson as writing to Dr. Brocklesby on July 21, 1784, "when accident recovers me from your immediate care" instead of "when accident removes me from your immediate care" (Boswell, *4*, 353; *Letters*, *3*, 185). See also below, p. 103, n. 22.

The mistake of the second "Samuel" Johnson, the rival translator of Sarpi's *History of the Council of Trent,* was also an easy one to fall into. If Johnson had told Hawkins that another person with the same name had engaged in the translation, Hawkins might well have assumed that the Christian names as well as the surnames were identical. On the other hand, if the account had reached him by way of one or more intermediaries, the change from John Johnson to Samuel Johnson was just such an embellishment as a lover of coincidence would have been unable to resist. It is regrettable that for his information on Johnson's translation Hawkins consulted the *Weekly Miscellany,* but, of course, he had no way of knowing that in the *Daily Advertiser* he would have discovered John Johnson's claim to the original rights in the translation.[9]

Hawkins' report of a Russian translation of the *Rambler,* error though it is, is certainly an excusable one, for Johnson's heart apparently was "dilated" with the news of the Russian translation.[10] "O! Gentlemen," Johnson announced at the Essex Head Club, "I must tell you a very great thing. The Empress of Russia has ordered the 'Rambler' to be translated into the Russian language: so I shall be read on the banks of the Wolga."[11] "I have since heard that the report was not well-founded," says Boswell in a footnote; but one wonders if Boswell would have added the footnote if Hawkins, in his second edition, had not reduced the story to an unfounded rumor.[12]

An error of greater magnitude is the statement that after the publication of Johnson's *Marmor Norfolciense* in May 1739, "warrants were issued and messengers employed to apprehend the author, who, though he had forborne to subscribe his name to the pamphlet, the

9. Boswell, apparently on Hawkins' authority, subscribed to the same error. See Ruhe, "The Two Samuel Johnsons."

10. *Life,* p. 290.

11. Boswell, *4,* 276–77.

12. *Life,* 2d ed., p. 290 n.

vigilance of those in pursuit of him had discovered. . . . To elude
the search after him, he, together with his wife, took an obscure
lodging in a house in Lambeth Marsh, and lay there concealed till
the scent after him had grown cold."[13] With the comment that this
"is altogether without foundation," Boswell pronounced what has
remained the final word on this episode: "Mr. Steele, one of the
Secretaries of the Treasury . . . informs me, that 'he directed every
possible search to be made in the records of the Treasury and Secretary of State's Office, but could find no trace whatever of any
warrant having been issued to apprehend the author of this pamphlet.' "[14]

It is not like Hawkins to invent a story of this kind, but Mr.
Steele's search would seem to have been thorough, and certainly
subsequent inquiry has turned up no evidence of a warrant against
Johnson. Yet it was a time, as Hawkins makes clear, when political
tempers were easily ruffled, and when the measures of government
to protect itself against criticism were likely to be decisive and
prompt. Not long before, *Gustavus Vasa* had been refused a license
for the stage; and near the end of June 1739 the publisher of the paper
Common Sense was imprisoned for attacking the Walpole administration.[15] In such an atmosphere a political writer had to proceed
with great care, particularly if he was as violently anti-administra-
tion as Johnson. That Johnson had something to fear seems certain
enough. In the May 1739 *Gentleman's Magazine* Edward Cave reprinted the Latin inscription from Johnson's pamphlet, with the
promise to his readers that the following month he would reprint
the English translation and the interpretation. But in June, while he
reprinted the translation, he held back the interpretation, which contained the really inflammatory part of the pamphlet. Cave knew a

13. *Life,* p. 72.
14. Boswell, *1,* 141–42.
15. *Daily Advertiser,* July 2, 1739. See also Clifford, pp. 215–16.

danger signal when he saw it. Surely, if an editor took the precaution of omitting the interpretation, it is not beyond belief that the author of so incendiary a work, fearing reprisal, would remove with his wife to the obscurity of a Lambeth Marsh lodging. As Clifford suggests, if warrants were not actually issued, Johnson may at least have heard rumors of them; or he may have felt that the natural course of government was to start proceedings against him.[16]

Many of Hawkins' other errors of fact are hardly significant enough to merit examination, and for most there is a simple explanation. The textual errors, however, must give us a moment's pause, for though Hawkins approached a text with more reverence than many of his contemporaries, he sometimes transcribed carelessly. In the stanzas on the death of Levett, for example, "letter'd ignorance" (for Johnson's "letter'd arrogance") is a plausible enough paradox, but the line demands the more subtle contempt of Johnson's original.[17] In the well-known letter to James Macpherson, Hawkins quoted Johnson as saying, "What would you have me retract? I thought your work an imposition; I think so still; and, for my opinion, I have given reasons which I here dare you to refute."[18] But Johnson wrote *imposture,* not *imposition,* and Hawkins' replacement has taken most of the bite from Johnson's retort. In Gilbert Walmesley's letter recommending Johnson and Garrick to the mathematician Colson, Hawkins has ascribed to Walmesley the inelegance of "If it should any ways lay in your way, doubt not but you would be ready to recommend and assist your countryman."[19]

16. Clifford, p. 215.
17. *Life,* p. 554. Since Hawkins' edition of Johnson's *Works* prints "letter'd arrogance," (*11,* 366), the error is probably in the proofreading.
18. *Life,* p. 491. Hawkins' source (William Shaw's *Authenticity of the Poems Ascribed to Ossian*) has "imposture." Again the proofreading would seem to be at fault.
19. *Life,* p. 39. Walmesley actually wrote, "If it should any ways lie in your way, I doubt not but you would be ready to recommend and assist your countryman" (Boswell, *1,* 102).

Such garbling is the less excusable since Hawkins, having noted that the letter was first printed in the *Gentleman's Magazine,* [20] seems to have taken his text from one of the numerous other printed versions of the letter. The *Gentleman's Magazine* would have provided an authentic text. [21]

Eighteenth-century practice in quoting texts was at best whimsical. Punctuation, spelling, capitalization, and paragraphing were by no means sacred—very few of the many letters in Boswell's *Life* are exact transcripts—and frequently we find words changed in accordance with the author or editor's ideas of how the letter should have been written. Thus Walmesley's "any ways" became "any way" in Cooke's *Life.* [22] As a result of these practices, one seldom finds two identical texts of the same letter; and, of course, when the original cannot be traced, it is not always easy to resolve the confusion.

A well-known letter still untraced is that written in 1739 by Lord Gower to a friend of Jonathan Swift in an abortive attempt to procure Johnson a Master's degree from Dublin University. The earliest known printing of the letter appears in one of the numerous editions of the *Beauties of Johnson,* a book apparently compiled by the same William Cooke who later wrote Johnson's life. [23] The letter

20. (Oct. 1765), p. 451. The printing in *Gent. Mag.* was really the second. See Clifford, p. 343, n. 44.

21. Boswell likewise ignored *Gent. Mag.* and took his text from Cooke's *Life.*

22. In his letter to Bennet Langton, March 8, 1766, Johnson wrote, "we have less of Burke's company." Boswell misread "less" as "loss" and so supplied *the* to go with it (Boswell, *2, 16; Letters, 1,* 185).

23. *The Beauties of Johnson* (5th ed., Pt. II, London, G. Kearsley, 1782), pp. ix–x. See Allen T. Hazen, "*The Beauties of Johnson,*" *MP, 35* (Feb. 1938), 289–95. When Cooke first printed the letter he dated it Aug. 1737; but the anonymous writer in the *European Magazine* (George Steevens, I believe) noted that since the letter mentioned the poem *London* it could not have been written in 1737, and so he corrected the date to 1738. Hawkins accepted this correction, but Boswell in his *Life* changed the year to 1739, and subsequent investigation has confirmed Boswell's date.

was later reprinted in Cooke's *Life,* in the anonymous *European Magazine* account, in Shaw's *Memoirs,* in Hawkins, and in Boswell, but no two of the versions are identical. Boswell, however, again took his text from Cooke,[24] but it is impossible to determine Hawkins' source, for in some respects his version is unlike any that preceded it. Apparently there are variants of the letter yet to be discovered.

Though there are numerous minor differences between Hawkins' text of this letter and Boswell's, one difference ought not to be overlooked. In Hawkins' version the letter opens with the following sentence:

> Mr. Samuel Johnson, (authour of London a satire, and some other poetical pieces,) is a native of this country, and much respected by some worthy gentlemen in his neighbourhood, who are trustees of a charity school now vacant, the certain salary of which is 60 l. per year, of which they are desirous to make him master.[25]

In Boswell the opening sentence is as follows:

> MR. SAMUEL JOHNSON (authour of *London,* a satire, and some other poetical pieces) is a native of this country, and much respected by some worthy gentlemen in his neighbourhood, who are trustees of a charity school now vacant; the certain salary is sixty pounds a year, of which they are desirous to make him master.[26]

While Hawkins' version hardly testifies to Gower's skill with the English language, after a moment's hesitation one finds the meaning clear enough: the salary offered by the school was sixty pounds a

24. Boswell's instructions to the printer may be seen in the original manuscript of the *Life.* His text was taken from the second edition of Cooke's *Life.*
25. *Life,* pp. 62–63.
26. Boswell, *1,* 133.

year, and the trustees were anxious to make Johnson master of the school. But the omission of the first "of which" in Boswell's version and the replacement of the comma after *vacant* with a semicolon have changed Gower's meaning considerably. The salary of the position remains sixty pounds a year, but instead of wishing to make Johnson master of the school, the trustees wished to make him master of sixty pounds a year!

Perhaps Boswell used Cooke's version for no better reason than that he did not wish to follow Hawkins'. Having attacked Hawkins frequently, he could hardly have wished it thought that he was making any more use of him than was absolutely necessary. Naturally the ideal use was as a whipping boy, yet there were times when Boswell could not deny himself the information which Hawkins temptingly held out to him. The account of the Ivy Lane Club, as Hill notes,[27] was undoubtedly derived from Hawkins. Possibly Boswell's statement that Pope expressed himself concerning Johnson's Latin translation of Pope's *Messiah* "in terms of strong approbation"[28] was prompted by a more explicit statement in Hawkins, for if Boswell had arrived at this information independently he would have said so, and Pope's reaction to the translation is not mentioned in any of the accounts of Johnson written before Hawkins'. For similar reasons we may conclude that Boswell kept his eye on Hawkins' *Life* when he described Johnson and Savage "wandering together whole nights in the streets."[29] Boswell's knowledge of the booksellers who contracted for the *Dictionary* would surely have come from Hawkins, who printed the names from the original contract,[30] and his comment on Johnson's bleak memories of the

27. Ibid., p. 190, n. 5.

28. Ibid., p. 61; *Life*, p. 13. Information on the translation and on Johnson's recollection of Market Bosworth may have been given to both writers by Dr. Taylor.

29. *Life*, pp. 53–54; Boswell, *1*, 163. Boswell, of course, did have a separate account of one of Johnson's wanderings from Sir Joshua Reynolds.

30. Boswell, *1*, 183; *Life*, p. 344 n.

ushership at Market Bosworth, as Reade notes, merely paraphrases Hawkins' own.[31] Perhaps, too, Boswell would not have noticed that Jonas Hanway was the only one of his critics that Johnson ever answered, had not Hawkins noticed it before him.[32]

In following Hawkins, of course, Boswell occasionally ran into error. Hawkins, as we have seen, seems to have steered him to the *Weekly Miscellany* for October 21, 1738, and into the error of identifying the rival translator of Sarpi as another *Samuel Johnson*. Another of Boswell's errors probably derived from Hawkins might easily have been avoided. In the first edition of his *Life*, Hawkins, confusing the two Cornelius Fords, one of them Johnson's uncle and the other his famous cousin Parson Ford, remarked: "In the autumn of the year 1725, he [Johnson] received an invitation from his uncle, Cornelius Ford, to spend a few days with him at his house." In the second edition Hawkins corrected the word "uncle" to "cousin" and rightly showed, for the first time, that part of Johnson's education had been directed by his richly gifted cousin.[33] Boswell, overlooking the correction in the second edition, copied Hawkins' error from the first and thus passed by a circumstance of Johnson's youth which must have had its effects upon Johnson until the day of his death.[34]

An editorial practice peculiar to Boswell's most famous editors, Croker and G. B. Hill, has had a significant effect on the reputations of Johnson's biographers. Croker and Hill's habit of quoting in the

31. Reade, 5, 79. Hawkins concluded his account of the Market Bosworth interlude by saying that "Johnson . . . resigned his office, and took leave of a place, which he could never after speak of but in terms of the utmost dislike, and even of abhorrence" (*Life*, p. 21). This is paralleled by Boswell's "he relinquished a situation which all his life afterwards he recollected with the strongest aversion, and even a degree of horrour" (Boswell, *1*, 85).

32. Boswell, *1*, 314; *Life*, pp. 346 ff.

33. *Life*, p. 8; 2d ed., p. 8.

34. Boswell, *1*, 49.

notes any statement by a contemporary of Johnson that tends to corroborate or illuminate Boswell, has helped perpetuate the myth not that Boswell is supreme, which is no myth, but that he is complete—that, with respect to Johnson, he is a biographical all-in-all. It has given impetus, in other words, to the belief that anything of interest about Johnson can be found in Boswell, that there is no need to look elsewhere. With the aid of this practice, Boswell has absorbed his rivals in a merger whereby, in the public mind at least, they have surrendered all rights in the legend that is Johnson. How many of those who know the anecdote in which Johnson handed Hawkins down to posterity as "unclubable" would look for it in Madame D'Arblay's *Diary* rather than in Boswell's *Life?* And if asked where could be found Johnson's opinion that a tavern chair is the throne of human felicity, who would not answer, "In Boswell's *Life*"? Of course he would be right. Through the auspices of Boswell's editors it could be found there. But unconsciously this person would be giving credit to Boswell that properly belongs to Hawkins. People have been doing this for years.

One cannot read the volumes of the late Mr. Aleyn Lyell Reade, or the recently published biography by James L. Clifford, without being impressed by the frequency with which these two men have been forced to call upon Hawkins to verify, to supplement, or to correct Boswell. For Boswell's account of Johnson's early life by no means superseded Hawkins'. Hawkins' account contains much that is not in Boswell, and where it coincides with Boswell's it frequently does so not by the same but by different, and therefore corroborating, testimony. Something else must be considered. Hawkins and Boswell on occasion disagree over the details of Johnson's early life, and often Hawkins has the better of the argument. At other times each provides a portion of the whole, so that the two must be read together.

Certain glimpses of Johnson in his youth, or of the effect which, even as a young man, he was having on his acquaintances, can be caught only in Hawkins' *Life:* Mr. Butt predicting that the young Johnson would some day be a great man; the Earl of Berkshire presenting Johnson with a guinea for some Latin verses; Johnson being denied readmission to Lichfield Grammar School when he returned from his sojourn with Parson Ford; the rebellious Johnson at Oxford refusing to answer the knock of the servitor come to check his presence, and then joining in the game of hunting the servitor "with the noise of pots and candlesticks"; the same Oxford student insolently complaining to his tutor that he had been "sconced" "two-pence for non-attendance at a lecture not worth a penny." These are glimpses into the dark early years of Johnson's life which one would not willingly relinquish. But they are only the beginning. In 1737 Hawkins plunges the nearly penniless Johnson and Garrick into the bewildering maze of London and finds them a benefactor in the bookseller Wilcox.[35] And then he comes to the 1740's, that decade when he first became acquainted with Johnson—when he himself was trudging many of the same paths as Johnson—and suddenly we have an account of Johnson and London life which Boswell himself cannot match: Cave and the *Gentleman's Magazine*, the writing of the Debates, politics, poverty, Osborne, the *Life of Savage*, the *Dictionary*, Lord Chesterfield, and the Ivy Lane Club, where took place one of the most delightful incidents in Johnson's career:

> Mrs. Lenox . . . had written a novel intitled, 'The life of Harriot Stuart,' which in the spring of 1751, was ready for publication. One evening at the club, Johnson proposed to us the celebrating

35. I am aware that, since it is not possible to corroborate these views of Johnson, Hawkins' accuracy in them may be questioned. To assess the validity of each would be a lengthy task. More important still, it would be an unnecessary one, for it has been done with great care by various writers, particularly Reade, who finds good reason to accept every one of them (see Reade, Pts. III, V, VI).

the birth of Mrs. Lenox's first literary child, as he called her book, by a whole night spent in festivity. Upon his mentioning it to me, I told him I had never sat up a whole night in my life; but he continuing to press me, and saying, that I should find great delight in it, I, as did all the rest of our company, consented. The place appointed was the Devil tavern, and there, about the hour of eight, Mrs. Lenox and her husband, and a lady of her acquaintance, now living, as also the club, and friends to the number of near twenty, assembled. Our supper was elegant, and Johnson had directed that a magnificent hot apple-pye should make a part of it, and this he would have stuck with bay-leaves, because, forsooth, Mrs. Lenox was an authoress, and had written verses; and further, he had prepared for her a crown of laurel, with which, but not till he had invoked the muses by some ceremonies of his own invention, he encircled her brows. The night passed, as must be imagined, in pleasant conversation, and harmless mirth, intermingled at different periods with the refreshments of coffee and tea. About five, Johnson's face shone with meridian splendour, though his drink had been only lemonade; but the far greater of us had deserted the colours of Bacchus, and were with difficulty rallied to partake of a second refreshment of coffee, which was scarcely ended when the day began to dawn. This phenomenon began to put us in mind of our reckoning; but the waiters were all so overcome with sleep, that it was two hours before we could get a bill, and it was not till near eight that the creaking of the street-door gave the signal for our departure.[36]

The fullness of Hawkins' account of the forties and early fifties is not again attained until he comes to Johnson's last days, when he was in almost constant attendance upon his dying friend. Here, of

36. *Life*, pp. 285–87.

course, Hawkins had a real advantage over Boswell, who had returned to Scotland in June of 1784 and was thus compelled to write of Johnson's death at second hand. In between, it is true, Hawkins could produce nothing to rival Boswell's records of Johnson's conversation (as indeed who could?), but we need not conclude that those thirty years in Hawkins' *Life* are no more than a desert waste between the two oases.

I have said that there are frequent occasions when Hawkins and Boswell are each partly correct and so must be read in conjunction if the truth (or most of it, since subsequent investigation has added much to our knowledge of Johnson) is to be arrived at. Hawkins knew, for example, that Johnson's tutor at Oxford, William Jorden, "in about a year's space, went off to a living which he had been presented to, upon giving a bond to resign it in favour of a minor," and he went on to say, mistakenly, that Johnson then became the pupil of Mr. Adams.[37] According to Boswell, Jorden remained Johnson's tutor all through Johnson's residence, which Boswell, like Hawkins, mistakenly says was about three years.[38] Reade attributes Boswell's error about Jorden to Boswell's knowledge that Adams never actually became Johnson's tutor.[39] Conversely, we may attribute Hawkins' error about Adams to Hawkins' knowledge that Jorden left Oxford after only about a year of Johnson's residence. Had Boswell and Hawkins known that Johnson's residence at Oxford terminated in December 1729, they could have worked out satisfactorily the problem of Johnson's tutor.

A mistake in Hawkins which Boswell noticed, though without mentioning Hawkins, is the attribution to Johnson of the translation of Crousaz's *Examen,* admittedly the work of Elizabeth Carter.

37. *Life,* p. 11.
38. Probably Dr. Adams misled both of them. See above, p. 46, n. 29.
39. Reade, 5, 56.

Johnson, as we have seen, had actually translated a work of Crousaz, and Boswell in his journal for June 4, 1781, had recorded that fact: "He told us that he had in one day written six sheets of a translation of Crousaz on Pope." In this form the sentence went to press, but when Boswell came to examine the proofs of his *Life* he deleted the last four words and substituted "from the French."[40] As L. F. Powell points out, Boswell was aware that Mrs. Carter had translated the *Examen,* and he failed to observe that in a letter to Cave quoted in the *Life,* Johnson had mentioned both the *Examen* and the *Commentary,* and had said of the *Examen,* "It will, above all, be necessary to take notice, that it is a thing distinct from the Commentary."[41]

Hawkins was not able to identify Johnson's hand in the *Commentary.* But though he misapplied Johnson's letter to the extent that he found in it evidence for Johnson's translation of the *Examen,* he was perfectly well aware of the distinction Johnson was making between the two works: "The reputation of the Essay on Man soon after its publication invited a translation of it into French, which was undertaken and completed by the Abbé Resnel, and falling into the hands of Crousaz, drew from him first a general censure of the principles maintained in the poem, and afterwards, a commentary thereon containing particular remarks on every paragraph."[42]

The account of Johnson's efforts on behalf of Dr. Dodd is another in which the information gathered by the two biographers may be

---

40. Boswell, *4,* 494–95.
41. Ibid., *1,* 137.
42. *Life,* p. 66. Curiously enough, careful attention to the anonymous *European Magazine* account would have saved both Boswell and Hawkins a great deal of trouble. Its author had noted that while it was believed that Johnson had translated the *Examen,* he had very definitely translated the *Commentary (European Magazine,* Jan. 1785). The feminine hand in the *Examen* seems to have been common knowledge in 1746, as poems addressed to the translator in *Gent. Mag.* attest, (Nov. 1746), p. 607; (Dec.) p. 664.

considered complementary.[43] Though Boswell did not turn up everything, he was much more successful than Hawkins in discovering what Johnson had written during the course of the attempt to obtain a pardon for Dr. Dodd. His list, if we count Johnson's letters to Dodd, numbers fifteen items, whereas Hawkins' numbers only four. But Hawkins' narrative is charged with a certain excitement by a running account of what was occurring (for sometimes the whole affair seems to resolve itself into a continuous flow of letters and petitions). Hawkins provides an interesting glimpse of Mrs. Dodd, who, he informs us, managed to persuade to sign the petition to the King, not just the jury that had found the true bill of indictment, but the very jury that had tried and convicted her husband! He gives us a further insight when he informs us (taking his account from Cooke) that when Johnson drew up for publication the *Occasional Papers by the Late William Dodd, LL.D.* and five hundred copies were printed for Mrs. Dodd's benefit, "she, conscious that they were not of her husband's writing, would not consent to their being published; and the whole number, except two or three copies, was suppressed."[44] Finally he allows us to glimpse two of the less widely publicized methods employed to save Dodd: the offer of 1,000 pounds to Akerman, the Keeper of Newgate, if he would permit Dodd to escape; and the attempt of a number of Dodd's friends who, "with bank-notes in their pockets to the amount of five hundred pounds, had watched for the whole evening, about the door of the prison, for an opportunity of corrupting the turnkey."[45]

The only apparent inaccuracy in Hawkins' account is his state-

43. For a full account of this affair see *Papers Written by Dr. Johnson and Dr. Dodd in 1777,* ed. R. W. Chapman, Oxford, Clarendon Press, 1926.
44. *Life,* p. 529.
45. Ibid.

ment that Johnson had never seen Dr. Dodd. Johnson informed Boswell that he had been in Dodd's company once.[46]

Hawkins' statement concerning the period of Johnson's composition of the Parliamentary Debates seems on the face of it less accurate than Boswell's, which was intended to correct Johnson's own statement. Hawkins asserted that the first debate composed by Johnson was on the proposal to remove Sir Robert Walpole, and that he "continued to write them till the passing the bill for the restraining the sale of spirituous liquors, which was about the end of the year 1743." Boswell, on the other hand, maintained that "his composition of them began November 19, 1740, and ended February 23, 1742-3."[47] The Corn Bill was ordered to be brought in to Parliament on November 19, 1740, but debate on it did not actually begin until November 25. And while it is true that of the Debates composed by Johnson, this was the first conducted in Parliament, it is not true, as Boswell's statement leads us to believe, that this was the first which Johnson composed. As Hawkins informs us, public interest in the attempt to remove Walpole was so keen and the debates on that occasion so spirited, that "the drawing them up required in Cave's opinion, the pen of a more nervous writer than he who had hitherto conducted them."[48] It was obviously an auspicious moment for a change to a writer of whose capabilities Cave was growing increasingly aware. Nor is it a refutation of Hawkins' statement that Johnson did actually report some of the debates which took place in Parliament before the debate on the proposal

46. Boswell, *3*, 140.
47. *Life*, p. 132; Boswell, *1*, 150.
48. *Life*, p. 96. For much of this discussion I am indebted to Medford Evans, "Johnson's Debates in Parliament," (unpublished doctoral dissertation, Yale, 1933), pp. 68–69. The debate on the proposal to remove Walpole took place in Parliament on Feb. 13, 1741, and Johnson's first report of it (his first published debate) appeared in *Gent. Mag.* for July 1741, after Parliament had adjourned.

to remove Walpole. The debates did not appear in the *Gentleman's Magazine* in strict chronological order, and it is not to be supposed that Cave, having once replaced Guthrie with Johnson, would go back to him; after Johnson had been assigned his first debate, the earlier debates, passed by momentarily, would naturally have become his responsibility also.[49]

Another incident in Johnson's life affords an opportunity to compare the accounts of Hawkins and Boswell. In December of 1731, Hawkins informs us, Johnson's father died, and in the following March, Johnson, having "the means of subsistence to seek . . . accepted of an invitation to the office of under-master or usher of a free grammar-school, at Market-Bosworth in Leicestershire." Johnson, he continues, unable to bear the barbarous treatment of his patron, Sir Wolstan Dixie, left the school the following July, after receiving twenty pounds from his father's estate on June 15. To give proof of the inheritance, Hawkins inserted Johnson's Diary entry of June 15, in both Johnson's Latin original and Hawkins' English translation.[50]

Of this episode Boswell wrote, "In the forlorn state of his circumstances, he accepted of an offer to be employed as usher in the school of Market Bosworth, in Leicestershire, to which it appears, from one of his little fragments of a diary, that he went on foot, on the 16th of July.—'*Julii 16. Bosvortiam pedis petii.*' " Boswell then

---

49. The statements of both biographers about the terminal date of Johnson's composition are misleading. If we read Boswell literally, we must conclude that Johnson stopped composing the Debates in Feb. 1743, when in fact he continued to compose them for another year. And Hawkins, through an error in syntax, informs us that the liquor bill was passed at the end of 1743, when he really intended to say that Johnson's composition ceased about that time. The bill was passed in Feb. 1743 but was not reported until the closing months of that year and the opening months of 1744. For information about a later debate identified as Johnson's, see D. J. Greene, "Some Notes on Johnson and the *Gentleman's Magazine*," *PMLA*, 74 (1959), 77.

50. *Life*, pp. 20–21.

refuted Hawkins' statement that Johnson had been an assistant to Anthony Blackwall, and went on to explain that the unpleasantness of the situation forced Johnson to leave in a very few months.[51] Like Hawkins, Boswell inserted Johnson's Latin Diary entry concerning his inheritance (which, of course, he translated anew), but with the date July 15 rather than June 15, as Hawkins had printed it.[52]

Boswell's vagueness about this episode should not escape our notice. He does not say definitely when Johnson accepted the ushership, but leaves us to assume that he took up his duties at Market Bosworth on July 16 and remained at the school a few months— apparently into the fall.

The problem has only recently been resolved, and Hawkins has been vindicated on almost every count. On this page of his diary (now in the Hyde Collection) Johnson noted in Latin that when he wrote "twenty" he should have written "nineteen" and that when he wrote "July" he should have written "June." Thus both Boswell and Hawkins were mistaken about the size of Johnson's inheritance, but Hawkins' date for the inheritance is correct, whereas Boswell has placed both that and the trip to Market Bosworth in the wrong month. Moreover, in the same Diary Johnson has made the following entry: "1731 = 32. Mar' 9no S.J. Bosvorthiam petivit. Julio 1732 Bosvorthiam reliquit." (He went to Market Bosworth on March 9, 1732, and left it the following July.) And so Hawkins was also right in saying that the Bosworth episode in Johnson's life lasted from March to July 1732.[53]

Most of the charges Boswell leveled against Hawkins, as I have tried to show, can be turned against Boswell himself. His book is by

51. Boswell, *1*, 84.
52. Ibid., 80.
53. For the diary entries see *Diaries, Prayers, and Annals*, ed. E. L. McAdam, Jr. (New Haven, Yale University Press, 1958), pp. 28–30.

no means without error; the errors in the first volume alone would comprise a notable list. He, too, does not always manage to extract the entire substance from his sources. And he is not an infallible reader of Johnson's hand. I think, moreover, that even the statement about Hawkins which I have made the occasion of this chapter can, with some justice, be turned against him: there is "such an inaccuracy in the statement of facts, as . . . is hardly excusable."

The letter of Lord Gower discussed above had been printed by biographers before Hawkins, but none had ascertained the location of the school of which Johnson was seeking the mastership. Accordingly, Hawkins' identification of the school fitted a key piece to the puzzle of this memorable episode:

> The publication of this poem [*London*] was of little advantage to Johnson, other than the relief of his immediate wants: it procured him fame, but no patronage. He was therefore disposed to embrace any other prospect of advantage that might offer; for, a short time after, viz. in August 1738,[54] hearing that the mastership of Appleby School in Leicestershire was become vacant, he, by the advice of Sir Thomas Griesly a Derbyshire baronet, and other friends, went to Appleby, and offered himself as a candidate for that employment; but the statutes of the school requiring, that the person chosen should be a Master of Arts, his application was checked. To get over this difficulty, he found means to obtain from the late Lord Gower, a letter to a friend of his, soliciting his interest with Dean Swift towards procuring him a master's degree from the university of Dublin.[55]

Boswell, of course, did not wish to rely upon Hawkins for so

54. Actually 1739. The error is doubtless due to Hawkins' belief that the correct date of Gower's letter was 1738. See above, p. 103, n. 23.
55. *Life,* pp. 61–62.

prominent a part of Johnson's biography, and apparently he set about trying either to prove Hawkins mistaken or to confirm the account independently so that he could attribute his information to someone other than Hawkins. Spurred by a note in Pope's hand which located the school in Shropshire, and by a letter from "Mr. Spearing, attorney-at-law" describing a school in Newport, Staffordshire, much like that mentioned in Gower's letter, Boswell concluded that Pope must have written *Shropshire* when he really intended *Staffordshire,* and so conjectured in his first edition that the school in Newport was the one in question. In the *Gentleman's Magazine* for May 1793, however, Mr. Henn, one of the masters of Appleby School, identified the school without reference to Hawkins, whose *Life* he apparently did not know, and thus in a subsequent edition Boswell was able, on Henn's authority, to identify the school for his readers.[56]

I think it is not being too severe to suggest that Boswell here overstepped the bounds of private pique. If we can condemn Hawkins for failing to credit Boswell with the first suggestion that Johnson's pension be increased, what are we to say of this ingenious evasion of the truth, or of the stubborn pride which could announce what is only a confirmation of Hawkins' discovery as though it were the first intimation of the truth?

Among unpardonable inaccuracies I think one might safely list the purposeful tampering with the evidence provided by Johnson's Diaries. Two of the foremost authorities on the Diaries, Donald and Mary Hyde, have found no reason to believe that Hawkins changed any of Johnson's entries.[57] To be sure, he interpolated one date, 1734, which turned out to be mistaken, but he made no attempt to conceal his interpolation. Boswell, however, had no such reverence

56. Boswell, *1, 132,* n. 1.
57. Donald and Mary Hyde, "Johnson and Journals," *The New Colophon* (New York, 1950), pp. 165–97.

for the Diaries. I have already mentioned his suppression of the fact that Johnson had considered remarrying, a fact he had learned from a surreptitious look into one of the Diaries Johnson was to burn before his death.[58] There is another, though somewhat different, act of omission. Boswell quoted, again from Johnson's burned Diary, an entry for July 13, 1755, containing a number of resolutions:

> 'Having lived' (as he with tenderness of conscience expresses himself) 'not without an habitual reverence for the Sabbath, yet without that attention to its religious duties which Christianity requires;
>
> 1. To rise early . . .'[59]

Boswell's transcript of Johnson's entry reveals that what he printed is only an abridgment of Johnson's original:

> Having lived hitherto in perpetual neglect of publick worship & though for some years past not without an habitual reverence for the sabbath yet without that attention to its religious duties which Christianity requires. I will once more form a scheme of life for that day such as alas I have vainly formed which when my mind is capable of settled practice I hope to follow,

58. Boswell, 4, 405. Boswell's omission of a much discussed clause from Johnson's last prayer ("forgive and accept my late conversion") might also be mentioned here. The clause (but not the prayer) had been omitted from the Reverend George Strahan's edition of the *Prayers and Meditations* (1785), and Hawkins, who printed the entire prayer (*Life*, p. 584), either failed to deliver the manuscript to Boswell or else had copied the prayer from Strahan's manuscripts and thus had none to deliver. At any rate, Boswell, possibly to escape a further indebtedness to Hawkins rather than to avoid printing a suggestive and controversial passage, copied his text from the *Prayers and Meditations* and so published it incomplete (4, 417). See Maurice J. Quinlan, "The Rumor of Dr. Johnson's Conversion," *Review of Religion* (March 1948), pp. 243–61. Boswell could also have found the full text of the prayer in *Works*, 11, 193.

59. Boswell, 1, 303.

To rise early . . .[60]

There is much more in this than the mere "tenderness of conscience" which Boswell carefully pointed out to his readers. The abridgment is a simple, almost unemotional statement of fact. It conveys nothing of the deep sense of guilt to be found in the original, nothing of the brooding agitation of a mind unsettled, unsure of itself. It is true, Boswell cannot be accused of changing Johnson's words, since he has printed nothing which Johnson did not actually write. But Boswell owed it to his readers to transcribe Johnson's feelings as well as his words, and his abridgment no more provides an accurate picture of Johnson's mind on July 13, 1755, than a pail of seawater does of a storm at sea.[61]

One more point of comparison. As Frederick Pottle remarks, "No portion of Boswell's *Life of Johnson,* as he foresaw, has been so unpopular with the commentators as that in which he attributes Johnson's agonies of remorse in his last days to the recollection of sexual irregularities into which he had been led by Savage years before."[62] Boswell wrote,

> His great fear of death, and the strange dark manner in which Sir John Hawkins imparts the uneasiness which he expressed on account of offences with which he charged himself, may give occasion to injurious suspicions, as if there had been something of more than ordinary criminality weighing upon his conscience. On that account, therefore, as well as from the regard to truth which he inculcated, I am to mention, (with all possible respect and delicacy, however,) that his conduct, after he

60. Hydes, "Johnson and Journals," p. 183.
61. Boswell also changed the date of Johnson's Diary entry for April 29, 1753, to April 23, but since there is no apparent reason for the change, it was doubtless made accidentally.
62. Frederick A. Pottle, "The Dark Hints of Sir John Hawkins and Boswell," *MLN,* 56 (May 1941), 325. Also in Hilles, ed., *New Light on Johnson.*

came to London, and had associated with Savage and others, was not so strictly virtuous, in one respect, as when he was a younger man. It was well known, that his amorous inclinations were uncommonly strong and impetuous. He owned to many of his friends, that he used to take women of the town to taverns, and hear them relate their history.—In short, it must not be concealed, that, like many other good and pious men, among whom we may place the Apostle Paul upon his own authority, Johnson was not free from propensities which were ever warring against the law of his mind,—and that in his combats with them, he was sometimes overcome.[63]

Professor Pottle goes on to comment that W. B. C. Watkins, in his book *Perilous Balance,* has done "real service by bringing out clearly the fact that Hawkins first made the charge, and that Boswell, though he wrote at greater length, really says no more than his predecessor."[64]

The passage in Hawkins which Watkins quotes is a brief one: "it is conjectured, that he would have been less troubled with those reflections, which, in his latest hours, are known to have given him uneasiness, had he never become acquainted with one so loose in his morals, and so well acquainted with the vices of the town as this man [Savage] appears to have been."[65]

I cannot see that this statement makes the same charge against Johnson that Boswell's makes. The dying Johnson, says Hawkins, would have been less troubled if he had never known Savage, who was loose in his morals and acquainted with the town's vices. He does not say, here or elsewhere, that Johnson was himself loose in his morals. On the contrary, he emphasizes again and again the

63. Boswell, *4,* 395–96.
64. Pottle, "The Dark Hints."
65. *Life,* p. 88; W. B. C. Watkins, *Perilous Balance* (Princeton, Princeton University Press, London, Oxford University Press, 1939), p. 50.

strong moral fiber that was Johnson's throughout his life. That Johnson was introduced by Savage to some of the town's vices seems unquestionable, but sexual promiscuity need not have been one of them. Savage had vices to spare: "an irregular and dissipated manner of life had made him the slave of every passion that happened to be excited by the presence of its object, and that slavery to his passions reciprocally produced a life irregular and dissipated."[66] The irregularity of Johnson's own life was, as we have seen, a constant source of anguish to him; in this regard, Savage was the worst possible companion he could have had, just as Sir Richard Steele, some years earlier, was a similarly bad companion for Savage.[67] Certainly if his acquaintance with Savage was responsible for Johnson's separation from his wife, as Hawkins said it was, Johnson would have had every reason to rue the acquaintance, particularly in those later years when his fondness for his wife matured into the stately reverence so movingly expressed in his *Prayers and Meditations.*

The truth is that Hawkins' comments about the relationship with Savage are much too explicit to be termed "dark hints." While he was aware that Johnson "reflected with as little approbation on the hours he spent with Savage as on any period of his life," he insisted that he was "not warranted to say that Johnson was infected with" the vices of the town.[68] If Johnson was guilty of sexual irregularity, Hawkins had no evidence of that fact. Savage's example, of course, "was contagious, and tended to confirm Johnson in his indolence and those other evil habits which it was the labor of his life to conquer."[69] But Hawkins knew perfectly well, just as Boswell did, that it was not the labor of Johnson's life to conquer the evil habit of sexual irregularity. To grant Savage's influence was not to ascribe

66. Quoted from Johnson's *Life of Savage,* in *Works, 3,* 366.
67. Ibid., p. 255.
68. *Life,* p. 54. See "The Dark Hints" (rev.) for a different interpretation.
69. *Life,* p. 86.

every one of his vices to his protégé; indeed, Hawkins' caution was admirable:

> How far his [Johnson's] conversations with Savage might in-
> duce him thus to delight in tavern-society, which is often a
> temptation to greater enormities than excessive drinking, can-
> not now be known, nor would it answer any good purpose to
> enquire. It may, nevertheless, be conjectured, that whatever
> habits he had contracted of idleness, neglect of his person, or
> indifference in the choice of his company, received no cor-
> rection or check from such an example as Savage's conduct
> held forth.[70]

Hawkins, who could leave Johnson's lemonade and coffee party for Charlotte Lennox with a feeling of guilt caused by its similarity to a debauch, would hardly be one to condone Johnson's regular indulgence in tavern life, particularly in the hard-drinking company of Savage. But did his indulgence in tavern life with Savage mean that Johnson had to be led into the vice of sexual irregularity? Of the female mind, says Hawkins, Johnson "conceived a higher opinion than many men, and though he was never suspected of a blameable intimacy with any individual of them, had a great es-teem for the sex."[71] It was never heard, he says at another point, that Johnson "entertained a passion for any one, or was in any other sense a lover, than as he was the author of amorous verses. [He] was a man too strict in his morals to give any reasonable cause of jealousy to a wife."[72] Do we need any other answer to our question? Johnson's life with Savage was simply not all that a good man would wish it to have been. He wrote in those days imprudent political attacks of which he later ceased to be proud; his habits of

70. *Life*, p. 88.
71. *Life*, p. 390.
72. *Life*, pp. 315–16.

indolence, late rising, neglect of his person, and indifference to his choice of company received no check; and these, plus his unhusbandly habit of walking the streets at night, alienated for a time the affections of his wife. Surely it is not surprising that reflections on this period of his life should trouble the dying Johnson, for though no man of his day had fewer sins to atone for, no man was more conscious of those which he had.[73]

73. Professor Pottle is convinced, nevertheless, that Hawkins was responsible for Boswell's charge concerning Johnson's sexual irregularity, and perhaps this is so. On May 7, 1785, Boswell met Hawkins on the neutral ground of Bennet Langton's home, and he recorded in his journal for that day: "Sir J. Hawkins and I did very well. Stood in a corner, and talked grave and earnest. He accounted for Johnson's fear of death: 'I have read his diary. I wish I had not read so much. He had strong amorous passions.' BOS. 'But he did not indulge them?' HAWK. 'I have said enough' " (*Private Papers, 16*, 84). And on July 8th the following year the two met again at Langton's and discussed a "delicate question" (ibid., p. 203). I do not know what Hawkins was suggesting, but I will venture a guess that he was not saying, however obliquely, "Johnson indulged his amorous passions indiscriminately when in the company of Savage." At any rate, Hawkins was revealing nothing new to Boswell when he announced that Johnson had strong amorous passions, for Boswell had long since learned from Mrs. Desmoulins just how strong those passions were ("Tacenda" in Yale Boswell Papers). Hawkins' own discovery of Johnson's amorous nature, however, must have come as something of a shock to him, since it is hardly likely that he, any more than most of Johnson's friends, had ever suspected that during much of his life Johnson had struggled painfully with powerful sexual desires.

But where in Johnson's Diaries could Hawkins have read of Johnson's strong amorous passions? No one can tell what Johnson confided to the two Diaries that Hawkins held briefly in his possession a few days before Johnson's death. Nor is it likely that we will ever know whether Hawkins had further Diaries, which were burned in the fire that demolished his house in Feb. 1785. Just what Hawkins was referring to when he said to Boswell, "I have read his diary," is therefore anybody's guess. It is possible he found some hint of a strong attachment to Mrs. Thrale, such as was described in Miss Balderston's article "Johnson's Vile Melancholy," in *The Age of Johnson*, New Haven, 1949. What seems to me more likely is that Hawkins had read the manuscript of Johnson's *Prayers and Meditations,* which in May 1785 Hawkins' friend the Reverend George Strahan was still preparing for publication. In spite of its title, the *Prayers and Meditations* is a diary. And it gives repeated evidence of the intensity of Johnson's amorous passions (see, for example, Clifford, p.

Watkins makes the curious suggestion that Boswell revealed this "sin of sufficient magnitude" in order to defend Johnson against "those who imagine that the sins, of which a deep sense was upon his mind, were merely such little venial trifles as pouring milk into his tea on Good-Friday."[74] While it is to be hoped that Boswell had some more sensible motive, the fact remains, whatever his motive, that in his *Life* alone we are confronted with the charge of Johnson's adultery, a charge for which not the slightest evidence exists, and against which all reason protests.

Boswell's own mistakes (some of them, as we have seen, rather more serious than Hawkins') should help us to see that it is not fair to Hawkins to judge his book primarily by its mistakes. As a pioneer, forcing his way into the wilderness of hidden facts, he deserves a liberal allowance for error, and it is to his credit that he compares so favorably with Boswell, who had four years to correct the mistakes of his predecessor. If it is our custom to judge Boswell not by counting his errors but by assessing his portrait of Johnson, then it is only reasonable that we should judge Hawkins in the same way. When we do so, we will find that he is one of the most accurate of biographers—that his portrait of Johnson is scarcely less vital than Boswell's, and that the two men, while employing dif-

---

315). What would have been more natural and just than for Hawkins to impute Johnson's fear of death, in part at least, to his consciousness of the lusts of his own flesh, for Johnson considered his desires sinful as well as his indulgences? I suspect that Hawkins might have gone on to specify other reasons for Johnson's fear of death, but when Boswell interrupted with a question that the puritanical Hawkins would have considered gross and impudent, Hawkins abruptly put an end to the conversation. Perhaps Boswell did base his charge of sexual irregularity on the May 7th conversation (it is impossible to know what "delicate question" the two men discussed in the second conversation) and on Hawkins' pronouncements in the *Life*. If he did, he has put a gloss on Hawkins' words for which I can see no justification.

74. Watkins, *Perilous Balance*, p. 50.

ferent techniques, have left striking memorials of the same great soul. It is this living quality of the portraits that Cowper was commending when he wrote, "I now think myself almost as much a master of Johnson's character, as if I had known him personally."[75] And it is for this quality, before its many others, that Hawkins' *Life* still merits our attention.

It is a quality which need not be labored here. Hawkins speaks well enough for himself. If the many extracts already quoted from his *Life* have not made it self-evident, perhaps those to follow will satisfy the most skeptical. Suffice it to say that the Johnson men know and love is the Johnson of Hawkins' *Life* as well as of Boswell's. Johnson is all there: the lover of London and its taverns, of friends (particularly old friends), of clubs and conversation; the shabbily dressed philosopher who could sit up talking half the night and then lie in bed far into the morning, too indolent to work except at the call of necessity and then working with a rapidity almost incredible; the scholar of wide reading and immensely varied knowledge; the incisive wit; the pensioner lavishing his bounty on beggars, vagrants, prostitutes, felons—careless of no one's comfort but his own; the melancholy soul tortured by his sins and dubious of a salvation that all his friends believed he could take for granted. Scholar, philosopher, Christian—Hawkins' theme was judiciously chosen, and it is our eternal good fortune that he was able to enrich it with the wealth of many years' acquaintance with eighteenth-century England's choicest spirit.

75. See above, p. 96.

Chapter Seven

SIR JOHN'S WAY

Mr. Throckmorton told me about three days since, that it [Hawkins'
Life] was lately recommended to him by a sensible man, as a book that
would give him more insight into the history of modern literature, and of
modern men of letters than most others. A commendation which I really
think it merits. Fifty years hence, perhaps, the world will feel itself ob-
liged to him.

—*William Cowper to Samuel Rose, Feb. 19, 1789*[1]

IN DEFIANCE OF WILLIAM COWPER, and in spite of the fact that it has
been rummaged again and again by writers and editors eager for
information about the eighteenth century, Hawkins' "miscellaneous
matter" (for it is here that Cowper would have found much of his
insight into modern literature and men of letters) has had few admirers since the early spring of 1787. "No book was ever so out-
rageously padded," one writer has complained,[2] and another, after
a sputter of adjectives brought on by reading Hawkins, has announced that the "digressions" are "neither illuminating nor
amusing."[3]

It would be easy to add to this company. But when one looks
for examples of praise, he finds that except for Cowper's encomium

1. *The Correspondence of William Cowper, 3,* 356.
2. Sir Edward Boyle, "Johnson and Sir John Hawkins," *National Review*
(March 1926), p. 86.
3. D. B. Wyndham Lewis, *The Hooded Hawk* (London, 1946), p. 183.

and that of Harold Nicolson,[4] he must settle for the begrudging admissions of Austin Dobson and one or two others, including, strangely enough, Hawkins' archrival James Boswell. In a footnote to his *Life,* Boswell wrote, "I do now frankly acknowledge, that, in my opinion, his [Hawkins'] volume, however inadequate and improper as a life of Dr. Johnson, and however discredited by unpardonable inaccuracies in other respects, contains a collection of curious anecdotes and observations, which few men but its authour could have brought together."[5] The praise, of course, is amply qualified. Boswell made sure that everyone knew the tree was a crab before he commended its apples. One may wonder, in fact, why Boswell should have bothered to commend Hawkins at all, unless he was suffering momentarily from pity for an enemy whom he had just been goring through a long paragraph. Whatever the reason, he took great pains with this footnote. In the manuscript of the *Life,* after the sentence just quoted, he originally wrote, "I read it at [first] with eagerness and often return to it with fresh hopes of amusement, which are not disappointed." But it was hardly safe to admit that he returned often to Hawkins' *Life of Johnson,* even if only in pursuit of amusement, and he struck the sentence from the manuscript.

The most unusual praise of the digressions, to use the term generally applied to Hawkins' miscellaneous matter, is contained in Austin Dobson's essay on Hawkins: "The abiding and original side of his labours is just those divagations and superfluities which disturbed the orderly eighteenth century spirit. . . . It is to these curious anecdotes that the reader, who knows all that he cares to know about Johnson, now turns."[6] Presumably there are some

4. See below, pp. 180–81.
5. Boswell, *1,* 27, n. 1.
6. Austin Dobson, "Sir John Hawkins, Knight, "*Old Kensington Palace and Other Papers* (New York, n.d.), p. 136.

people who know all that they care to know about Johnson, or at least think they do, for even the satiated are likely to find Johnson at times compelling their attention. Dobson, of course, hardly expected us to conclude that these readers would follow Hawkins from cover to cover for the sake of the "divagations and superfluities." So conscientious a pursuit would lead to the disappointing discovery that too much of the book concerns the life of Johnson, and is therefore thoroughly distracting, annoying, and digressive.

Dobson's comment, however, emphasizes once again what one of the main problems of Hawkins' *Life* has been. For it is not enough to insist that the "digressions" are interesting. A reader who sees no connection between them and the life of Johnson will inevitably find them tedious, no matter how he might react to them if he were to read them separately, as much of the public did in 1787. Thus anyone who sets out to study the digressions must consider not only whether they are important in themselves, but whether they have a definite bearing on the life of Johnson—in short, whether they are the insipid babbling of a garrulous old man or whether they are an integral and significant part of the type of biography which Hawkins undertook.

Out of its 600 pages, not more than half can truthfully be described as having any direct bearing on the life of Johnson.[7]

It is unfortunate that when Sir Edward Boyle penned this estimate of Hawkins' *Life* he did not explain what he meant by "direct bearing on the life of Johnson." One can only guess at his meaning, and the obvious guess is that he had in mind only those parts which might be termed the narrative of Johnson's life. To say that Johnson wrote *Taxation No Tyranny*, and to explain the circumstances under which it was written, would not be digressive; but to include excerpts

7. Boyle, "Johnson and Sir John Hawkins," p. 86.

from the essay, or more than a brief criticism of it, would. To say that Johnson was given the job of writing the Debates for the *Gentleman's Magazine* and to assess the value, for Johnson, of this political activity, would not be digressive; but to give the history of Parliamentary reporting would. The formation of the Ivy Lane Club would be a proper part of Johnson's biography; but writing sketches of each of the other members would obviously mean cultivating the weeds at the expense of the flower.

If we were to interpret Sir Edward Boyle in this way, we would be forced to agree that he is mathematically precise. Only about half of Hawkins' book would seem to have any direct bearing on Johnson's life;[8] and although the anonymous charge that the book contained hardly enough for a sixpenny pamphlet[9] could be promptly dismissed as a facetious exaggeration (along with Boswell's statement that only "a very small part of it relates to the person who is the subject of the book"),[10] the 300 pages of foreign matter could surely be considered enough to "overload the memory" of Dr. Johnson, just as Arthur Murphy and Dr. Robert Anderson, at decent intervals, said they were.[11] It would be a strange biography indeed, with one-half of it about Johnson and the other half about a sixteenth-century breakfast, an eighteenth-century feud, the liturgy of Edward VI, Magna Charta, Dr. John Hill, Beauclerk, Goldsmith, Chamier, the gravity of physicians, general warrants, Richardson, Fielding, Smollett, and Sterne—and a hundred other persons and things.[12] It would be very easy for us to share the annoyance of Hawkins' critics.

8. See below, Appendix, A.
9. See above, p. 25.
10. See above, pp. 31–32.
11. Robert Anderson, *The Life of Samuel Johnson, LL.D.* (3d ed. Edinburgh, 1815), p. 3; Arthur Murphy, *An Essay on the Life and Genius of Samuel Johnson, LL.D.*, in *Works of Samuel Johnson* (London, 1824), *1*, 4. Murphy's essay was first published in 1792.
12. See below, Appendix, B.

It would be easy, that is, provided we interpreted the word "digression" as strictly, or nearly as strictly, as Sir Edward Boyle must have done in order to arrive at his figures. But is there any reason for us to interpret it so strictly? Hawkins, it goes without saying, did not. But that he was not, on the other hand, totally insensitive to the dangers of digression is evidenced by the number of times he explains why he is inserting some matter which he fears that his readers may think digressive. He follows his account of the fugitive pieces of the *Harleian Miscellany,* for example, with Johnson's preface, "which being very short, may itself be deemed a fugitive piece, and is therefore here inserted."[13] Of course, one can always find an excuse for a digression. But Hawkins' excuses suggest not so much a feeling of guilt on his part as an eagerness to win his readers over to an acceptance of his own idea of what was relevant to the life of Johnson. What, then, did Hawkins consider relevant that Sir Edward Boyle would probably have rejected?

First of all, he must have decided somewhere in the course of his work that any of Johnson's writings were admissible to his biography. "I shall need, as I trust," says Hawkins, about to quote the final paragraph of the *Life of Savage,* "no excuse for inserting so fine a specimen of style and sentiment."[14] For where was Johnson to be found if not in his works? The political virtuosity of *The Patriot* and *Taxation No Tyranny,* the Parliamentary eloquence of the Debates, the great good sense of the *Rambler* and the *Idler* could be much more effectually demonstrated by the works themselves than by Hawkins' exposition of them. In our own day Hawkins would not have to fight for this principle, for no one would disagree with him. Porson's indictment of Hawkins for quoting Johnson's works when they were readily available in the set of which the *Life* comprised the first volume we may accordingly dismiss on

13. *Life,* p. 146.
14. *Life,* p. 155.

the grounds that Hawkins was not merely writing an introduction but was writing a biography which he quite naturally wished to be complete in itself. The only real question is whether or not he showed sufficient restraint in quoting Johnson's works, particularly the Parliamentary Debates. His inclusion of four of the Debates, preempting among them twenty pages of text and four of footnotes, we may with reason wonder at, although Hawkins no doubt could have ably defended their inclusion. Because these were the only works about which Johnson had had any real misgiving,[15] Hawkins had made the regrettable decision to exclude them from his edition of the *Works,* so that they were available only in the back files of the *Gentleman's Magazine.* And yet his admiration of them was such that he could say,

> Never were the force of reasoning or the powers of popular eloquence more evidently displayed, or the arts of sophistry more clearly detected than in these animated compositions. Nor are they more worthy of admiration for these their excellencies than for that peculiarity of language which discriminates the debates of each assembly from the other, and the various coloring which he has found the art of giving to particular speeches. The characteristic of the one assembly we know is Dignity; the privilege of the other Freedom of Expression. To speak of the first, when a member thereof endowed with wisdom, gravity, and experience, is made to rise, the stile which Johnson gives him is nervous, his matter weighty, and his arguments convincing; and when a mere popular orator takes up a debate, his eloquence is by him represented in a glare of false rhetoric, specious reasoning, an affectation of wit, and a disposition to trifle with subjects the most interesting. With great judgment also does Johnson adopt the unrestrained

15. Boswell, *4,* 408.

oratory of the other house, and with equal facility imitate the deep-mouthed rancour of Pulteney, and the yelping pertinacity of Pitt.[16]

To withhold the Debates after such an encomium would have been all but impossible. And yet it is hardly necessary to say that to illustrate Johnson's versatility more than one Debate was necessary. Excerpts, of course, might have been satisfactory, but Hawkins refused to be satisfied with part of an argument (which is really not an argument at all), and not seeing, apparently, why anyone could deplore the inclusion of Johnson's works, he did not bother to tell his readers what Fielding told his, that when they came to a part they disliked they were at liberty to skip ahead till they found one more to their liking. Hawkins did not think that the speeches of Lord Hardwicke and Lord Chesterfield would try his readers' patience. But wary of overquotation, he inserted the much shorter speeches of Pitt and Horatio Walpole in the footnotes, where the reader could ignore them if he pleased. The planning here is obvious, however: two speeches from each of the Houses to illustrate the "Dignity" of one House and the "Freedom of Expression" of the other, with the speeches delivered by four men of very different characters and interests to illustrate Johnson's "various coloring."[17]

Actually, even in the eighteenth century few if any persons would have contended seriously that extracts from an author's works were not admissible to his biography. Johnson's *Lives of the Poets* abound with excerpts, and Boswell himself allotted space, among other works, to Johnson's legal opinions, perhaps the most tedious of his

16. *Life,* pp. 99–100.
17. Hawkins may also have wished to print the speeches of Pitt and Chesterfield because both were well known and universally accepted as the work of the speakers themselves. In 1900 the Chesterfield speech was published as Chesterfield's own (The World's Great Classics, *British Orators, 1,* 161–75). Still more recently, the *Pelican Book of English Prose* has printed excerpts under Chesterfield's name.

productions. There is really no argument here; a literary biographer can hardly carry out his task without frequent quotation, and there are times when he may consider it necessary, as Hawkins did, to quote at length. Thus, while some may wish that Hawkins had shown greater restraint, it would be incorrect to say that Johnson's works have no direct bearing on his life; and so we may add some thirty-five pages to the "not more than half" of Hawkins' biography which Sir Edward Boyle considered relevant to Johnson's life.

Admission of Johnson's works should make admissible some other pages which, for the sake of paring down Hawkins' narrative to Sir Edward Boyle's figures, I have suggested he must have considered digressive. I refer to the account of William Lauder's forgery of various modern Latin poets in order to give the impression that Milton had plagiarized from them. In this attempt Johnson was intimately, though innocently, involved, but in order to prove Johnson's innocence it was essential that Hawkins trace the progress of Lauder's attempt from the beginning, so that it might be seen how, over a long period, Lauder had managed to dupe not merely Johnson but the British public generally. Thus in 1750 when Johnson wrote the preface to Lauder's diabolical *Essay on Milton's Use and Imitation of the Moderns,* he was not a party to the scheme; he was interested only in propagating what his misplaced faith in Lauder assured him was the truth.[18]

Johnson's part in Lauder's scheme is best comprehended when we know something of the history of that scheme, and it was for similar reasons that Hawkins traced the history of various other projects and institutions. Johnson's achievement as a lexicographer, for example, may be measured with some accuracy only if we know what had been done by lexicographers before him. The London

18. See Warren Mild, "Johnson and Lauder: A Reexamination," *MLQ,* *14* (1953), 149–53.

133

literary scene into which Johnson hurled himself in 1737 may come alive for us if we can picture the organization around which much of Johnson's early activity revolved—the *Gentleman's Magazine,* with the penurious but capable Edward Cave encouraging his correspondents, building up his empire, and fighting off the attacks of the rival *London Magazine.* And one of Johnson's major contributions to the magazine, the Parliamentary Debates—the chief fruit of nearly three years of his life—can be best understood if we know the history of Parliamentary reporting, for Johnson's manner of reporting, with all the disguises attendant upon the invasion of Parliamentary prerogative, is likely to puzzle an age like Hawkins' or ours, which will not tolerate a legislature that acts in secret.

Certainly these accounts are relevant to the life of Johnson. While they may not always contribute to the essential narrative of Johnson's life, it can hardly be doubted that they aid greatly in making that narrative comprehensible and vivid. Let us see if the same may not be said of the accounts of Johnson's contemporaries.

That Hawkins considered the lives of Johnson's contemporaries relevant to his biography we need not doubt. They provided no "escape to scenes more congenial to his disposition."[19] His accounts of them were not the mumbled reminiscence of senile garrulity; on the contrary, like an artist's background, they gave his biography much of the depth and color which a full-length work required. When the reviewers attacked him, Hawkins might have found support in Johnson's friend, the learned Dr. Samuel Parr: "Dr. Parr said, he had once begun to write a life of him [Johnson]; and if he had continued it, it would have been the best thing he had ever written. 'I should have related not only everything important about Johnson, but many things about the men who flourished at the same time.' "[20]

19. See above, p. 25.
20. J. Wilson Croker, ed., *Johnsoniana* (Philadelphia, 1842), p. 339.

Parr would have done as Hawkins did. Both men recognized the
central position of Johnson, and both perceived that he could be
displayed to best advantage in the midst of his contemporaries, like
a diamond set among smaller diamonds. One is almost ashamed to
seek excuses for Hawkins for writing about the friends of a man
who said that he considered every day lost in which he did not
make a new acquaintance,[21] or for writing about those who flourished at the same time when Johnson was so keenly alive to the
accomplishments of his contemporaries. Johnson prided himself on
living in the world,[22] and no biography of him could be adequate
that did not present that world. "No less than Boswell, Hawkins
writes a 'life-and-times,'" wrote Donald Stauffer.[23] And it was because he was writing a life-and-times that he found not only the
accounts of Johnson's contemporaries but also the accounts of eighteenth-century customs, institutions, and professions relevant to his
book. When we view the book in this light, we see that very little
of it can justly be termed digression. We have long since accepted
the fact that this "miscellaneous matter" has a place in a biography
which pretends to give the facts of a person's life and also to place
him in his milieu. As with Johnson's works, we can see that Hawkins' reasoning was sound, and it is only his practice which sometimes makes him vulnerable to criticism. Hawkins, to be sure, did
not always exercise restraint. The third hundred pages of the book
contain all too little of the narrative of Johnson's life. The account
of eighteenth-century doctors and the medical profession extends
for eighteen of these pages. The account of the Admirable Crichton,
including a quotation from the *Adventurer,* extends for fifteen. The
account of the men who made good use of their time and yet still

21. Boswell, *4, 374.*
22. Ibid., *1, 427; 4,* 161, n. 3.
23. Donald A. Stauffer, *The Art of Biography in Eighteenth Century England*
(Princeton, Princeton University Press, 1941), p. 408.

managed to mix in the world extends for thirteen and includes, in quick succession, appreciations (or depreciations) of Thomas Birch, John Campbell, John Hill, Henry Fielding, Tobias Smollett, Samuel Richardson, and Laurence Sterne, until one has almost forgotten what Hawkins' original purpose was.

None of these accounts is wasted, however. The account of the medical profession, even though Hawkins himself could label it "digression," can unquestionably claim a place in the biography of Johnson, among whose earliest literary efforts were several medical biographies, who numbered many medical men among his intimate acquaintance, and who expressed throughout his life the warmest admiration for that profession. The account of the Admirable Crichton was proffered because Hawkins felt impelled to demonstrate Johnson's good faith in presenting to the public as truth something which was, on the face of it, incredible. Johnson's devotion to truth is one of Hawkins' recurrent themes. And the account that extended from Birch to Sterne served the dual purpose of providing an object lesson and drawing a picture of the hard-working world of letters. What people have found objectionable in Hawkins, besides the length of some of his accounts, is that he had to stop—to leave his narrative of Johnson momentarily—each time he wished to fill in some aspect of eighteenth-century life, so that his book has seemed to move along jerkily, like a car under the unsteady guidance of a novice driver. Hawkins, of course, did not have the experience of earlier biographers of his type to guide him. His problem was one he had to work out for himself. Nor did he have the endowment of Boswell, whose problem was solved for him almost automatically. With his unique genius for reconstructing scenes and conversation, Boswell could let his picture of Johnson's times grow out of the conversation, or he could present it as an integral part of some dramatic sequence in which Johnson played the central role.

For all this, Boswell occasionally found it advisable to do exactly

what Hawkins did (witness, among others, his accounts of Akerman and Wedderburne),[24] and no one has thought his biography
the worse for it.[25] Boswell's full title, in fact, shows that his purpose
was essentially the same as Hawkins': *The Life of Samuel Johnson
LL.D. Comprehending an Account of His Studies and Numerous Works,
in Chronological Order: a Series of His Epistolary Correspondence and
Conversations with Many Eminent Persons; and Various Original Pieces
of His Composition, Never Before Published: the Whole Exhibiting a
View of Literature and Literary Men in Great-Britain, for Near Half a
Century, During Which He Flourished.* Hawkins' *Life,* wrote William
Cowper, was recommended for the insight it would give into the
history of modern literature and modern men of letters. Here, al-
ready, was a remarkable "view of literature and literary men in
Great-Britain, for near half a century."[26]

For if Hawkins lacked some of Boswell's subtlety, he was nevertheless frequently much more subtle than he has been given credit
for being. The Debates, for example, besides evidencing Johnson's
abilities afford a picture of the political ferment of London, particularly at the important time when Johnson began composing the
Debates. Dr. Birch's "Circuit of London," one of those pieces
which the 1787 periodicals found eminently reprintable, not only
helps to characterize one of Johnson's friends but serves the useful

24. Boswell, *4,* 431–32; *1,* 386–87.
25. It might be noted, however, that the dust jacket of the Modern Library
abridgment of Boswell's *Life* encourages purchasers with the following: "To
give the modern reader the spirit and substance of Johnson's life and times,
Bergen Evans . . . has winnowed out the obscurities and irrelevances of the
full text and kept its essence."
26. Curiously enough, the age which could be so hard on the digressor had
an undeniable fondness for digression. Johnson digressed frequently in the
Lives of the Poets, as with his account of Gilbert Walmesley in the life of
Edmund Smith. And the same Arthur Murphy who hacked away at Hawkins'
"miscellaneous matter" in the *Monthly Review,* devoted ten pages of his brief
Essay on the Life and Genius of Johnson to an account of Father Lobo's discovery
of the head of the Nile!

function of fixing graphically in the reader's mind the limits of London in mid-century:

> I heard him once relate, that he had the curiosity to measure the circuit of London by a perambulation thereof: the account he gave was to this effect: He set out from his house in the Strand towards Chelsea, and having reached the bridge beyond the water-works, he directed his course to Marybone, from whence pursuing an eastern direction, he skirted the town, and crossed the Islington road at the Angel. There was at that time no city-road, but passing through Hoxton, he got to Shoreditch, thence to Bethnal green, and from thence to Stepney, where he recruited his spirits with a glass of brandy. From Stepney he passed on to Limehouse, and took into his rout the adjacent hamlet of Poplar, when he became sensible that to complete his design he must take in Southwark: this put him to a stand; but he soon determined on his course, for taking a boat he landed at the red house at Deptford, and made his way to Say's court, where the great wet-dock is, and keeping the houses along Rotherhithe to the right, he got to Bermondsey, thence by the south end of Kent-street to Newington, and over St. George's fields to Lambeth, and crossing over to Millbank continued his way to Charing cross, and along the Strand to Norfolk street, from whence he had set out. The whole of this excursion took him up from nine in the morning to three in the afternoon, and, according to his rate of walking, he computed the circuit of London at about twenty miles. With the buildings erected since, it may be supposed to have increased five miles, and if so, the present circumference of this great metropolis is about half that of ancient Rome.[27]

The account of Lauder's forgery reveals much about eighteenth-

27. *Life*, pp. 207-8 n.

century taste and eighteenth-century charlatanism, and much about Johnson himself. The account of Cave and the *Gentleman's Magazine*, as I have mentioned, sets the London literary scene upon which Johnson first made his entrance. We could hardly wish these omitted. And there are many more as useful and interesting.

The brief Latin excerpts, it is true, we would not wish to defend. Ingulphus' account of how he was "apposed" will never get us out of bed a moment earlier than usual. We would gladly give up Hawkins' pretentious disquisition on the proportions of columns. But, on the whole, his sins of this sort are venial. For the clearest idea of his accomplishment we should measure his *Life* against the lives of Johnson that preceded it, particularly those of Cooke and Shaw, which are most nearly comparable to it; and it is as much the "miscellaneous matter" that makes the difference between them as it is the greater fullness and intimacy of Hawkins' information about Johnson. In the earlier lives one reads about Johnson. But in Hawkins' *Life* one lives in Johnson's world, and sees it through the eyes of a man whose curiosity and experience were wide, whose observation was keen, and whose judgment, though frequently prejudiced, was invariably honest. Hawkins' biography is a record of life, as the earlier biographies were not. And it is a record made possible by the very matter which the eighteenth-century wits and some more recent critics have chosen to laugh to scorn.

Doubtless no two lists of Hawkins' digressions would agree. What seems relevant to one person will seem irrelevant to another, for in a biography of this sort the question of what constitutes a digression is bound to be a highly subjective one. If we can make allowances for the length of some of Hawkins' accounts, however, and consider only the question of whether or not a section contributes in some way to our understanding of Johnson, I do not see how any list can differ very greatly from my own.[28] Such sins of

28. See below, Appendix, B. What I consider the true digressions I have marked with an asterisk.

digression as are left are not really sufficient to detract from Hawkins' accomplishment. At most, some forty pages can properly be termed digressive. It is worth noting, moreover, that nearly all of these sins are committed in the footnotes, where an author is traditionally licensed to indulge an occasional whim.

Chapter Eight

THE SEEDS OF JUDGMENT

To judge rightly of an author, we must transport ourselves to his time, and examine what were the wants of his contemporaries, and what were his means of supplying them.

—Johnson's Life of Dryden, *in* Works, 3, 378

"A REPORT GOT ABROAD," Miss Hawkins tells us, "that I had written the Life; but I furnished no more than the reviews of the works connected with the subject."[1] The first part of Miss Hawkins' assertion need not detain us, for the report fits readily into the complex mill of abuse through which the *Life* was run. But a student of Hawkins would be derelict indeed if he permitted the second part to go unchallenged; he is not eager to grant co-authorship to the young Laetitia-Matilda Hawkins. Fortunately, Miss Hawkins has been honest enough to qualify her claim:

> In reviewing the Scotch Tour, I had contrasted, in rather handsome terms, the prejudices of Johnson with the candid good-humour of Pennant; and for this, Sir J. received the very polite thanks of the latter in a bookseller's shop. He could not avow the fact—his revision of what I had done acquitted him of any thing unfair, and he very honourably brought the acknowledgments to me.[2]

1. *Memoirs*, 1, 160.
2. Ibid. Thomas Pennant published his *Tour in Scotland* in 1771.

141

While we would welcome some knowledge of the extent of Sir John's revision, it is significant that in the daughter's opinion the revision was sufficient to acquit her father of "any thing unfair."

Perhaps, however, something more than mere revision may be salvaged for Sir John. While a fond father may have been willing to relinquish the criticism of a work like the *Journey to the Western Islands* to an ambitious but inexperienced daughter, it is hardly likely that he would have permitted her to review *London* and the important political works—*Marmor Norfolciense,* the *Compleat Vindication of the Licensers of the Stage,* the Parliamentary Debates, and the four political tracts of the seventies. With all of these Hawkins' own political prejudices were too intimately involved for him to lose the opportunity to have his say. The political principles of the first three were anathema to an admirer of Sir Robert Walpole; and it was one of Hawkins' major projects to demonstrate, not only that Johnson had succumbed to the very cant against which he repeatedly warned, but that Johnson came himself to see that the blasts against Walpole were the stock-in-trade of an opposition eager to be returned to office. With respect to the Debates and the later political tracts, Hawkins' prejudices were as much on the side of Johnson as they had earlier been against him. The exciting days of Johnson's Parliamentary reporting had made a vivid impression, as Hawkins' book attests, but it is only Sir John's own intimate acquaintance with this period which could have brought it so unmistakeably back to life. As for the later tracts, Hawkins had reason to take pride in Johnson's political change of heart, since Johnson— the canting decrier of standing armies and corruption in government—had come to think politically in much the same way as Hawkins himself. Thus Hawkins' pleasure in the later tracts was not merely in discovering opinions which coincided perfectly with his own, though that was great indeed. It was a pleasure sweetened by the thought that the blot of Johnson's earlier work had finally been erased. Surely it is too much to believe that the politically astute Hawkins would have been willing to surrender all this to his daughter, or that she herself would have been capable of savoring the later political tracts with quite the relish apparent in the book.[3]

Hawkins might have been willing to trust some of the other reviews to his daughter. Her mention of the Scotch Tour makes it more than likely that she wrote at least the first draft of that review. I suspect her hand also in the reviews of *Rasselas* and the *Idler*, but just where it was guided by her father's it is difficult to ascertain. No doubt Hawkins left parts of his daughter's reviews very much as they came to him. We have already seen him taking material bodily from the *New and General Biographical Dictionary* and the *Gentleman's Magazine*, to mention only two of his sources. Such practice was time-saving: obviously the elderly Hawkins had little inclination to do again what had already been done for him. And there is no reason to think that his practice with his daughter's reviews would have been appreciably different.

A part of Hawkins' criticism of Johnson's works which almost no reviewer neglected was the short first paragraph of his comments on *Rasselas*. Considered as a specimen of our language, he wrote, *Rasselas* "is scarcely to be paralleled: it is written in a style refined to a degree of immaculate purity, and displays the whole force of turgid eloquence."[4] Is "turgid eloquence" praise or censure? queried Arthur Murphy,[5] and few can resist a smile at the hyperbole of a style refined to a degree of "immaculate purity." But these are just the excesses one might expect of an over-zealous young lady making her first public attempt at criticism. No doubt Miss Hawkins (if she

---

3. Miss Hawkins herself (*Memoirs*, 1, 90–92) notes her father's hand in the final paragraph of the comments on *The False Alarm* (*Life*, pp. 463–64). Nevertheless, there are parts of these reviews which Miss Hawkins could have written. See below, p. 153.

4. *Life*, p. 367.

5. *Monthly Review* (May 1787), p. 374.

was responsible) had in mind Johnson's own statement of one of his goals in the *Rambler:* "I have laboured to refine our language to grammatical purity."[6] As for "turgid eloquence," the reader of Miss Hawkins' *Memoirs* is startled to discover her saying that in the *Journey to the Western Islands* her father seemed to recognize all the comprehensiveness of Johnson's mind "and the turgid compression of his style."[7] Was she unconsciously echoing what she herself had written years before?[8]

A thorough analysis of the comments on *Rasselas,* however, confronts one with certain difficulties. Except for this first paragraph, it is not possible to find any characteristics of style that allow passages to be confidently assigned to the father or to the daughter. Some of the other reviews in the book are hardly more than summaries; the fourth paragraph of the "examen" of *Rasselas* begins a summary, and if any part of the examen may be considered inferior in style to the rest it is certainly this. One could wish, momentarily, that when Miss Hawkins claimed the reviews for herself she was claiming only the summaries of Johnson's works, but her remarks about the *Journey to the Western Islands* make it clear that she contributed more than a summary of that.

Parts of the examen of *Rasselas,* at least, would seem to have been written by Hawkins. The comments on Johnson's fear of insanity reveal genuine insight. Johnson, says Hawkins, styles insanity "one of the dangers of solitude, and perhaps to this dread and this opinion was his uncommon love of society to be attributed."[9] And the com-

---

6. *Works,* 7, 395.

7. *Memoirs,* 1, 89.

8. The sentence with which Hawkins introduced this review is also worth a moment's notice: "As none of his [Johnson's] compositions have been more applauded than this, an examen of it in this place may not be improper, and the following may serve till a better shall appear." Is there a suggestion here that the examen had "appeared" to Hawkins?

9. *Life,* p. 370.

ments on Johnson's superstition reveal a wisdom and sensitivity we would expect in the father but would be much surprised to discover in the daughter:

> His superstitious ideas of the state of departed souls, and belief in supernatural agency, were produced by a mental disease, as impossible to be shaken off as corporal pain. What it has pleased Omnipotence to inflict, we need never seek to excuse; but he has provided against the cavils of those who cannot comprehend how a wise can ever appear a weak man, by remarking, that there is a natural affinity between melancholy and superstition.[10]

The discussions of Johnson's superstition and his fear of insanity are exceedingly delicate ones, and it is impossible to believe that Hawkins could have permitted his daughter to conduct them without such strict supervision that her share in them would indeed have been insignificant.

Examination of the other reviews is no more conclusive. While each contains something which Miss Hawkins might have written, it is a rare review that does not furnish some acute observation far beyond her range. The father was always at his daughter's shoulder. Nevertheless, if we except the reviews of Johnson's political works, Miss Hawkins' claim of authorship would seem substantially correct. Probably the first drafts of the reviews were written by her (with her opinion undoubtedly influenced by her father's) and revised sufficiently by Hawkins to make them virtually his own work, though at the same time some sentences and even some paragraphs may have been left exactly as his daughter wrote them.

---

10. *Life*, p. 370. Alvin Whitley remarks ("The Comedy of *Rasselas*," *ELH*, March 1956, p. 49) that "Hawkins seems to have been the first and almost the last to realize that *Rasselas* is a 'general satire' of mankind."

Hawkins' criticism (as I will now consider it), though not always distinguished, is more than adequate for its purpose. In a biography, first of all, it was desirable that he acquaint his readers with the works that he was to discuss. It was for this reason that he summarized much of *Rasselas* and quoted pertinent passages from the works themselves. It was for this reason, also, that he provided a history of periodical essays and of dictionaries, for Johnson's writings could more readily be appreciated if they could be compared to others like them.

With this background, Hawkins was at liberty to proceed with his remarks, and his method is what we should expect from a man so intimately associated with Johnson. In accordance with Johnson's own counsels, he praises with alacrity and censures with respect. He finds, for example, that the precepts of *Irene* are excellent and its language correct, but "it wants those indispensable qualities in the drama, interest and pathos. . . . We read it, admit every position it advances, commend it, lay it by, and forget it: our attention is not awakened by any eminent beauties, for its merit is uniform throughout: all the personages, good or bad, are philosophers."[11] With good judgment he limits his remarks to the more general characteristics of the work in question, for detailed, esoteric criticism had no place in a biography that hoped to reach a large audience of widely varying intellectual capacities and interests. Thus he objects to Johnson's edition of Shakespeare on the ground that Johnson made only a few textual emendations, "some scattered remarks on particular passages,"[12] and some general observations (in all, far less than the public had expected), but he does not analyze Johnson's emendations or remarks as a critic with a more select audience would have done.

Finally, keeping his role of biographer always in mind, Hawkins studies Johnson's works with a view to understanding Johnson him-

11. *Life,* pp. 200–1.
12. *Life,* pp. 441–42.

self. He finds him in *Rasselas,* as we have seen, steeped in adversity, superstitious, melancholy, fearful of insanity. He finds him in the *Journey to the Western Islands* prejudiced against "Scotland as a country, and the Scots as a people," but not against individuals, for his compliments to them are "judicious, elegant, and well conceived, and express the sense of gratitude proportioned to the favours he experienced."[13] He finds in the Debates a great versatility, in the *Rambler* a wide knowledge and a matchless wisdom, and in the *Dictionary* an erudition the discerning will always ponder with amazement.

No method, of course, could guarantee Hawkins against mistakes in judgment. As with the Debates, he does not always introduce Johnson's works with acceptable dispatch. The three-page account of the *Voyage to Abyssinia,* while commendably more restrained than Arthur Murphy's,[14] might well have been abridged. Nor are Hawkins' critical strictures beyond reproof. Contemning Johnson's political principles of the thirties as he did, he was able to prepare what should have been a convincing case against Johnson's early political satires, but a total inability to appreciate Johnson's tactics all but lost the decision for him and made him appear ridiculous even in victory:

> Of all the modes of satire, I know none so feeble as that of uninterrupted irony. The reason of this seems to be, that in that kind of writing the author is compelled to advance positions which no reader can think he believes, and to put questions that can be answered in but one way, and that such an one as thwarts the sense of the propounder. Of this kind of interrogatories the pamphlet I am speaking of seems to be an example; 'Is the man without pension or place to suspect the

13. *Life,* p. 484.
14. See above, p. 137, n. 26.

impartiality or the judgment of those who are entrusted with the administration of public affairs? Is he, when the law is not strictly observed in regard to him, to think himself aggrieved, to tell his sentiments in print, to assert his claim to better usage, and fly for redress to another tribunal?'

Who does not see that to these several queries the answer must be in the affirmative? and, if so, the point of the writer's wit is, in this instance, blunted, and his argument baffled.[15]

Thus the *Marmor Norfolciense* was arraigned not merely on the valid charge of its political cant but on the unreasonable one of its uninterrupted irony. Against the *Compleat Vindication of the Licensers of the Stage* Hawkins could bring still a third charge. For it was written in defense of the theater, an institution which Hawkins' experience as a magistrate had persuaded him was immoral: "a playhouse, and the regions about it, are the very hot-beds of vice: how else comes it to pass that no sooner is a playhouse opened in any part of the kingdom, than it becomes surrounded by an halo of brothels?"[16] His dismissal of the edition of Shakespeare (though not of the preface) as a work which would not greatly add to Johnson's literary reputation touched Edmond Malone in a sensitive spot. "It certainly c[oul]d not," wrote Malone, apparently for Boswell's benefit, "in the opinion of such a blockhead as this writer who knows nothing of what he has done for Sh[akespeare]."[17] Hawkins' pronouncement in his discussion of the *Lives of the Poets* that Johnson did not possess a "truly poetic faculty" again elicited Malone's contempt: "because [to quote Hawkins] he had but one eye & had no relish for the beauties of nature—he was not a poet—His eye

.

15. *Life*, p. 79.
16. *Life*, p. 76.
17. See below, Appendix, C, p. 190. Hawkins' judgment, nevertheless, was standard for his day. While the preface was acclaimed, disappointment in the edition was widespread.

c[oul]d not in a fine frenzy roll[.] How perfectly absurd! This proves that he could not write a descriptive poem like Thompson's Seasons . . . but it proves nothing else."[18]

Naturally those judgments of Hawkins with which his critics disagreed were remembered. But it must not be thought for this reason that he was always, or even a large part of the time, singular in his judgments. In most of his reviews there is little enough to shake one's head about. They are competently done, and at least one of them is distinguished.[19] If their style is sometimes choppy (the result, I suspect, of the imperfect collaboration between father and daughter), there is on the other hand an attention to individual passages which frequently compels our admiration. Though they seldom rise to very great heights, they seldom descend to the banal and the obvious. They are, in short, unobtrusive and appropriate: sufficiently muted so that Johnson is not obscured by his works, and

18. Ibid., p. 194. Admirers of Johnson's poetry naturally take offense when they are informed that Johnson lacked a truly poetic faculty. But Hawkins was himself an admirer of Johnson's poetry, and was perfectly aware of the paradox of his remark: "This may seem a strange doubt, of one who has transfused the spirit of one of Mr. Pope's finest poems into one written by himself in a dead language, and, in two instances, nearly equalled the greatest of the Roman satyrists" (*Life*, p. 534). Hawkins was merely trying to account for what he considered the "frigid commendation which Johnson bestows on Thomson, and other of the descriptive poets, on many fine passages in Dryden, and on the Henry and Emma of Prior." And he came to the conclusion that because of Johnson's bad eyesight, "all his conceptions of the grandeur and magnificence of external objects, of beautiful scenes, and extensive prospects, were derived from the reports of others, and consequently were but the feeble impressions of their archetypes." Thus Johnson lacked the poetic faculty, "that power which is the result of a mind stored with beautiful images, and which exerts itself in creation and description." If Hawkins' paradox of the outstanding poet who lacked the poetic faculty is offensive, it is worth reminding ourselves that Johnson, great as he was, did have limitations both as poet and as critic. Hawkins found a limitation in Johnson's lukewarm appreciation of "the grandeur and magnificence of external objects, of beautiful scenes, and extensive prospects," and he attributed it, understandably, to Johnson's physiological handicap.

19. See below, pp. 156 ff.

sufficiently stressed so that Johnson will be remembered as one of
the great English writers. Critics have always agreed, for example,
that *Irene,* while containing much of interest, is not a particularly
good drama; that the diction is "cold and philosophical" and that
"the characters cause no anxiety."[20] Surely readers of the *Journey to
the Western Islands* will allow "that every body must have regretted
the omission, had he [Johnson], for any reason withheld so entertaining a series of reflections."[21] Probably very few readers of the
Life of Savage can fail to appreciate Hawkins' high regard for it or
to share his conviction that its major theme is "that idleness, whether
voluntary or necessitated, is productive of the greatest evils that
human nature is exposed to."[22] Finally, who could wish for a more
sympathetic answer than this to the cavils of those who would attack Johnson for occasionally making the *Dictionary* a vehicle of
personal prejudice:

> moved by party-prejudice, he has imposed significations on a
> few words that are indefensible. Let these be imputed to a mind
> agonized, at various periods during the prosecution of this
> laborious work, with indigence, with sorrow, and pain; and
> let the piteous description of his circumstances and feelings,
> which the preface contains, induce us to bury our resentment
> of a few petulant expressions, in the reflection, that this stu-
> pendous compilation was undertaken and completed by the
> care and industry of a single person.[23]

While these scattered comments from the *Life* provide a sampling
of Hawkins' criticism, we can study his method and assess his
achievement with greater precision if we look more closely at two

20. *Life,* pp. 199, 201.
21. *Life,* p. 482.
22. *Life,* p. 155.
23. *Life,* p. 343.

or three of his critiques. About half of the six pages devoted to
London, for example, describe, with the aid of two of Johnson's
letters, the arrangement for the printing of the poem, for the publication of Johnson's first original work was a notable event. The
rest, in one way or another, is intended to illuminate the poem itself. The parallel between the London of Johnson's poem and the
Rome of Juvenal's prompts a brief note on the influence of Pope,
who had written similar imitations. The effects of Johnson's year in
London—of the poverty symbolized in his Exeter Street lodging[24]
and of the "vulgar complaints" adopted by him from the weekly
publications—are considered at greater length, since these determined the major themes of the poem. And the topical and personal
quality of *London* is further underlined by Hawkins' recognition of
Richard Savage in the character Thales, who bids farewell to London in the poem.[25]

24. Actually Johnson had left Exeter Street before he wrote *London.* But
Hawkins' point remains valid.

25. Boswell's objection to Hawkins' identification of Thales (Boswell, *1,*
125, n. 4) has touched off numerous discussions of the question. Essentially I
am in agreement with the conclusions reached in the most recent of these
(*Young Sam Johnson,* pp. 207–8). The parallels between Thales and Savage are
convincingly close; yet Johnson insisted that he had not met Savage when the
poem was written, and Savage did not actually set out from London until
July 1739, more than a year after the poem was published. Neither objection,
however, is insuperable. Johnson could not have been ignorant of the circumstances of a poet as notorious as Savage; in fact, at the very moment *London*
was in the presses Johnson demonstrated his concern for Savage by addressing
a Latin couplet to him (*Gent. Mag.,* April 1738). As for the second objection,
Clifford suggests that when Johnson was writing the poem Savage may already have been talking to his friends about leaving London. Hawkins, however (basing his statement, perhaps, on Johnson's *Life of Savage*), is quite explicit. The subscription was first moved at the beginning of 1738, shortly after
the death of Queen Caroline, "but as it was some time before the subscription
could be completed, his retirement thither was retarded" (*Life,* pp. 55–56).
While there are mistakes in Hawkins' account, there is good reason to accept
this. Such arrangements seldom proceed according to plan, and Savage was
hardly one to be packed off from London in a hurry. Johnson himself says
that there were "many alterations and delays" (*Works, 3,* 343). The death of

It is natural that Hawkins should concentrate on the vulgar complaints against the ruling Whig faction, since (as we have just seen) it was partly these complaints which rendered *Marmor Norfolciense* and the *Compleat Vindication of the Licensers of the Stage* so obnoxious to him. But Hawkins' insight into Johnson's political furor has not led him to slight those other aspects of the poem which contribute to the reader's appreciation. Nor has it blinded him to the poem's merit. Johnson's parallel between the corruptions of Rome and London has been drawn, he informs us, with "great judgment,"[26] and the poem as a whole is "spirited."[27] Indeed, no less a personage than Alexander Pope commended it highly and was "very importunate" to know the author's name.[28] Thus, Hawkins concludes, did *London* procure Johnson fame, though no patronage.

By the decade of the seventies Johnson's work had procured him the patronage of a government with many of whose policies Johnson was in sympathy. Thus his enemies attempted to write off his political tracts of that period as nothing more than a grateful acknowledgment of the government's bounty. The attack against Johnson was heated, and Hawkins had no patience with it. This time it was Johnson's detractors who were the friends of faction, for Johnson's arguments, he thought, were cogently and reasonably urged. And on the arguments alone, concludes Hawkins wisely, must the case rest, since even if Johnson's motives could be proved they would have no real weight in the matter; "arguments alone are the weapons of controversy."[29]

Queen Caroline, moreover, was the obvious cue for Savage's friends to rush to his aid, for the Queen's death was much more than a personal blow to Savage. It meant that once again he was penniless.

26. *Life*, p. 56.
27. *Life*, p. 60.
28. Ibid.
29. *Life*, p. 501.

Reflecting this opinion, Hawkins' reviews of the four tracts[30] consisted largely in a delineation of Johnson's arguments. In fact, not until Hawkins had described all four did he comment upon them at length. Nevertheless, it is the four pages of comment which invite our attention. Essential though the fourteen pages of description were to Hawkins' plan, the tasks of summarizing Johnson's tracts and of recording the events which moved him to the labor of writing were routine ones which Miss Hawkins may well have spared her father. The comment, on the other hand, demanded the vigor of a mind steeped in the politics of a period when Miss Hawkins was an adolescent.

For all his insistence upon Johnson's arguments, Hawkins' discussion of the four tracts is as much a defense of Johnson's motives as it is a monument to his achievement. For Johnson's Toryism had not been hastily pieced together to please his patrons in the Tory ministry. Johnson was a Tory because his sturdy powers of reasoning and his profound "knowledge of the principles of civil policy"[31] had made him a staunch friend not of the ministry but of "both the ecclesiastical and civil establishment of his country."[32] Thus "he thought it his duty, as a good subject, when the legislative authority was denied, to refute the arguments of such as resisted it."[33]

That Johnson did refute their arguments, Hawkins was not for a moment in doubt. Johnson not only entered the lists with superior weapons but used them with every imaginable skill. Without being acrimonious, his tracts "abound in wit" and delight the ear. More important still, they convince the understanding, for with "respect

---

30. *The False Alarm; Thoughts on the Late Transactions Respecting Falkland's Islands; The Patriot; Taxation No Tyranny.*
31. *Life,* p. 500.
32. *Life,* p. 501.
33. Ibid.

to logical precision, and strength of argument," says Hawkins, they "defy all comparison."[34]

It may seem like blind reaction in Hawkins that he should extol the "logical precision" and "strength of argument" of *The False Alarm* and *Taxation No Tyranny*. In the one Johnson showed his willingness to see Colonel Luttrell returned to Parliament even though the electors had cast their votes preponderantly for Wilkes; in the other he argued Parliament's right to tax the colonists without the representation they insisted upon. Even so ardent an admirer as Boswell was compelled to express his dissatisfaction with Johnson for his stand on these issues.

But Hawkins' support of Johnson was far from a blind one. Like Johnson, he saw no reason to be jealous of the Crown's authority. By 1770 the English constitution had been so amended by concessions "made by the crown to the people" that less was "to be feared from princes or their ministers, who are ever responsible for their conduct, than from artful and designing men . . . furnished with the fascinating powers of popular eloquence."[35] Thus those who supported Wilkes understood neither the constitution nor the politics of the country,[36] and Hawkins did not hesitate to brand them, along with those who supported the Americans, the "friends of sedition and rebellion."[37] Similarly, appreciation of Johnson's arguments in *Taxation No Tyranny* was dependent upon a knowledge of the constitution:

> The principle assumed by Johnson, that 'the supreme power of every community has the right of requiring from all its subjects such contributions as are necessary to the public safety, or public prosperity,' is as self-evident, as that obedience is due

34. *Life,* p. 499.
35. *Life,* p. 502.
36. *Life,* p. 501.
37. *Life,* p. 499.

from children to parents, and is not refuted by the assertion, that the consent of those who are required thus to contribute, is necessary, for, were it so, what becomes of the right? Neither is the position, that taxation and representation are correlative, to be admitted as a principle of the English constitution, seeing it does not, nor ever did, exist as a part of it; and that the far greater number of the subjects of England, men who are not freeholders to a certain amount, copyholders, who are a third of the landholders in this kingdom, and all women, are unrepresented in parliament, and bound by laws enacted by the representatives of others, but in no sense of themselves. In cities, and boroughs, the representation is often of the meanest of the people; in London, for instance, where a mechanic, if he be a liveryman, has a vote, and a freeholder, wanting that qualification, though assessed ever so high to the land-tax, has none.[38]

As Greene persuasively demonstrates,[39] this is not a mere quibble. Johnson's precise reasoning, founded upon an intimate knowledge of the English constitution, was proof against any appeal to the law. To be sure, Hawkins is not likely to convince us that the government was right to acknowledge Colonel Luttrell's election or to reject the demands of the colonists. But in putting the question in constitutional terms, he has made it clear that Johnson's arguments were not merely an eruption of antipopular and anti-American feeling. Of course, Johnson had his prejudices. But one comes away from Hawkins' discussion with a new appreciation of a political stand which has too often been dismissed as a mere collection of Tory prejudices. Hawkins' great service is that he shows the rational basis of Johnson's Toryism. Even Boswell, who attacked so much else in Haw-

38. *Life,* pp. 502–3.
39. Greene, pp. 214–19.

kins, never openly took exception to his statements concerning Johnson's political principles. This is the more noteworthy since he did not share Johnson's (and Hawkins') dislike for Wilkes and the Americans, and since he considered some of the later tracts rather more acrimonious than they might have been. Of the events behind the earlier works he had, naturally, no personal experience. Indeed, his discussion of the political attitude expressed in the poem *London* is hardly more than an echo of one of Hawkins' recurrent themes: ". . . candour obliges us to allow, that the flame of patriotism and zeal for popular resistance with which it is fraught, had no just cause. There was in truth, *no* 'oppression'; the 'nation' was *not* 'cheated.' "[40]

Between Johnson's political writings of the thirties and of the seventies lay the Debates. These, as we have seen, were introduced to Hawkins' readers by an account of the subterfuges once attendant upon Parliamentary reporting and by the insertion of four of the speeches, two each from the House of Lords and the House of Commons. In this work Hawkins was not interested in studying Johnson's political principles; indeed, being reports, the Debates were not properly vehicles for Johnson's opinions at all. Hawkins' interest was rather in Johnson's ability to capture the flavor of the two houses and of the individual speakers: the Debates were "worthy of admiration . . . for that peculiarity of language which discriminates the debates of each assembly from the other, and the various coloring which he has found the art of giving to particular speeches."[41] These were works of art decidedly different from the tracts of the seventies, and Hawkins approached them with all the fondness with which age turns over the memories of old associates and heroes.

Boswell, however, was quite unwilling that Hawkins should have the Debates his way. "I must observe," he wrote, "that although

40. Boswell, *1*, 131.
41. *Life*, pp. 99–100.

there is in those debates a wonderful store of political information, and very powerful eloquence, I cannot agree that they exhibit the manner of each particular speaker, as Sir John Hawkins seems to think. But, indeed, what opinion can we have of his judgement, and taste in publick speaking, who presumes to give, as the characteristicks of two celebrated orators, 'the deep-mouthed rancour of Pulteney, and the yelping pertinacity of Pitt.' "[42]

Boswell seems very sure of himself here. But since evidence can be adduced to support Hawkins' characterizations of Pitt and Pulteney, perhaps there is reason to question the judgment and the taste in public speaking of Boswell rather than of Hawkins. Part of the evidence has been carefully provided by Hawkins himself. In the remarkable speech of Pitt opening with the ironic "The atrocious Crime of being a young Man," Pitt continues at length in a hurt defense of his youth and conduct until he shouts against his accusers, "I will exert my Endeavours at whatever Hazard, to repel the Aggressor, and drag the Thief to Justice, whoever may protect them in their Villainy, and whoever may partake of their Plunder." But such yelping was too free even for the House of Commons, and Mr. Winnington interrupted Pitt with a call to order: "I do not, Sir, undertake to decide the Controversy between the two Gentlemen, but . . . no Diversity of Opinion can justify the Violation of Decency, and the Use of rude and virulent Expressions; Expressions dictated only by Resentment, and uttered without Regard to—" Here, however, Winnington was himself interrupted by Pitt, who pertinaciously insisted upon holding the floor through another three paragraphs.[43]

One wonders what better evidence Boswell could have wished.[44]

42. Boswell, *1*, 152.
43. *Gent. Mag.* (Nov. 1741), pp. 569–70. *Life*, pp. 126–28 n. Thomas Winnington (1696–1746) was Leader of the House of Commons.
44. Perhaps Malone's name should be added to Boswell's, since Malone's comments (See Appendix, C, p. 193) suggest that Boswell's attack upon this part of Hawkins' criticism may have been prompted by Malone.

Hawkins did not maintain that *all* of Pitt's speeches revealed his "yelping pertinacity." But when such a characteristic was in evidence, Johnson was perfectly capable of capturing it in his report. "With equal facility" could he imitate the "deep-mouthed rancour of Pulteney," which Hawkins felt no need to exemplify. Medford Evans, in his study of the Debates, finds Pulteney "always bitter." He "hardly ever speaks without showing his mastery of sarcasm at the expense of foregoing arguments."[45] Consider, for example, the opening sentence of one of his speeches delivered during the Debate on the Bill for Raising Seamen: "I cannot discover for what Reason the Bill before us is so vigorously supported, but must observe that I have seldom known such vehement and continued Efforts produced by mere publick Spirit, and unmingled Regard for the Happiness of the Nation."[46] Or this, delivered during the same debate: "Observation, Sir, has inform'd me, that to remove the Detestation of the Emperor's Service, it is not necessary to raise the Wages of the Seamen, it is necessary only to secure them; it is necessary to destroy those hateful Insects that fatten in Idleness and Debauchery, upon the Gains of the Industrious and Honest."[47] This is rancor indeed, and "deep-mouthed" describes it well. But if Hawkins is correct about Pitt and Pulteney, then it is quite possible that he is correct in going so far as to say that the Debates exhibit the manner of each particular speaker. As Greene notes, it must of course be recognized that speeches composed by Johnson all have the Johnsonian ring. His own style naturally went with him. But Johnson's stamp of authorship did not prevent the speeches from having many marks of the speakers themselves. Evans notes that Chesterfield is always witty, Carteret always quotes Latin, Hardwicke's speeches "abound in quasi-philosophical observation," and Wal-

45. Evans, "Johnson's Debates in Parliament," p. 252.
46. *Gent. Mag.* (Oct. 1741), p. 517.
47. Ibid. (Sept. 1741), p. 465.

pole, the best characterization, is "always placable, always confident, never pretentious."[48] And Greene, who has performed the valuable service of analyzing the Debate on the Mutiny Bill, finds that General Wade

> makes a point of being a ' plain soldier". . . . Sandys and Gybbon, two perpetual opposition gadflies, are made to look a little ridiculous: Hawkins' account applies perfectly to them —'When a mere popular orator takes up a debate, his eloquence is by him [Johnson] represented in a glare of false rhetoric, specious reasoning, an affectation of wit, and a disposition to trifle with subjects the most interesting.' The Tory backbenchers Carew and Cornewall, act like backbenchers. . . . Sir John Barnard injects some of his businessman's common sense into the mass of verbiage. . . . The hero of the piece is certainly Pulteney, whose speech represents a level of intelligence and polished style far above the others, combined at the same time with a shrewd awareness of the realities of practical politics. . . .[49]

Greene's example is not an isolated one. A glance at the Debate on the Question of Raising Regiments shows that General Wade makes much the same impression: "I, who claim no other Title than that of an old Soldier, cannot hope to prevail much by my Oratory, it is enough for me that I am confident of confuting those Arguments in the Field, which I oppose in the Senate."[50] Gage follows with a "glare of false rhetoric" and specious reasoning. An alarmist, he announces dramatically that "Every Gentleman, pays to the Government more than two thirds of his Estate by various Exactions," and that the "Weight of Imposts . . . has already . . .

48. Evans, p. 253.
49. Greene, p. 122.
50. *Gent. Mag.* (Jan. 1743), p. 15.

depress'd our Commerce, and over-borne our Manufactures, and if it be yet increased . . . every wise Man will seek a milder Government, and enlist himself among Slaves that have Masters more wise or more compassionate."[51] In reply, the dryly humorous Sloper expresses the highest satisfaction from Gage's observations, and assures him that his "accurate Computations cannot but promise great Improvements of the Doctrine of Arithmetic."[52] The speech of Sir William Yonge contains the most weighty matter, gleaned in his tenure as Secretary at War.[53] In short, if every speech is not highly individualized, the reason is not that Johnson did not distinguish but that Parliamentary Debates are likely to be similar in the first place. A point well or badly reasoned will sound much the same in one speech as in another. But where a distinction was to be made, Johnson, as Hawkins says, was quite capable of making it. Johnson's readers must have come to expect one manner from General Wade and quite different manners from Gage and Sloper, or from Yonge, Pulteney, and Chesterfield. For it is highly questionable that the arguments alone would have been responsible for the tremendous popularity of the Debates. The mere fact that the magazine published a key to the names at the end of the year suggests that the speakers themselves were partly, if not largely, responsible. But they could hardly have sustained the public interest if they were all alike. As an artist, dealing in speakers as well as in speeches, Johnson was duty-bound to make distinctions both of character and of oratory.

The remainder of Hawkins' description of the Debates can also be defended. The characteristic of the House of Lords was dignity and of the House of Commons, freedom of speech; and certainly the most unrestrained oratory, as in the speech of Pitt, was to be

51. Ibid., pp. 19–20.
52. Ibid., p. 21.
53. Ibid., pp. 3–9.

found in the House of Commons. Johnson studied his men well. Indeed, he must have poured every energy into this major work of three years of his life. When one reads, as Greene styles it,[54] the quietly dramatic speech of Sir Robert Walpole ending the Debate on the motion to remove him from office,[55] one finds it easy to accept Hawkins' picture of Johnson shutting himself up in his room at St. John's Gate, where he raised his imagination to a fervor bordering upon enthusiasm, and permitted no one to approach but the compositor or Cave's boy, who gathered up the pages as he tumbled them out the door.[56]

Finally, one of Hawkins' silences deserves a moment's notice. In his *Essay on the Life and Genius of Samuel Johnson*, Arthur Murphy recorded that Johnson said of the Debates, "I saved appearances tolerably well; but I took care that the WHIG DOGS should not have the best of it."[57] And Boswell thought that Horace Walpole might have been prejudiced against Johnson for the manner in which he had treated Sir Robert Walpole in the Debates. But, as Greene, Evans, and Hoover[58] all show, nearly all the most active men in Parliament during the early forties were Whigs. If Johnson took care that the Whig dogs should not have the best of it, in reality no one was likely to have the best of it. By the time Johnson came to compose the Debates, it is clear, the fever of his partisanship had broken, and he was able to view with some detachment not only the Whig members of Parliament but even those in the ruling faction of Whigs. Sir Robert Walpole himself, the prime target of *Marmor Norfolciense*, is tendered great respect, so that even if Horace Walpole had known that Johnson was the composer of the Debates,

54. Pp. 127–28.
55. *Gent. Mag.* (April 1743), pp. 180–83.
56. *Life*, p. 99.
57. *John. Misc.*, 1, 379.
58. Benjamin Beard Hoover, *Samuel Johnson's Parliamentary Reporting*, Berkeley and Los Angeles, University of California Press, 1953.

he could not have been prejudiced against him for the reason Boswell suggested. Hawkins' silence with regard to Johnson's bias in the Debates was not therefore the result of a failure to see what was obvious to others. Hawkins merely read the Debates a little more carefully than most people did. After all, it was the boast of the *Gentleman's Magazine* that it was impartial, and if Johnson had failed to live up to that boast, it is a safe guess that Hawkins would have noticed it.

Hawkins, no doubt, will never rank among the foremost critics of his day. The seeds of judgment simply did not thrive in his mind as they did in Johnson's. But when his comments on Johnson's political works are studied as a whole, it is clear that there was a flowering of his judgment which might well have impressed an audience less hostile to him. What emerges from these comments is a picture of Johnson's political development which no other biographer was capable of providing. Boswell's remarks on Johnson's early political position are slight indeed, a mere echo of Hawkins'. His attempt to read Johnson's Tory prejudices into the Debates is misguided and distracting. He relinquishes the opportunity to study Johnson's position in the later tracts in order that he may express his dissatisfaction, in part, with Johnson's matter and manner. While Boswell is frequently proud of Johnson's Toryism, the reader who is "trying to get a coherent picture of Johnson's political position"[59] has sometimes a feeling of bafflement, of talking at cross-purposes, for to Boswell's generation the word "Tory" meant something different from what it meant to Johnson's. "Sir John Hawkins," concludes Greene, "who belonged to Johnson's own generation and used a similar terminology for political discussion, is much easier to follow."[60]

59. Greene, p. 13.
60. Ibid.

This is an advantage not to be overlooked. For not only was Johnson constantly preoccupied with politics, but his political writings form almost as sizable a part of the body of his work as his biographical or purely moral. The changing grounds of Johnson's political belief were the stuff of his biography, but they were not intelligible to everyone. Hawkins' own political awareness, and his long and intimate acquaintance with Johnson, made him a useful person to record so significant a change. True, there is altogether too much in the description of the later tracts which Miss Hawkins might have written for her father. But where would one have found another man to pen the incisive comments on Johnson's political works? Hawkins could transport himself to Johnson's times—even to the distant decade of the thirties—because he had been on the scenes himself. A bit part in the *Gentleman's Magazine* of those days brought the whole political stage within view of a young man who kept his wits about him. This is the more significant, since almost none of Johnson's works but these require, for appreciation, a thorough knowledge of the setting which occasioned them. Thus in his criticisms of Johnson's other works Hawkins might equal, but he could not always hope to improve upon, his contemporaries. With the political works the advantage was all his own.

Chapter Nine

QUARTER SESSIONS JARGON

*A very kind mediating lady of his [Hawkins'] acquaintance once wished
to recommend to him for a wife her niece, afterwards the celebrated Mrs.
Barry, the actress: he was not very likely to be drawn in; but if he had
wavered, the method taken to secure him would have saved him. The
young lady was a visitor in the house at the same time with himself. As
a correct young man, it was to be presumed that industry and attention to
religion would meet his approbation. Miss S—— was therefore at work
with "The Practice of Piety" by her, and as he was known to be fond of
music, she was desired to sing; and she sung as he used to describe it, about
"mutal love."*[1]

*Another lady was put forward by her friends in the year 1745, but
unfortunately, the poor girl in her zeal for the House of Brunswick,
talked of the veterian corps, and he broke the meshes.*

—*Miss Hawkins' Memoirs, 1, 168*

OBVIOUSLY MISS S—— and the other lady would have been ill-
matched with the young John Hawkins, at least until he could find
time to mend their tattered English. And mend it he would have
done, if we may judge from his concern for the language in later
years. Indeed, much of the hilarity at the expense of Hawkins' own
style had its source in his censure of the speakers of Parliament and

1. Words and music of a song "Mutual Love" were printed in the *Universal
Magazine* (Jan. 1748), p. 38, when Hawkins was still a bachelor.

in his condemnation of Addison's style as feeble and inane.[2] These at least seemed to justify the effusions of the critics, who liked their public to think that they were only returning measure for measure. With respect to Parliament Hawkins, commenting on the unsuccessful attempt of Mr. Thrale to win Johnson a seat in the House of Commons, remarked somewhat pompously,

> Had it succeeded, and Johnson become a member of the house of Commons, as he was one of the most correct speakers ever known, he would undoubtedly have exhibited to that assembly a perfect model of senatorial eloquence; and might probably have prevented the introduction therein of a great number of words, phrases, and forms of speech, to which neither dictionaries, nor the example of any English writer of authority, have given a sanction.[3]

Although there is much truth in Hawkins' statement, it is difficult not to be amused by the thought of Johnson taking up his post in Parliament as guardian of the language's purity.[4] Of prime interest, however, is the list of "words, phrases, and forms of speech" to which Hawkins took exception: "Such as these: a truism—reciprocity—living in habits of friendship—a shade of difference—that line of conduct—sentiments in unison—blinking the question—I am bold to say—I should then commit myself—and others equally affected and singular. See the speeches in the public papers for the last seven years."[5]

2. *Life*, pp. 270–71. "Yet I am not willing," wrote Hawkins, "to deprive him [Addison] of the honour implied in Johnson's testimony, 'that his prose is the model of the middle style'; but if he be but a mediocrist, he is surely not a subject of imitation; it being a rule, that of examples the best are always to be selected."

3. *Life*, p. 513.

4. Horace Walpole (probably more out of scorn than amusement) inserted two exclamation marks next to this passage in his copy of the *Life*.

5. *Life*, p. 513 n.

To indict Parliament for seven years of affectation and singularity, and in such general terms às merely to refer his readers to the public papers, was challenge enough. But when Hawkins printed his list, he immediately set the critics thumbing through his own volume for words, phrases, and forms of speech sufficiently affected or singular to be relegated to the same group of outcasts. And they did not have far to search. The reviewer for the *Critical Review* gathered a bouquet of what he called "rhetorical flowers" from the first seventy-six pages alone:

p. 12   he read by fits and starts
    17   non attainment of a degree
    20   mansion house adjacent thereto
    22   almost stagger our belief
    29   the patrons thereof and the fame whereof
    32   letter herein-before inserted
    68   Pope stood a dead mark
    69   W[arburton] betook himself to studies
    70   took it into his head
         he had already tried his hand
    76   how it comes to pass
         B[rooke] with his eyes open, and the statute
         staring him in the face[6]

And Edmond Malone, doubtless for Boswell's benefit, compiled a similar list under the heading "His own bad style":

p.   2   if any *shall please* to make it
     3   bailif—the duties of that *exalted station*
    11   *which* he had been presented *to*
         twitted
    21   preferring the chance of the *wide* world
    34   register of the E[cclesiastical] C[ourt] of the
         b[isho]p *thereof*

6. *Critical Review* (June 1787), p. 424 (not quoted in the exact form of the original).

50 adventurer in the wide world
52 for want *thereof*
386 he w[oul]d often *huff* Garrick
     he *took to* the profession of the law
394 which he found in a spare leaf thereof
533 Oldys was the man *of all others* best qualified[7]

Today only the purist is likely to be disturbed by the preposition
at the end of a clause. Some of Hawkins' clichés might even pass as
useful idioms. But many of the examples gleaned by Malone and
the reviewer cannot readily be explained away. The "whereof's"
and "thereto's" and "herein-before's" had undoubtedly seeped into
Hawkins' style from the muddy rills of Quarter Sessions jargon.
Perhaps "stood a dead mark" is a trifle more elegant than "took it
into his head," but Hawkins might well have improved upon both.
To be sure, these compilations might easily be shrugged off as inadequate sampling from a book of 600 pages. Yet one would still
have to face the many parodies of Hawkins' style and its almost
universal condemnation by the critics. Such agreement can hardly
be ignored. For, though many critics may not have been qualified
to assess the accuracy of Hawkins' portrait of Johnson, every one
of them was qualified to pass judgment on an English style.

Indeed, had the critics chosen to examine Hawkins' style system-
atically, they would have discovered many more impurities than
the Quarter Sessions jargon which they gathered up in quantity.
This was only the most obvious and the most easily ridiculed, so
that a critic who wished merely to amuse his readers had no occasion
to probe any further. One or two critics, however, did notice certain other peculiarities of Hawkins' style. He used the intensive
rather too frequently as the simple personal pronoun: "myself can
attest"; "himself was the author of them all." He spelled the pret-

7. See below, Appendix, C, pp. 190–91. A third list was compiled by Philo
Johnson for the *European Magazine* (May 1787), p. 310.

erit of the verb "to read" as "red."[8] In the first edition he spelled
"ancient" five times in the accepted manner and once as "antient,"
but in the second edition, whether at his bidding or someone else's,
the proportion was exactly reversed.[9] At worst, however, these are
harmless whims worthy of mention only because they did not
escape the eyes of the critics. The more serious defects of Hawkins'
style cannot be perceived unless we look intently at an occasional
passage from the *Life*, for a few words chosen at random are hardly
representative of a style.

A sentence from the account of Johnson's folio attack upon the
bookseller Osborne provides a good starting point: "Johnson, while
employed in selecting pieces for the Harleian Miscellany, was
necessitated, not only to peruse the title-page of each article, but
frequently to examine its contents, in order to form a judgment of
its worth and importance, in the doing whereof, it must be supposed, curiosity might sometimes detain him too long, and whenever it did, Osborne was offended."[10] Apparent, first of all, is the
great length of the sentence. While long sentences were characteristic of the period, skillful writers, by a judicious use of pauses, were
careful to vary the rhythm of a sentence and grant the reader an
opportunity not merely to catch his breath but to keep the sentence
in perspective. In this passage Hawkins is not so thoughtful of the
reader. The many pauses are of equal length, so that one is likely
to find himself reviewing the sentence in order to grasp its meaning.
True, the monotony of unvaried rhythm might be less oppressive
if the language were vivid. But one glance suffices to show that
Hawkins' language in this sentence, far from being vivid, is almost

8. On the margin of page 162 of his copy of the *Life*, Horace Walpole
spelled it *redde*. And in the *St. James's Chronicle* for April 15–17, 1787, "A
Selector" lauded Hawkins' attempt to distinguish between the two forms of
the verb.

9. Johnson's *Dictionary* does not list "antient."

10. *Life*, p. 150.

anemically pale. There is no need to point, with his critics, to the offense of a single "whereof"; one might argue, in fact, that the "whereof" is an acceptable substitute for "of which." What oppresses most is the high frequency of Hawkins' verbals. So much that is passive and dependent—the two gerunds, the four participles, and the skein of three infinitives, in addition to two dependent clauses—saps the little vitality of the two independent clauses, and the sentence expires with the inept "whenever it did, Osborne was offended."

Hawkins' account of Johnson's feat of strength on the stage at Lichfield is disfigured in somewhat the same way. When Johnson, as we are told, momentarily vacated his seat on the stage, a Scots officer, who disliked him, persuaded an innkeeper to take it.

> Johnson, on his return, finding his seat full, civilly told the intruder, that by going out it was not his intention to give it up, and demanded it as his right: the innkeeper, encouraged by the officer, seeming resolved to maintain his situation, Johnson expostulated the matter with him; but finding him obstinate, lifted up the chair, the man sitting in it, and, with such an Herculean force, flung both to the opposite side of the stage, that the Scotsman cried out, 'Damn him, he has broke his limbs;' but that not being the case, Johnson having thus emptied the chair, and Mr. Walmsley interposing, he resumed his seat in it, and with great composure sat out the play.[11]

That Hawkins could end this anecdote so deftly is only the more reason to regret the clumsiness with which the rest of it is told. This time the length of the sentence is not particularly oppressive; Hawkins has provided an adequate number of stops. It is the many verbals, predominantly participles, which subvert the style and ren-

11. *Life,* p. 439 n.

der the story monotonous. Moreover, while the use of verbals is itself a mannerism with Hawkins, he has compounded his eccentricity by lodging many of the participles in absolute phrases: "the innkeeper . . . seeming resolved"; "the man sitting in it"; "that not being the case"; "Johnson having thus emptied"; "Mr. Walmsley interposing." So deadening is this construction that one almost overlooks the fact that the phrase "with such an Herculean force" would be much more effectively placed after the verb which it modifies than before.

Quite often Hawkins uses parenthetical phrases and clauses to the consternation of the reader, who is awaiting the very matter which the parenthesis delays. That facetious gentleman, he tells us,

> Mr. Foote, who, upon the strength and success of his satyrical vein in comedy, had assumed the name of the modern Aristophanes, and at his theatre, had long entertained the town with caricatures of living persons, with all their singularities and weaknesses, thought that Johnson at this time was become a fit subject for ridicule, and that an exhibition of him in a drama written for the purpose, in which himself should represent Johnson, and in his mien, his garb, and his speech, should display all his comic powers, would yield him a golden harvest.[12]

Between the subject "Mr. Foote" and the verb "thought" we find not only a subordinate clause with a compound predicate but an interruption of the clause by three parentheses. As its objects, "thought" has two noun clauses, the first of which is quickly dispatched. The subject of the second, however, is separated from the verb by a parenthetical phrase and by a further subordinate clause, the two verbs of which are separated from each other by a lengthy parenthesis. In short, by the time the reader has reached the final

12. *Life*, pp. 438–39.

verb, he is not at all sure whether it belongs to the main clause, to one of the noun clauses, or to the clause within the clause.

Passages like these (which could be multiplied) attest convincingly to the shortcomings of Hawkins' style. Obviously, much of what he wrote can be read with little delight. It does not follow, however, that little of what he wrote can be read with much delight. It is one of the faults of Hawkins' *Life* that the style is uneven, but it could not be uneven unless the bad were varied with the good. Long though most of his sentences are, they do not always pall. His rhythms are not invariably the monotonous ones of the passage quoted from the account of Johnson and Osborne:

> Though born and bred in a city, he [Johnson] well understood both the theory and practice of agriculture, and even the management of a farm: he could describe, with great accuracy, the process of malting; and, had necessity driven him to it, could have thatched a dwelling. Of field recreations, such as hunting, setting, and shooting, he would discourse like a sportsman, though his personal defects rendered him, in a great measure, incapable of deriving pleasure from any such exercises.[13]

Or, to choose from another part of the book:

> Bred to no profession, without relations, friends, or interest, Johnson was an adventurer in the wide world, and had his fortunes to make: the arts of insinuation and address were, in his opinion, too slow in their operation to answer his purpose; and, he rather chose to display his parts to all the world, at the risque of being thought arrogant, than to wait for the assistance of such friends as he could make, or the patronage of some individual that had power or influence, and who might have the kindness to take him by the hand, and lift him into notice.[14]

13. *Life*, p. 469.
14. *Life*, pp. 50–51.

Though here, as elsewhere, Hawkins' manner is highly formal, both passages are developed in clear, simple, and readable language. They contain no legal jargon, no intrusive parentheses, no excessive number of verbals. Even the expression to which Malone objected ("adventurer in the wide world") may be defended as properly descriptive of Johnson, who, with the spirit of an adventurer, trusted his wits to guide him through the hazardous London expanse. And the image which closes the second passage is both vivid and graceful, a fitting representation of Hawkins' esteem for the patron of letters.

Hawkins' language, in fact, is frequently vivid. He was constantly in search of the word, phrase, or image (for his book is filled with imagery) that would best convey his meaning—"the deep-mouthed rancour of Pulteney and the yelping pertinacity of Pitt." Such palpable hits are not isolated in Hawkins; there are many of them. If playhouses are not hot-beds of vice, how is it that as soon as one opens "it becomes surrounded by an halo of brothels?" "The placing Garrick under the tuition of Johnson . . . resembles that politic device of country house-wives, the placing one egg in the nest of a hen to induce her to lay more." Chesterfield's *Letters to His Son* are "this institute of politeness." The authors of the *Universal History* in forty folio volumes were "miners in literature" who "worked, though not in darkness, under ground; their motive was gain; their labour silent and incessant." Characterizations frequently bring out notable turns of phrase. "Cave had no great relish for mirth, but he could bear it." Dr. John Hill obtained his diploma from "one of those universities which would scarce refuse a degree to an apothecary's horse." At the Hague, Lord Chesterfield rubbed off the "college rust" and acquired "the polish of gaming."[15]

Of course, Hawkins' legal jargon was sometimes a bar to vividness, for no sensitive reader can take pleasure in a run of "whereof's"

15. For the references in this paragraph see *Life*, pp. 100, 76, 35–36, 188, 219, 45, 211, 178.

and "herein-before's." On the other hand, it would be a disservice to Hawkins not to note that nowhere does he use his jargon in such volume as parodies like Arthur Murphy's implied. Murphy's parody is the grossest of exaggerations, a collection of the impurities from the whole mass rather than from any of its parts. While one page might yield two or three specimens for such a collection, subsequent pages are likely to yield none at all. Moreover, Murphy's concentration on words of this sort tends to obscure the question of Hawkins' style in other ways. "Whereof," "thereof," and "therein" do not always set a legal seal upon the style. When they appear with no greater frequency than we find them in Hawkins, they leave an impression more of formality than of anything else. One becomes accustomed to them as to the long sentences. It is rather expressions like "non attainment of a degree" (to which the reviewer for the *Critical Review* objected) which bear, unequivocally, the legal mark. The combined effect of these expressions, the long sentences, the "whereof's" and "thereof's," and an antiquated diction ("he regretted not"; "these his assistants"; "Johnson bethought himself")[16] is too often an exaggerated formality which smacks less of the magistrate's bench than of the drawing room of elderly Puritan affluence.

This is the style's frequent, not its invariable characteristic. A glance at some of the many passages quoted throughout this study will reveal not only the extent of Murphy's distortion but also the ability of Hawkins to make telling use of the language. The anecdote of the party for Mrs. Lennox is vividly and imaginatively recounted.[17] The comment on Osborne's treatment of Johnson is succinct and eloquent.[18] On the whole, in fact, Hawkins' style speaks for itself, and I have dared to quote from the *Life* repeatedly

16. *Life,* pp. 17, 204, 198.
17. See above, pp. 108–9.
18. See above, pp. 76–77.

and at length because I believe that the virtues of his style are no less prominent than its vices.

Yet, while one insists upon its virtues, one is forced to confess that all too much of the hilarity at its expense was justified. Hawkins' artistry was simply not on a level with his perception and his judgment. His is not a style refined to a degree of immaculate purity, not a style which displays the whole force of "turgid eloquence," not a style to devote one's days and nights to. It is often too stiffly formal, too legal, too dryly antiquated—a style, in short, like the man himself. But if, like him, it contains a few coarse fibers, like him it is capable of sound and sustained effort. For it did not have to be the easy, familiar style of Philo Johnson, Arthur Murphy, or James Boswell in order to carry out its task. It is even quite as good as the styles of some of the men who found it so hilarious.

Chapter Ten

CONCLUSION

"Hawky," writes Boswell to Temple, "is no doubt very malevolent. Observe how he talks of me, as if quite unknown!" But, had Boswell realized it, he had something more important than mere misprisal to fear from Sir John Hawkins: he had, to no slight extent, to fear comparison.

—Harold Nicolson, The Development of English Biography, *p. 97*

FOR MANY PEOPLE not only Johnsonian biography but all biography begins and ends with Boswell's *Life of Johnson.* It is understandable that it should be so. Nowhere else are scenes from a great man's life so dramatically and fully recorded; nowhere else has the biographer so perfectly suited his methods to the needs of his subject. And yet (it is a curious paradox) if for some reason the world had been deprived of this biography of biographies, the man who is its subject would still be one of the most fully and intimately known of English literary figures.

Were there no Boswell's *Life,* our first-hand knowledge of Johnson would still be abundant. There would be, first of all, the biographical evidence of Johnson's own works. There would be Miss Burney's *Diary* and the minor but useful sketches of his life. There would be the invaluable contributions of Mrs. Piozzi and Boswell himself—Boswell's *Journal of a Tour to the Hebrides* (if we may consider it apart from the *Life*) with its intimate, revealing, and endlessly interesting picture of Johnson during a significant period of his life; Mrs. Piozzi's *Anecdotes,* nearly as interesting, a series of film strips where Boswell's is a full reel, but supplementing the picture, extending it, and varying it with shots from a new perspective; and her *Letters to and from the Late Samuel Johnson,* a notable start for a notable collection.

Finally, there would be Hawkins' *Life,* a biography which by any standard must be considered full length; which is, in fact, one of the fullest of eighteenth-century biographies and one of the few of length written by a man personally acquainted with his subject. Had we no more than these we would be rich indeed. Johnson, both as man and as writer, would still command his followers. His personal habits, his wit and eloquence, his wide reading, his incomparable memory and knowledge, his friends and clubs, his frailties, his great moral and physical strength, his warm generosity, his fears, his youth, his death—all these would be carefully documented. Of what other writer before the nineteenth century would we know so much? Yet these things about Johnson would be known to us not primarily through Boswell's *Tour,* or Mrs. Piozzi's *Anecdotes,* or Fanny Burney's *Diary,* or Johnson's own works and letters. Our most important source for Johnsonian biography would unquestionably be Hawkins' *Life.*

As we have seen, the wits flared up, sometimes with real brilliance, the moment that Hawkins ignited them. But without Boswell to lend encouragement, doubtless the wit would have dimmed and gradually died, and in the cooler air of the nineteenth century lovers of Johnson might have been able to recognize, with William Cowper, that Hawkins was a biographer any literary figure would be honored to have: "I . . . can not but regret *that our bards of other times* found no such biographers as these. They have both been ridiculed, and the wits have had their laugh; but such a history of Milton or Shakespeare, as they have given of Johnson—O how desirable!"[1] Had Boswell's *Life* not cast its shadow on Hawkins', surely it should be clear that the chances of Cowper's prediction[2] being realized were excellent. In fifty years the world might well have considered itself in Hawkins' debt.

Nevertheless, not fifty years but three times fifty have passed, and the world has not yet acknowledged its debt. Indeed, it is only because Hawkins remains in the shadow, all but unseen, that this study was undertaken. Its purpose is to find him a place in the light. For not the abuse of his contemporaries or the defects of his own style or the superior achievement of his rival can obscure the fact that Hawkins' biography has still an extraordinary value and a wide appeal.

For Johnsonian scholars Hawkins remains, and will continue to remain, a primary source not merely for miscellaneous information about Johnson, but for information about every period of his life. Where Hawkins' *Life* contains the only surviving record, as in the accounts of the Ivy Lane Club and of various incidents of Johnson's youth, his early years in London, and his dying months (to mention only a part), one can hardly say it has been superseded. And Hawkins' facts and interpretations must command the Johnsonian's respect. It is no longer possible to assume that when Boswell and Hawkins differ, Hawkins is almost certain to be mistaken. If time has convicted him on some counts, it has vindicated him on others. As with other biographers, the utmost care and industry could not always secure him from error. But his integrity remained uncompromised. His purpose was always to narrate and to interpret to the best of his ability. It was never to distort or fabricate in order to delude his readers with a false estimate of his knowledge and understanding. "I was never much conversant with the history of the

1. Letter to Samuel Rose (June 20, 1789), quoted from *The Correspondence of William Cowper*, 3, 352.
2. See above, p. 126.

stage"³ is an admission a scholar will appreciate. In Hawkins he is dealing with a fellow 'scholar, whose judgment and insight he learns quickly to respect.

For the Johnsonian, moreover, Hawkins affords an interesting glimpse into the development of Johnsonian biography. To many it is a glimpse which may be surprising. For Boswell so eclipsed his predecessors that it is natural to think of his *Life* as the fountainhead of all Johnsonian knowledge. A study of Hawkins shows inevitably, however, that, just as Hawkins was indebted to his predecessors, so Boswell was indebted to his. Tyers, Cooke, Steevens, Shaw, Boswell (in the *Tour to the Hebrides*), and Mrs. Piozzi not only supplied Hawkins with much useful information but together provided a rule against which he could frequently measure his own performance. How much more valuable a rule did Hawkins provide for Boswell! If the actual amount of information which Boswell specifically copied from Hawkins is small, the extent to which he used him is incalculable. Hawkins' statements were always of interest to Boswell, and not merely because he was determined to waste no opportunity to prove Hawkins wrong. Where Hawkins went wrong, Boswell had an incentive to go right. Where Hawkins was right, Boswell had a reassuring check on his own work. And where Hawkins had information unknown to him, Boswell took every care to verify it⁴ and, if possible, to arrive at the same information independently, so that he might present his account unencumbered with debt.⁵

Similarly, the development in biographical method is interesting. The early lives of Johnson printed a number of letters, particularly Walmesley's letter to Colson, Gower's to the friend of Jonathan

---

3. *Life,* p. 193.
4. In the manuscript of the *Life,* for example, Boswell made the following notation: "Inquire as to the authenticity of the story in Hawkins p. 43 of £5 being borrowed by him & Garrick from Wilcox."
5. As with the account of Appleby School. See above, pp. 116–17.

Swift, and Johnson's letters to Macpherson and Lord Thurlow. They printed what scraps of Johnson's conversation they could glean, and dated and described what works of his they could identify. One finds in them also some rudimentary criticism of Johnson's works. Hawkins merely expanded and systematized their method. He printed a few more of Johnson's letters, and he added to the store of Johnson's conversation. He described Johnson's works more thoroughly and accurately than had been done before, and he made his criticism an integral and vital part of his biography. Finally, he went one step further and placed Johnson in his milieu.

Boswell's introduction of long, dramatic conversations was the final step in the development of Johnsonian biography. Essentially the purposes of the two men were alike. Boswell, like Hawkins, described and criticized Johnson's works and placed Johnson in his milieu. But unlike Hawkins, he was unwilling to let anything about Johnson escape him, no matter how trivial it seemed.[6] He printed every one of Johnson's letters he could find. And with his matchless journalistic skill, he was able to record, sometimes in a few pages, more of Johnson's conversation than all the Johnsonians before him had been able to collect among them; and whereas others had generally recorded isolated statements, Boswell was able to reconstruct whole conversations in the form of dramatic dialogue. This was a major advance. Yet (granting all this) one cannot escape the conclusion that his book would have suffered notably if the pioneers in the same field had not done their work before him.

In addition to the Johnsonians, Hawkins' *Life* has an abiding interest for anyone with a fondness for the eighteenth century. Indeed, few other works set us down with such advantage in the very life of the times. Many of Hawkins' accounts—of Edward Cave and the *Gentleman's Magazine,* for example, of the *Historical Register,* of

---

6. Hawkins, for example, passed over some of the numerous Johnsoniana in *Gent. Mag.,* including a few of Johnson's letters.

Samuel Dyer, Dr. Birch, Garrick, and Mrs. Williams—have no counterparts. We can be grateful for his insights into the political control of the eighteenth-century hospitals or into the opposition which threw itself relentlessly against Sir Robert Walpole. To be sure, Hawkins' Puritanism will always make him a target for devotees of the theater (among others), but the stiffness of his Puritan cloth did not by any means invariably hamper his movements. It is, in fact, his wide range which gives the book so much of the spirit of the times and which will continue to attract scholars, whether they are seeking information on such varied writers as Richardson, William Lauder, Paul Whitehead, and Mark Akenside, or on such remarkable institutions as the Sun Fire Office and the Ivy Lane Club.

But Hawkins' appeal cannot be limited to Johnsonians and to students of the eighteenth century. For all readers he affords the perpetual delight of Johnson himself. Through Hawkins, just as through Boswell, we can think ourselves "almost as much a master of Johnson's character"[7] as if we had known him personally. Hawkins opens the curtain upon the full stage of Johnson's richly diversified career. It could be contended, wrote Nicolson, that Hawkins gives a more complete and convincing picture of Johnson than Boswell does himself:

> It is from Hawkins and not from Boswell that we get the picture of the middle period from 1749 to 1756, when Johnson was forming himself as a dictator at the King's Head in Ivy Lane. . . . It is from Hawkins that we obtain, even upon the later period, certain sidelights which Boswell failed to observe or understand. It is Hawkins, and not Boswell, who advances the interesting and acute supposition that Johnson was at heart a coward, and that in his later years he was tortured by some specific remorse. There is little in Boswell about the gentler side of Johnson; no picture so illustrative of this aspect as that

7. See above, p. 96.

of Johnson watering his flowers in Bolt Court. Hawkins, again, is far more intelligent and penetrating on the subject of John- son's strange seraglio; on his dread of returning home at night to find Mrs. Williams sitting up for him with some grievance against Francis Barber.[8]

The comparison must not be pushed too far. Boswell remains supreme. But one thing is clear: all the accusations against Hawkins cannot alter the fact that he drew a picture of Johnson identical in nearly all essentials with that which survives in other records. Haw- kins was not a butcher brutally hacking away at his dead friend. He was not inexcusably inaccurate. His "miscellaneous matter," though often long-winded, is a major achievement of his work. And though his faults of style cannot be overlooked, he was neither the club- footed stylist nor the imbecile critic his contemporaries laughingly held him to be.

An appeal to Johnsonians, to lovers of the eighteenth century, to anyone with the wit to appreciate a wise and vivid portrait of a great soul—few books can boast so much. "Such a history of Milton or Shakespeare—O how desirable!" But we have seen what hap- pened. Competition was the lot of Hawkins' life. As a magistrate he was overshadowed by Sir John Fielding. His edition of Walton's *Compleat Angler* fought its way to popularity over the mangled text of Moses Browne's edition. His *History of Music* was felled by the wits and by the popular Dr. Burney, the first volume of whose history was published in the very same year. But all this was child's play. The book which is indispensable to our knowledge of one of England's outstanding figures was hooted and buffeted and then tossed into the ring with the towering giant of biography. Un- seconded, unable to retaliate, Hawkins' *Life* passed quickly into a seclusion from which it has never emerged. It is a strange fate for a book that has so much to offer.

8. Harold Nicolson, *The Development of English Biography* (London, 1933), pp. 96–97.

APPENDIX

A. The "narrative" of Johnson's life, including the criticism of Johnson's works. Numbers refer to pages in Hawkins' *Life*.

1-18, 19-23, 26-29, 32-40, 42-45, 49-55, 55-65, 66-67, 69-72, 78-90, 96-97, 99-100, 122-29, 132-34, 145-46, 149, 150-55, 156-71, 175-77, 188-89, 190-96, 198-202, 203-6, 219-20, 250-54, 255-56, 257-59, 264-66, 269, 271-77, 281-82, 283, 284, 285-94, 309, 312-21, 325-29, 340-47, 349-75, 377, 379, 380-82, 383-84, 385-86, 387-88, 389-96, 400-1, 403-5, 406-11, 412-16, 423-26, 435-64, 466, 468-71, 472-73, 478-80, 480-87, 488, 490-93, 494, 499-502, 503-7, 508, 512-15, 515-18, 520, 524, 527, 528-50, 551-54, 556-74, 575-91.

B. Hawkins' "Miscellaneous Matter." Asterisks indicate what I consider the true digressions.

*4-5 n.	Edward the Confessor's cure for the King's Evil quoted in Latin from Stow's *Annals*.
*13-14 n.	Pope's praise of Smart.
*14-15 n.	Difference between those who practice in civil law and those who practice in common law.
18-19	Justification of college servitors.
*19 n.	The clergy abandoning their duties to the lowest of their order.
23-26	Outline of the *Voyage to Abyssinia*.
29-32	Predecessors of the *Gentleman's Magazine*.
*31 n.	Origin of the term "Grub Street writers."
41-42	The story of *Irene*.

182

45–49	Account of Edward Cave.
46–49 n.	Cave's associates on the *Gentleman's Magazine*.
55	Anecdote of Garrick and Fleetwood.
65–66	Johnson's opinion of Crousaz quoted from his *Life of Pope*.
*67–69	Pope and Warburton.
72–78	Background of the Licensing Act; Hawkins' opinion of theaters and plays; comment on *Gustavus Vasa*.
*73 n.	A Quaker woman tried before Hawkins.
*87–88 n.	The history of taverns.
90–92	"Ad Urbanum" quoted with an English imitation.
92–94	The feud between the *Gentleman's Magazine* and the *London Magazine*.
*93–94 n.	Newsham's printing of a scurrilous letter.
{ 94–96 { 97–99	Background of the reporting of the debates.
100–22	Speeches of Hardwicke and Chesterfield.
124–28 n.	Speeches of Horatio Walpole and Pitt.
129–32	Defense of Sir Robert Walpole.
134–48	Extracts from the Harleian Catalogue.
143–45	Plan of the Harleian Catalogue.
146–49	Proposals for the Harleian *Miscellany*.
149–50	Account of Osborne.
155	Paragraph from the *Life of Savage*.
156	Fielding's comment on the *Life of Savage*.
157–60 n.	Accounts of Amhurst and Samuel Boyse.
171–75	Account of early dictionaries.
*171 n.	Anecdote of the lexicographer Cooper.
*172–74 n.	Preface to John Baret's dictionary quoted.
176–85	Account of Lord Chesterfield.
*185–88	Letter of Henry Sidney to his son.
188	Further account of Lord Chesterfield.
189–90	Chesterfield's characterization of Johnson.
*192 n.	Anecdote of Sir Thomas Robinson.

*479 n.	Note on Icolmkill.
*480	The Norderys and the Suderys.
487–88	Extract from Pennant's account.
488–90	Johnson's opinion of the authenticity of Ossian.
493–94	Extract from *The Patriot*.
494–99	*Taxation No Tyranny* quoted and summarized.
*500 n.	Anecdote of Hogarth.
502–3	Remarks on the political system.
*503 n.	A nobleman who was opposed to the American War.
*505–6 n.	Extract from Magna Charta.
507–8	The "madness of the people."
508–12	Defense of general warrants.
*509–10 n.	The government's preventing artificers from leaving England.
*511 n.	Watches returned to England because of bad workmanship and material.
513 n.	Barbarisms in Parliamentary language.
514	Reasons for liking Sir Robert Walpole.
518–20	Johnson's prologue to *A Word to the Wise* quoted.
*518–19 n.	That English vengeance does sometimes war with the dead.
520–21	Account of Dr. Dodd.
521–23	Remarks on fashionable humanity.
523–24 n.	Account of Selwin and his creditors.
524–26	Johnson's letters for Dr. and Mrs. Dodd quoted.
527–28	Johnson's observations on Dr. Dodd quoted.
*531 n.	Precedents in law.
*541 n.	Two learned Puritan divines.
*542 n.	Note on Howell.
550–51	Johnson's epitaph for Mr. Thrale quoted.
554–56	Johnson's verses on Dr. Levett quoted.
*565–66 n.	Anecdote of the infidel Annet.
*573 n.	Brocklesby's charity and Hobbes on self-love.
574–75	Johnson's translation of Horace quoted.

Appendix, C

*580 n.   Introductory professions of faith.

591-95   Johnson's will.

596-602   Postscript concerning Francis Barber and Heely.

C. Malone's Comments on Hawkins' *Life*[1]

1. His [Hawkins'] inaccuracy.

From the numerous cancelled Leaves one w^d expect great accuracy—sed e contra—

p. 4   Time sh^d have been given

6   duck.—false

9   account of Corbet—false

10   father p^d for his commons—not true

12   no authority quoted for Meekes at college

13   False that he was idle at College
Messiah an imposition [four words undecipherable].
acc^t not true.

16   Oxonio rediit misinterpreted.

26   published in an 8vo vol. 1733-4.
No—at London, in 1735.

33   Mrs. J[ohnson] fortune 800L. False

60   50 [L.] for 3rd Sat[ire] of Juv[enal]. False.

150   the Story of Osborne false as told.

161   did not apply at College—*False*.

162   Acc^t of Johnson, C. Cibber & Chesterfield—

313   Johnson's *not* a love match.

1. Photographs of the originals in the William Salt Library, Stafford, England, have been kindly supplied me by Professor James L. Clifford. Malone's elusive handwriting, the tattered condition of the originals, and the photographic reproduction make the deciphering of Malone's notes almost always difficult and at times impossible. On the whole, I have followed Malone's order; and I have retained his six headings. However, where he has inserted entries out of position or sideways in the margins, I have placed them where I thought they belonged. I have also made occasional minor changes in punctuation.

327 he had a rem[ainin]g interest in the Rambler which
he sold.
He never sold—he had it to the last.

328 [Comment about Hawkins' quarrel with Frank Barber is undecipherable.]

346 Dr. Kenrick author of Lexiphanes. Not so

421 Story abᵗ G[oldsmith] confinement and sale of Vicar
of Wakefield—false.

425 Garrick never admitted to Club *false*
Hist of the authors secession from the Club false; and
he knows its false

530 his faculties impaired in 1774—No one [page torn]
this [page torn]

2. His bad taste and misrepresentation of Johnson and his writings.

367 Rasselas is scarcely to be paralleled it is written in a
style refined to a degree of immaculate purity & displays the whole force of *turgid* eloquence

386 Wretched taste in producing two specimens of Johnson's humour, wᶜʰ are no specimens.

431 Wretched taste in a story of Garrick

440 Forced by Sʳ J. Reynolds to work at Shaksp.—A
[lie?] probably—as his Letters to T. Warton prove.
The work had been printing from 1760.[2]

441 On publication of S[hakespeare] little appeared to
have been done—a few conjectural emendˢ of the
text & some scattered remarks—
J. did more than all the preced[ing] ed[itors] together

442 "From the apparent meagreness of the work, the
paucity of the notes &c" some atonement is made by
the pref[ace].

445 We are not to suppose that the publication of S. a

2. Malone also labeled this entry "inaccuracy."

work undertaken without any impulse, & executed with reluctance, c^d greatly add to the lit. rep. of Johnson.

It certainly c^d not in the opinion of such a block-head as this writer who knows nothing of what he has done for Sh.

If the motives he assigns for this partic[ular] work not adding to his rep were just. viz. being written with^t impulse &c—then no work of his c^d ever have gained him any reputation; for by this writers own acc^t *every* work that he ever engaged in was so executed. And that and [only that?] is the truth.

473 His absurd judgment ab^t his *Journey* to the Hebrides.

479 His abuse of Johnson because he does not rigmarole like himself & give an acc^t of St. Colomb.

484 His misrepresentation of Dr J. as abusing the people he had been hospitably entertained by—& because he has called a barren country by its proper name— See Dempster Letter [word undecipherable].

[Pennant?] in his [word undecipherable] on Scot. did not forget that his book was to be reviewed by some hireling Scots.

487 & [praise?] of such a bookmaker as Pennant.

3. His own bad style.

2 if any *shall please* to make it—

3 bailif—the duties of that *exalted station*—

11 *which* he had been presented *to*
    twitted

21 preferring the chance of the *wide* world—

34 register of the E[cclesiastical] C[ourt] of the b[isho]p *thereof*

50 adventurer in the wide world—

52 for want *thereof*

386   he w^d often *huff* Garrick

        he *took to* the profession of the law

394   which he found in a spare leaf thereof

533   Oldys was the man *of all others* best qualified

4. His illiberal and unconstitutional notions.

18   approves of literary men being degraded by being levelled with common servants in colleges.

19   to justify the practice &c—we have an example &c —So that the *propriety* does not depend on the reason of things, but on a *precedent.*

131   "the most popular minister that ever directed the councils of this country—" he means Pitt—but having talked of his "yelping pertinacity" in a preceding page—he has not liberality enough to name him.

391-2   A cancel to [word undecipherable] Dr. Taylor.

        He had not the spirit to quote this at first—but afterwards, having some petty quarrel with Taylor, he inserted that at the insertion of which every man must be pleased—while he despises the man who had not the spirit to do it for the love of truth, & was meanly induced to make this a vehicle of [mere?] sentiment.

408   A most base and illiberal charge ag^t D^r J without any authority quoted, for which the author ought to be pilloried.

        "He would frequently by letters recommend those to credit, who c^d obtain it by no other means, & thereby enabled them to contract debts, which he had good reason to suspect they neither c^d nor ever w^d pay."

419   Because Goldsmith on Ld Northumberland offering to assist him in Ireland, generously declined it in favour of his brother, H. represents him as saying to

Ld Northum, "I c^d say nothing but that I had a brother there a cler[gy]man that stood in need of help. As for myself, I have no dependence on the promises of great men. I look to the booksellers for support— They are my best friends, & I am not inclined to forsake them for others."—These words it is evid^t were spoken by G[oldsmith] to Sir J. H. as one of the grounds of his refusal of L^d N's offer; but he has printed them in such a manner as to make the reader believe they were spoken to [Lord Northumberland].

421   in his dealings with the booksellers he [Goldsmith] is s^d to have acted very dishonestly—When the fame of a dead man is thus attacked proof sh^d be adduced.

536   "By a kind of arithmetical process subtracting from his excellencies he has endeavoured to sink Shaks. in the opinion of his numerous admirers, & to persuade us ag^t reason and our own feelings that the former are annihilated by the latter—"

540   His [Johnson's] transl^n of Sal[lust] Bell[um] Cat[ilinarium] so flat & insipid its appearance w^d be a disgrace to his memory.

5. Rigmarole.

29   Gentleman's Mag. being men[tione]d—a digr[essio]n on Magazines.

40   Irene being ment^d—a long quot. from Knolles.

43   w^d have given M^r G[arrick]'s history, had not M^r Th[omas] D[avies] done it.

46   *good hands* in G[entleman's] M[agazine].—so gives characters of them all.

100   Johnson's speeches in G. M. being ment^d he gives 20 pages of them.

134   Harl[eian] Catal[ogue] men^d so gives you 12 pages chiefly of *Oldys's* writing [word undecipherable].

177–89   Ld Chesterfield being chosen by J. as a patron for his
Dict.—12 pages on him.

205   active and idle authors being men^d he gives an acc^t
of 15 pages of the former.
then of all his club—15 more.
then 3 physicians being among them, a hist of
Schomberg, Akenside, Secker.

294   Crighton [*sic*] being men^d in Adventurer 15 pages on
him.

329   Mentioning that Ld Melcombe selected his acquaintances, he gives a long character of them, & of all
those who were his followers with whom J. *c^d have
been* acquainted, had he accepted the invitation,
which he did not—10 pages.

6. Absurdity.

100   he [two words undecipherable] deepmouthed rancour of Pulteney & the yelping pertinacity of Pitt.
So far from thus discriminating was he [Johnson],
that all the speeches are alike.

173   He does not tell that it was rendered in this manner
in order to level it to the capacity of a schoolboy.

195   Comparison of Gar[rick]'s Prol[ogue] & Johnson's
on totally different subjects.

205   Johnson's waste of time—
Tho' J. charged himself with this, his biographer
has no right to do so—He did more than 99 men
in 100. He might say like Pope, in answer, was I
born for nothing but to write.

258   No one equall to Johnson in humour *except* old Tarle-
ton—a low comedian of [old Drury?] who performed
the part of the clown & the fool in old plays and
[remainder of line undecipherable].

313   if Johnson's fondness for his wife not *dissembled* it was
a lesson he·had learned by *rote*.

He knew nothing of her b[eau]ty for he never saw
her face—& he merely laboured to make himself
think highly of her by writing mem^s—This is dear
Tetty's book &c

316   Johnson's mel[ancholy] from death of his wife like
the affection of Milton which c^d excite such pleasing
images as Methought I saw my late espoused Saint—
Certainly not like the affection of a man who married
three wives & was a tyrant to them all—

Johnson to the last hour of his life had the same tenderness for T[etty].

354   Whenever it [tea] appeared, he was almost raving—

406   Southwell a man of wonderful parts—very common
parts.

534   because he had but one eye & his sight in that not
very good & had no relish for the beauties of nature
—he was no poet—His eyes c^d not in a fine frenzy
&c.

How perfectly absurd! This proves that he c^d not
write a descriptive poem like Thompson's Seasons
(from actual obser^{vtn}) but it proves nothing else.

535   frigid encomium on fine passages in Dryden—
Where? never—

This [not?] of the imaginative faculty—the cause
of his not relishing Henry & Emma—[&c?] is his
not approving the [word undecipherable].

588   His ridiculous acc^t [of John]sons making a few
punctures [paper torn].

D. List of Cancellations from Hawkins' *Life of Johnson*[1]

7–8   In p. 8 *l*.16 *originally*—"*in* a living."

19–20 In p. 13 [19] *l*.14 after *him* stood originally—"though his brother Nathaniel had made room for him by his death."

Originally p. 19—though he had the example of his Uncle Ford before his eyes, whose profligacy was enough to have effaced [undecipherable words seem to indicate that the original of this part of the text was just as it is now]—nor beheld the beneficed clergy &c gentlemen at large, meeting card assemblies and in all publick recreations and amusements; affecting as well in the colour as in other particulars of their dress the garb of the laity, and exclaiming as one is known to have done, ag[ains]t the canon which prohibits the Clergy from wearing white stockings. I say, not knowing, &c but lamented that the race was extinct. Vid—74 of the Canons of 1607.

21–22   In p. 22 *l*.[12] *objects* changed to *subjects*.

33–34   In p. 33 *l*.4 originally "a brewer."

169–70 In p. 169 *l*.5 after "*language*" stood, "till the republication of it by Mr. Whalley in 1753."

269–70 In p. 269 *l*.3 Instead of *March* stood *April*.

275–76 In p. 275 *l*.20 originally—that he had inserted *verbatim*.

311–12 In p. 311—"and informed himself of." Originally—"made himself acquainted with."

321–22 Note originally thus.

After what has been said of his defect of sight, it

1. The originals of these sheets, in the handwriting of Edmond Malone, are in the William Salt Library, Stafford, England. Professor James L. Clifford has kindly supplied me with photographs of them. In transcribing, I have made a few minor changes of punctuation not affecting the text.

may perhaps be questioned, how he could discern beauty; but his method was, as he has been heard to describe it, by examining the features singly could [two words undecipherable] in the whole countenance.

327–28 In p. 328 note: Instead of "*was very attentive to the conduct of his servants,*" stood originally "kept a strict eye on this his favourite"—

331–32 In p. 332—for "who wrote" stood—"the author of."

391–92 Twice cancelled

In original copy— *l*.16 &c stood thus.

This was the first intimation I ever received that any such casual emolument was to be derived from the profession of an author; but others have since occurred to me which shewed that this was not the only instance of the kind; and I reckon his Introduction to the London Chronicle and to the World Displayed, his Prefaces to the Preceptor & to Rolts Dict[ionar]y of Commerce, as also, his Ded[icatio]n of Kennedy's Scripture Chronology, Payne's Introduction to the Game of Draughts & many other books in the number. For the ded[n] to his present majesty of Adams's book on the use of the Globes, one of [the remainder of the sentence is undecipherable].

The Note stood thus.

Some of these have been preached in St. James Chapel, and many I myself have heard in another place, one in particular which Johnson also heard, he being in the same church at the time it was preached. By the method and style of it, I judged it to be of his composition; I told him so, and he did not deny it. In his Diary I find the name of one Clergyman whom he assisted.

In the first Cancel the above paragraph was struck out from the text & instead of it this substituted:

"This was the first intimation I ever received that any such casual emoluments were to be derived from the profession of an author; but others have since occurred which shewed that this was not the only instance of the kind, and for the ded^n to his present Majesty of Adams's book on the uses of the Globes, he was as himself informed me &c."

The note on Dr. Taylor was changed thus.

Some of them I myself have heard in the Church of St. Margaret Westminster, one in particular which Johnson also heard, he being present at the time it was preached. By the sentiments & the style of it I judged it to be of his composition. I afterwards told him so & he was silent. In his Diary I find this note—"77 Sep. 22 Concio pro Tayloro."

461–62   [No indication of what change was made.]

511–12   in p. 511 last line originally stood—in these of cambrick & paper and in printing, in sculpture and other arts of design.

513–14 l.11 of 513—originally—he might probably have introduced a style of debate more weighty & less declamatory than that which then prevailed, and banished from it a great number &c.

In the note *originally*—"and others which occur in the printed [speeches?].

527–28   In l.1 of 527 originally.

To this petition &c.

549–50   In 549 l.24—originally—of manors, of lands, & other things exposed to sale &c.

577–78   In p. 577 l.3 originally—"Aegri Ephemeris, in which the words Nox insomnis occur more frequently than any others."

BIBLIOGRAPHY

1. Hawkins' Works

   A General History of the Science and Practice of Music, London, Novello, 1853.

   The Life of Samuel Johnson, LL.D., London, J. Buckland, 1787; 2d ed. rev. and corrected, London, J. Buckland, 1787. Another ed., Dublin, Chambers, 1787.

   With John Stanley: *Six Cantatas for a Voice and Instruments,* London, 1742?; 2d Series, London, 1746?

   The Works of Samuel Johnson, LL.D. Together with His Life, and Notes on His Lives of the Poets, by Sir John Hawkins, London, J. Buckland, 1787.

   Walton, Izaak, *The Complete Angler, or Contemplative Man's Recreation,* 4th ed. by Sir John Hawkins, London, Rivington, 1784.

2. Manuscript Materials

   Boswell, James, manuscript of Boswell's *Life of Johnson,* Sterling Memorial Library, Yale University.

   —— paper marked "Tacenda," Sterling Memorial Library, Yale University.

   Hawkins, Sir John, letter to Thomas Cadell, Feb. 26, 1785, Pierpont Morgan Library, New York City.

   Lysons, Samuel, a scrapbook of Johnsonian clippings from eighteenth-century newspapers, with some comments in

Lysons' hand, in the possession of James L. Clifford, New York City.

Malone, Edmond, comments on Hawkins' *Life of Johnson,* the William Salt Library, Stafford, England.

—————— list of cancellations from Hawkins' *Life of Johnson,* in the handwriting of Edmond Malone, the William Salt Library, Stafford, England.

Walpole, Horace, marginal notes in Walpole's copy of Hawkins' *Life of Johnson,* in the possession of W. S. Lewis, Farmington, Connecticut.

3. Eighteenth-Century Periodicals

The County Magazine, for the Years 1786 and 1787, Vol. 1, Salisbury and London, 1788.

The Critical Review: or, Annals of Literature, Vol. 63, London, 1787.

The Daily Advertiser, London, 1739.

The Dublin Chronicle, Dublin, 1787.

The English Review of Literature, Science, Discoveries, Inventions, and Practical Controversies and Contests, Vol. 9, London, 1787.

The European Magazine, and London Review, Vols. 6–10, London, 1784–87.

The General Evening Post, London, 1785.

The Gentleman's Magazine, Vols. 8–58, London, 1738–88.

The Lady's Magazine; or Entertaining Companion for the Fair Sex, Vol. 18, London, 1787.

Lloyd's Evening Post, and British Chronicle, for the Year 1785, Vol. 56, London, 1785.

The London Chronicle, or Universal Evening Post, Vols. 56–62, London, 1784–87.

Bibliography

The London Packet; or, New Lloyd's Evening Post, London, 1784–85.

The Monthly Review; or, Literary Journal, Vols. 76–77, London, 1787.

The Morning Chronicle and London Advertiser, London, 1787.

The New Annual Register, or General Repository of History, Politics, and Literature, for the Year 1787, London, 1788.

The New Town and Country Magazine; or General Repository of Knowledge and Pleasure, Vol. 1, London, 1787.

Olla Podrida, No. 13. Saturday, June 9, 1787.

The Political Magazine, and Parliamentary, Naval, Military and Literary Journal, Vol. 12, London, 1787.

The St. James's Chronicle; or, British Evening-Post, London, 1784–87.

The Scots Magazine, Vol. 49, Edinburgh, 1787.

The Town and Country Magazine; or Universal Repository of Knowledge, Instruction and Entertainment, Vol. 19, London, 1787.

The Universal Magazine of Knowledge and Pleasure, Vols. 65–78, London, 1775–87.

Walkers Hibernian Magazine or Compendium of Entertaining Knowledge, Dublin, 1787.

The Whitehall Evening-Post, London, 1785.

4. Articles and pamphlets

Balderston, Katherine C., "Johnson's Vile Melancholy," *The Age of Johnson, Essays Presented to Chauncey Brewster Tinker* (New Haven, Yale University Press, 1949), 3–14.

Boyle, Sir Edward, "Johnson and Sir John Hawkins," *National Review,* 87 (1926), 77–89.

Bibliography

Bronson, Bertrand, review of Scholes' *Life and Activities of Sir John Hawkins, MLN,* 69 (1954), 521–24.

Chalmers, Alexander, "Sir John Hawkins," *The General Biographical Dictionary,* new ed. London, 1814.

Chapman, R. W., and Hazen, Allen T., "Johnsonian Bibliography: A Supplement to Courtney," *Proceedings of the Oxford Bibliographical Society,* 5, 1939, 119–66.

Clifford, James L., "The Complex Art of Biography," *Columbia University Forum,* 1 (1958), 32–37.

Dobson, Austin, "Boswell's Predecessors and Editors," *A Paladin of Philanthropy* (London, Chatto and Windus, 1899), 137–72.

———— "Sir John Hawkins, Knight," *Old Kensington Palace and Other Papers* (New York, Oxford University Press, n.d.), 112–39.

Fifer, C. N., "Dr. Johnson and Bennet Langton," *JEGP,* 54 (1955), 504–6.

Greene, D. J., "Some Notes on Johnson and the *Gentleman's Magazine,*" *PMLA,* 74 (1959), 75–84.

Hazen, Allen T., "*The Beauties of Johnson,*" *MP,* 35 (1938), 289–95.

Hyde, Donald and Mary, *Dr. Johnson's Second Wife,* privately printed, 1953; in *New Light on Johnson,* ed. F. W. Hilles, New Haven, Yale University Press, 1959.

———— "Johnson and Journals," *The New Colophon* (1950), 165–97.

Mild, Warren, "Johnson and Lauder: A Reexamination," *MLQ,* 14 (1953), 149–53.

Miller, C. A., *Sir John Hawkins Dr. Johnson's Friend-Attorney-Executor-Biographer,* Washington, privately printed, 1951.

Osborn, James M., *Dr. Johnson and the Contrary Converts*, New Haven, privately printed (Yale University Press), 1954. Also in Hilles, ed., *New Light on Johnson*.

Pottle, Frederick A., "The Dark Hints of Sir John Hawkins and Boswell," *MLN*, *56* (1941), 325–29. Also in Hilles, ed., *New Light on Johnson*.

Powell, L. F., "Johnson's Part in the *Adventurer*," *RES*, *3* (1927), 420–29.

Quinlan, Maurice J., "The Rumor of Dr. Johnson's Conversion," *Review of Religion*, *12* (1948), 243–61.

Ruhe, Edward L., "The Two Samuel Johnsons," *NQ*, new ser. *1* (Oct. 1954), 432–35.

"Sir John Hawkins, Kt." (review of Scholes' *Life and Activities of Sir John Hawkins*), *TLS*, Jan. 30, 1953.

Stevenson, Robert, " 'The Rivals'—Hawkins, Burney, and Boswell," *Musical Quarterly*, *36* (1950), 67–82.

Whitley, Alvin, "The Comedy of *Rasselas*," *ELH*, *23* (1956), 48–70.

Wood, Frederick T., "Pirate Printing in the Eighteenth Century," *NQ*, *159* (Nov. 20, 1930), 381–84; (Dec. 6), 400–3.

5. Books

Anderson, Robert, *The Life of Samuel Johnson, LL.D. with Critical Observations on His Works*, 3d ed. Edinburgh, Doig and Stirling, 1815.

An Asylum for Fugitive Pieces, III, 2d ed. London, J. Debrett, 1795.

Boswell, James, *Boswell's Life of Johnson together with Boswell's Journal of a Tour to the Hebrides and Johnson's Diary of a Journey into North Wales*, ed. George Birkbeck Hill, rev. and enlarged by L. F. Powell, Oxford, Clarendon Press, 1934–50.

—— *Boswell's London Journal,* ed. Frederick A. Pottle, New York, McGraw-Hill, 1950.

—— *Letters of James Boswell,* ed. Chauncey Brewster Tinker, Oxford, Clarendon Press, 1924.

—— *The Private Papers of James Boswell from Malahide Castle in the Collection of Lt-Colonel Ralph Heyward Isham,* ed. Geoffrey Scott and Frederick A. Pottle, privately printed, 1928–34.

Burney, Frances (Madame D'Arblay), *The Diary and Letters of Madame D'Arblay,* ed. Austin Dobson, London and New York, Macmillan, 1904.

Campbell, Thomas, Dr. *Campbell's Diary of a Visit to England in 1775,* ed. James L. Clifford, Cambridge, Cambridge University Press, 1947.

Carter, Elizabeth, *Letters from Mrs. Elizabeth Carter to Mrs. Montagu,* London, Rivington, 1817.

Clifford, James L., *Johnsonian Studies 1887–1950: A Survey and Bibliography,* Minneapolis, University of Minnesota Press, 1951.

—— *Young Sam Johnson,* New York, McGraw-Hill, 1955.

[Cooke, William], *The Beauties of Johnson,* London, G. Kearsley, 1781; 5th ed. Pt. II, London, G. Kearsley, 1782.

—— *The Life of Samuel Johnson, LL.D.,* London, G. Kearsley, 1785; 2d ed. London, G. Kearsley, 1785.

Courtney, William Prideaux, *A Bibliography of Samuel Johnson. Revised and Seen through the Press by David Nichol Smith,* Oxford, Clarendon Press, 1915.

Cowper, William, *The Correspondence of William Cowper,* ed. Thomas Wright, New York, Dodd, 1904.

Davies, Thomas, *Memoirs of the Life of David Garrick, Esq.,* London, pub. by the author, 1780.

Egmont, John Percival, *Faction Detected, by the Evidence of Facts,* 2d ed. London, J. Roberts, 1743.

Evans, Medford, "Johnson's Debates in Parliament," unpublished doctoral dissertation, Yale University, 1933.

Fielding, Henry, *The Works of Henry Fielding, Esq. with an Essay on His Life and Genius, by Arthur Murphy, Esq.,* new ed. London, J. Johnson, 1808.

Francis, Barber [pseud.], *More Last Words of Dr. Johnson,* 2d ed. London, Rich, 1787.

Greene, Donald Johnson, *The Politics of Samuel Johnson,* New Haven, Yale University Press, 1960.

The Hamwood Papers of the Ladies of Llangollen and Caroline Hamilton, ed. Mrs. G. H. Bell, London, Macmillan, 1930.

Hawkins, Laetitia-Matilda, *Anecdotes, Biographical Sketches and Memoirs,* London, Longman, 1823.

—— *Memoirs, Anecdotes, Facts, and Opinions,* London, Longman, 1824.

Hilles, F. W., ed., *New Light on Johnson,* New Haven, Yale University Press, 1959.

Jerningham, Edward, *Edward Jerningham and His Friends: A Series of Eighteenth Century Letters,* ed. Lewis Bettany, London, Chatto and Windus, 1919.

Joe Miller's Complete Jest Book, unabridged ed. New York, Henderson, 1903.

Johnson, Samuel, *Diaries, Prayers, and Annals,* ed. E. L. McAdam, Jr., New Haven, Yale University Press, 1958.

—— *A Dictionary of the English Language,* London, J. Harrison, 1786.

—— London, J. Jarvis, 1786.

Bibliography

——— *The Letters of Samuel Johnson, LL.D.*, ed. George Birkbeck Hill, New York, Harper, 1892.

——— *The Letters of Samuel Johnson with Mrs. Thrale's Genuine Letters to Him*, ed. R. W. Chapman, Oxford, Clarendon Press, 1952.

——— *Papers Written by Dr. Johnson and Dr. Dodd in 1777*, ed. R. W. Chapman, Oxford, Clarendon Press, 1926.

——— *Prayers and Meditations*, 2d ed. London, Cadell, 1785.

Johnsonian Miscellanies, ed. George Birkbeck Hill, New York, Harper, 1897.

Johnsoniana: or, Supplement to Boswell, ed. J. Wilson Croker, Philadelphia, Carey and Hart, 1842.

Krutch, Joseph Wood, *Samuel Johnson*, New York, Holt, 1944.

Lewis, D. B. Wyndham, *The Hooded Hawk or the Case of Mr. Boswell*, London, Eyre and Spottiswoode, 1946.

Murphy, Arthur, "An Essay on the Life and Genius of Samuel Johnson, LL.D.," *The Works of Samuel Johnson*, I, London, T. Tegg, 1824.

A New and General Biographical Dictionary, new ed., enlarged and improved, London, W. Strahan, 1784.

Nichols, John, *Biographical Anecdotes of William Hogarth*, 2d ed., enlarged and corrected, London, J. Nichols, 1782.

——— and John Bowyer Nichols, *Illustrations of the Literary History of the Eighteenth Century*, London, Nichols, Son, and Bentley, 1817–58.

Nicolson, Harold, *The Development of English Biography*, London, Hogarth Press, 1933.

Orations of British Orators, The World's Great Classics, New York, Colonial Press, 1900.

Osborn, James M., *John Dryden: Some Biographical Facts and Figures*, New York, Columbia University Press, 1940.

Bibliography

Percy, Thomas, *The Correspondence of Thomas Percy and Edmond Malone*, ed. Arthur Tillotson, Baton Rouge, Louisiana State University Press, 1944.

Prior, Sir James, *The Life of Edmond Malone*, London, Smith, Elder, 1860.

Probationary Odes for the Laureateship: with a Preliminary Discourse, by Sir John Hawkins, Knt., London, J. Ridgway, 1785.

Reade, Aleyn Lyell, *Johnsonian Gleanings*, eleven parts, privately printed, 1909–52.

Reynolds, Sir Joshua, *Portraits*, ed. F. W. Hilles, New York, McGraw-Hill, 1952.

Scholes, Percy A., *The Life and Activities of Sir John Hawkins*, London, Oxford University Press, 1953.

Shaw, William, *An Enquiry into the Authenticity of the Poems Ascribed to Ossian*, 2d ed. London, J. Murray, 1782.

——— *Memoirs of the Life and Writings of the Late Dr. Samuel Johnson*, London, J. Walker, 1785.

Simmons, Walter Lee, "Sir John Hawkins, Knight," unpublished doctoral dissertation, Ohio State University, 1938.

Stauffer, Donald A., *The Art of Biography in Eighteenth Century England*, Princeton, Princeton University Press, 1941.

Twining, Thomas, *Recreations and Studies of a Country Clergyman of the Eighteenth Century*, London, J. Murray, 1882.

Tyers, Thomas, *Biographical Sketch of Dr. Samuel Johnson*, London, n.p., 1785, rep. by the Augustan Reprint Society, No. 34, Los Angeles, 1952.

Waingrow, Marshall, "Five Correspondences of James Boswell Relating to the Composition of the Life of Johnson," unpublished doctoral dissertation, Yale University, 1951.

Watkins, W. B. C., *Perilous Balance*, Princeton, Princeton University Press, 1939.

INDEX

Adams, George (d. *1773*), mathematical instrument-maker, his *Treatise on the Globes*, 196
Adams, Dr. William (*1706–89*), Master of Pembroke College, 46 and n., 110 and n.
Addison, Joseph (*1672–1719*), essayist and critic, 68, 165 and n., 185
Akenside, Mark (*1721–70*), poet and physician, 180, 184, 193
Akerman, Richard (*ca. 1722–1792*), Keeper of Newgate, 112, 137
Allen, Edmund (*1726–84*), printer, 50
American War, 187
Americans, 154, 155, 156
Amhurst, Nicholas (*1697–1742*), poet and political writer, 52–53, 91, 183
Anderson, Dr. Robert (*1750–1830*), biographer of Johnson, 129
Anne, Queen (*1665–1714*), 44
Annet, Peter (*1693–1769*), deistical writer, 187
Appleby School, 116–17, 178 n.
Artificers, 187
Aston, Mary (Molly) (*1706–ca. 1765*), 51–52
Asylum for Fugitive Pieces, 26 n.
Augustan Reprint Society, 47 n.

Balderston, Katherine, 123 n.
Baldwin, Henry (*ca. 1734–1813*), printer of *St. James's Chronicle*, 5 n., 6–7, 15

Barber, Francis (*ca. 1745–1801*), Johnson's servant, 15, 50, 58, 81, 181, 188; Hawkins' attack on, 59, 189
Baret, John (d. *ca. 1580*), lexicographer, 183
Barker, Dr. Edmond (*1721–ca. 1780*), physician, 94 n., 184
Barnard, Sir John (*1685–1764*), Lord Mayor of London, 159
Barry, Mrs. Ann Spranger (formerly Mrs. Ann Street), actress, 164
Bath, William Pulteney, Earl of (*1684–1764*), MP, 132, 157 ff., 172, 193
Bathurst, Dr. Richard (d. *1762*), physician, 22 and n., 91, 92, 94 n., 184
Beauclerk, Hon. Topham (*1739–80*), friend of Johnson, 4, 45, 91, 129, 186
Beggars, 79–83
Bell, Jane (Mrs. John) (*ca. 1710–1771*), 186
Berkshire, Henry Bowes Howard, 4th Earl of (*1686–1757*), 108
Birch, Dr. Thomas (*1705–66*), writer, 14 n., 47 n., 66, 136, 180, 184; his circuit of London, 18, 137–38
Birmingham, 38
Blackwall, Rev. Anthony (*1674–1730*), classical scholar, 98, 115
Bolingbroke, Henry St. John, 1st Vct. (*1678–1751*), 69

207

Index

Cadell, Thomas (*1742–1802*), bookseller and publisher, 2 and n., 11–12

Campbell, Archibald (*ca. 1726–1780*), his *Lexiphanes*, 22, 98, 99, 189

Campbell, Dr. John (*1708–75*), writer, 53, 54, 66, 91, 136, 184

Campbell, Dr. Thomas (*1733–95*), writer, 63

Carew, Thomas (*ca. 1702–1766*), MP, 159

Carlyle, Thomas (*1795–1881*), 36, 55

Caroline, Queen (*1683–1737*), consort of George II, 151 n.

Carter, Elizabeth (*1717–1806*), poetess and writer, 95 and nn., 110–11, 111 n.

Carteret, John, Vct., afterwards 1st Earl Granville (*1690–1763*), 158

Catherine II, Empress of Russia (*1729–96*), 100

Cave, Edward (*1691–1754*), printer and publisher, 17, 88, 108, 134, 139, 161, 183; has Johnson write Debates, 113–14; Hawkins' relations with, 40, 41 and n.; no relish for mirth, 172; publishes Debates, 41–42; reprints part of *Marmor Norfolciense*, 101–2

Chamier, Anthony (*1725–80*), Undersecretary of State, 91, 129, 186

Chapman, R. W., 47 n.

Charlemont, James Caulfeild, 1st Earl of (*1728–99*), 96

Charles II (*1630–85*), King of England, 44 n.

Chatham, William Pitt, 1st Earl of (*1708–78*), 132 and n., 160, 172, 183, 191, 193; characterized in Debates, 157–58

Chesterfield, Philip Dormer Stanhope, 4th Earl of (*1694–1773*), 15,

48, 90, 108, 132 and n., 158, 160, 183, 188, 193; *Letters to His Son*, 172

Chesterfield, Philip Stanhope, 5th Earl of (*1755–1815*), 59–60

Cibber, Colley (*1671–1757*), dramatist and actor, 188

Clarendon Press, viii

Clifford, James L., vii, 72 n., 188 n., 195 n., *Young Sam Johnson*, vii, 36 n., 102, 107

Cock Lane Ghost, 69, 70

Collins, William (*1721–59*), poet, his "Song for Shakespeare's *Cymbeline*," 40–41, 41 n.

Colman, George, the Elder (*1732–94*), dramatist, 20

Colson, John (*1680–1760*), Lucasian Professor at Cambridge, 102, 178

Common Sense, 101

Constitution, English, 154–55

Cooke, William (d. *1824*), writer, 178; *Beauties of Johnson,* 3 n., 103 and n.; *Life of Johnson,* v, 3 and n., 94, 98, 103, 104, 139, used by Hawkins, 46, 50–51, 50 n., by Boswell, 103 n., 104 n., 105

Cooper, Thomas (*ca. 1517–1594*), lexicographer and divine, 183

Copyright laws, 15 and n., 49–50

Corbet, Andrew (*1709–41*), schoolfellow of Johnson, 188

Cornewall, Velters (*1696–1768*), MP, 159

Cotton, Charles (*1630–87*), poet and writer, 2

County Magazine, 16, 17–18, 24

Cowper, William (*1731–1800*), poet, 96, 125, 126, 137, 176–77

Crichton, The Admirable, 135, 136, 185, 193

Index

Index

Mag., 18, *London Chronicle*, 16, *New Town and Country Mag.*, 18, *Political Mag.*, 16, 17, 18, *St. James's Chronicle*, 15–16, *Scots Mag.*, 16, 18, *Town and Country Mag.*, 18, *Universal Mag.*, 16–17, 18; parodied and satirized by *Critical Review*, 26, by *More Last Words of Dr. Johnson*, 30, by Murphy, 26, by Porson, 29–30, by *St. James's Chronicle*, 15–16, 26 and n. Praised by *European Mag.*, 26, by Dr. Horne, 27–28, by public, 18–19, by "A Selector," 15, by *Universal Mag.*, 17 n.; reviewed in *County Mag.*, 24, *Critical Review*, 20 ff., *English Review*, 20, *European Mag.*, 21, *Gent. Mag.*, 19, 20 n., *Monthly Review*, 20 ff., *New Annual Register*, 24; ridiculed in newspapers, 28–29;

EVALUATION: accounts, compared with Boswell's, of Appleby School, 116–17, Gower letter, 104–5, Johnson's composition of Debates, 113–14, 114 n., period at Oxford, 110, translation of Crousaz, 110–11, work for Dr. Dodd, 111–13, incident of Market Bosworth School, 114–15, Savage's influence on Johnson, 119–23. Appraisals of, by Mrs. Carter, 95, by Cowper, 96, 125, 126, 176–77; one of fullest 18th-century biographies, 176; present reputation, 177, second only to Boswell's, vii. Hawkins' criticism: of Addison's style, 165 and n., Miss Hawkins' part in, 141–45, Hawkins' method, 146–47, 150, of Johnson's Debates, 156–62, of *Dictionary*, 150, of edi-

tion of Shakespeare, 148 and n., or *Irene*, 150, of *Life of Savage*, 150, of *London*, 151–52, 151 n., of poetic faculty, 149 n., of political tracts, 147–48, 151–52, 151 n., of *Rasselas*, 143–45, 146, Malone's attack on, 148, of parliamentary style, 165. Digressions: attacked by Boyle, 128–29, by Lewis, 126, discussed, 126–40, extent of, 129 ff., list of, 182–88, praised by Boswell, 127, by Dobson, 127–28, purpose of, 134–36; honesty of, 83–84, 84 n. Inaccuracies in: in ascribing Crousaz translations, 99, avoidable errors, 97–99, justification of, 97, in reading Johnson's handwriting, 99, second Samuel Johnson, 100, 106, textual errors, 102–5. Interest in: for all readers, 180–81, for Johnson scholars, 177–78, for those concerned with 18th century, 179–80; principles of biography in, 67–70, 83–86. Style of: defects, 167–71, 173, formality, 173, 174, strengths, 171–72

HAWKINS' ATTITUDES, toward Johnson's: grief at loss of mother, 58, 59, indolence, 65–67, 67 n., love for wife, 58, 70–73, 72 n., "ostentatious bounty," 59–61, 81–83, personal habits, 57, 61–65; political principles, 69–70, 142–43, 147, 151–56; toward living persons, 93–95, the dead, 88, 91–92, 94 n., earlier biographies, 94, the theater, 148, uninterrupted satire, 147–48

Hawkins, Laetitia-Matilda (*ca. 1760–1835*), daughter of Sir John, 12 n., 45, 95; her part in writing *Life*,

lationship with Savage, 119–23, 151 n.; returns to London, 45; visits Mrs. James Harris, 61; Walmesley recommends him to Colson, 102–3;

Characteristics and Personal Traits
ability to read, 75; asperity, 76; compassion, 76; dress, 62–65; fear of insanity, 144; ferocity, 81; gratitude, 75; handwriting, 99 and n.; imbecility, 81; indolence, 57, 65–67; infirmness of mind, 57; knowledge, 171; limitations as poet and critic, 149 n.; manner of eating, 61–62; melancholia, 147; modesty, 75; physical disabilities, 65; piety, 75; professional qualifications, 75; pusillanimity, 81; sexual desires, 123 n.; slovenliness, 57, 62–65; spirit, 75; superstition, 57, 69, 145; taste for tea, 57, 58;

Attitudes and Opinions
Americans, 156; beggars, 82; copyright laws, 15 n.; departed souls, 145; ecclesiastical appointments, 44; Garrick, 58 and n.; Gray, 84; Hawkins, 45–46; Dr. Levett, 80 n.; the medical profession, 136; Milton, vi, 58, 69, 84; Pelham, 43; the poor, 79–82; Scotland and Scots people, 147; use of sizars and servitors, 59 and n.; Robert Walpole, 43–44, 43 n., 44 n., 142; Whigs, 161–62; Wilkes, 156. His devotion to truth, 136; fondness for his wife, 22, 58, 70–73, 72 n., 122; principles of biography, 68, Toryism, 153, 154–56, 162;

Writings
"Adversaria": as Hawkins' source, 38;
A Compleat Vindication of the Licensers of the Stage: Hawkins' criticism of, 148; "vulgar prejudices," 69; mentioned, 44, 142;
Debates in Parliament: characterizations in, 157–60; Hawkins' criticism of, 156–62; Johnson's versatility in, 147; method of composition, 41–42; period of composition, 43, 113–14, 114 n.; treatment of Whigs in, 161–62; mentioned, 108, 134, 137, 142;
Diaries: Boswell's use of, 117–19, 119 n.; Hawkins pockets one of them, 7 n., 10, 84 n.; his possession of, 1; as his source, 38; Johnson's amorous nature revealed in, 123 n.; Malone's description of, 10 n.; Steevens', 5; mentioned, 4;
A Dictionary of the English Language: definition of *pension,* 77–79, 79 n., of *imbecility,* 82 n.; Hawkins' criticism of, 150; Jarvis edition, vi; Johnson's erudition in, 147; original contract for, 38; praised by critics, v; mentioned, 74, 98, 108;
The False Alarm: Hawkins' criticism of, 152–56; mentioned, 142, 143 n.;
The Idler: Miss Hawkins' help with review of, 143;
Irene: confusion in date of, 98; Hawkins' criticism of, 150;
A Journey to the Western Islands of Scotland: review by Miss Hawkins, 141, 143, 144; Johnson's prejudice in, 147;

Index

Index

Index

chief accountant of the Bank of England, 94

Payne, William, writer, his *Introduction to the Game of Draughts*, 196

Pearce, Dr. Zachary (*1690–1774*), Dean of Winchester, Bishop of Rochester, 44 and n.

Pelham, Hon. Henry (*ca. 1695–1784*), MP, 43

Pembroke College. *See* Oxford University

Penn, William (*1644–1718*), founder of Pennsylvania, 184

Pennant, Thomas (*1726–98*), traveler and naturalist, 141 and n., 186, 187

Pepys, Samuel (*1633–1703*), diarist, 38

Percy, Dr. Thomas (*1729–1811*), Bishop of Dromore, 12, 34, 88

Philo Johnson (pseud.), 20–22, 21 n., 22 n., 25, 34, 88, 89 n., 91, 167 n., 174

Pierpont Morgan Library, viii, 12 n.

Piozzi, Hester Lynch (Mrs. Thrale) (*1741–1821*), friend of Johnson, 14 n., 17 n., 30, 32, 37, 45, 123 n., 178; Hawkins' treatment of her, 93 and n., 95; *Anecdotes of Samuel Johnson*, vi, 24 n., 52 n., 73, 94, 95 n., 175–76, used by Hawkins, 46, 51–52, 55; *Letters to and from the Late Samuel Johnson*, 176

Pitt, William, the Elder. *See* Chatham, Earl of

Plagiarism, 37, 49–51

Playhouses, 148, 172

Politian, Angelus (*1454–94*), Italian scholar, 46 n.

Political Magazine, 16, 17, 18

Pope, Alexander (*1688–1744*), 49, 84, 90, 117, 166, 182, 183, 193; commends *London*, 152; influence on Johnson, 151; *Essay on Man*, 99, 111; *Messiah*, 105, 149 n., 188

Poppy, Ned (character in *The Guardian*), 25

Porson, Richard (*1759–1808*), Greek scholar, 29–30, 31, 54 n., 130

Potter, Rev. Robert (*1721–1804*), poet, 19

Pottle, Frederick A., 119–20, 121 n., 123 n.

Powell, Lawrence F., 40, 111

Practice of Piety, 164

Prior, Matthew (*1664–1721*), poet and diplomatist, his "Henry and Emma," 149 n., 194

Probationary Odes for the Laureateship, 9–10, 9 n.

Psalmanazar, George (*ca. 1679–1763*), literary impostor, 91

Pugh, John, author, his *Memoirs of the Life of the Late Jonas Hanway*, 19

Pulteney, William. *See* Bath, Earl of

Quarter Sessions (Middlesex), 2, 11

Raleigh, Sir Walter (*ca. 1552–1618*), naval commander and author, 47 n.

Reade, Aleyn Lyell, his *Johnsonian Gleanings*, 36 n., 107, 108 n., 110

Resnel, Jean-François du B. (*1692–1761*), translator of Pope, 111

Reynolds, Frances (*1729–1807*), sister of Sir Joshua, 45–46, 46 n., 64

Reynolds, Sir Joshua (*1732–92*), portrait painter, 5, 23 n., 36, 88, 189; gives materials to Boswell, 34, 105 n.; offended by Hawkins, 10; *Portraits*, 90 n.

Richardson, Samuel (*1689–1761*),

219

Index